Praise For

The Muslim Next Door

"[W]ho do I read if I only have a limited amount of time and want to know what and why Muslims believe what they believe? ***The Muslim Next Door*** is an excellent place to start. Sumbul Ali-Karamali presents Islam as a living and lived faith. She combines scholarship with an engaging and accessible style and frank self-criticism that crystallizes the faith and commitment of a majority of mainstream Muslims in its unity and diversity."

—Dr. John L. Esposito, Director of the Center for Muslim-Christian Understanding at Georgetown University

"This book easily ranks as one of the best three books published on the Islamic faith in the English language since the tragedy of 9/11. It is a profoundly eloquent, consistently reliable, comprehensive, insightful, and often brilliant testament of what it means to be a Muslim and what the religion of Islam is all about. Refreshing in its honesty, accessibility, and humility, and truly impressive in scope and depth, this is an indispensable book. Indeed this book is a necessary read not just for those who are interested in learning about Islam, but even more so for those who believe that they have learned all there is to know about Islam."

—Dr. Khaled Abou El Fadl, Professor of Islamic Law, UCLA School of Law

"There are few books that I would genuinely recommend to everybody I know, and you are holding one of them. Sumbul Ali-Karamali has written a lovely, lyrical, and learned book about living Islam. Whether you are an expert in the subject or a novice, a skeptic or a believer, you will find this book a treasure."

—Dr. Eboo Patel, Executive Director, Interfaith Youth Core

"Sumbul Ali-Karamali has written a book which is gripping, comprehensive and essential. With wit, honesty, and scholarship, she offers an account of what being Muslim means in a polarized world where the fault line is as grave as it is prejudiced. A masterpiece of simplicity that offers a groundbreaking testimony that will find its way to every household, in the U.S. and beyond, for Muslims and non-Muslims alike."

—Chibli Mallat, Ph.D. in Islamic Law; Professor of Law and Politics of the Middle East, SJ Quinney College of Law, University of Utah

"Sumbul Al-Karamali has a gift for explaining the ins and outs of Islam in a language understandable by all. As a practicing Muslim, she puts a human face on a religion that is grossly misunderstood and often feared in America. I recommend this book to anyone who wants to learn more about Islam from someone who lives it."

—FIROOZEH DUMAS, AUTHOR OF *FUNNY IN FARSI* AND
LAUGHING WITHOUT AN ACCENT

"A beautiful book. At a time when most Americans are bombarded with misinformation about Islam and, in particular American Muslims, Ali-Karamali has written an elegant corrective. For anyone who truly wants to know what Muslims believe, this is the perfect book."

—REZA ASLAN, AUTHOR, *NO GOD BUT GOD:
THE ORIGINS, EVOLUTION, AND FUTURE OF ISLAM*

"Sumbul Ali-Karamali has produced an intelligent, sensitive and highly readable study of Islam as it is experienced and interpreted by most Muslims. An important work that challenges the distorted views of the extremists and the prejudices of Islamophobes."

—DR. ALI ASANI, PROFESSOR OF THE PRACTICE OF INDO-MUSLIM
LANGUAGES AND CULTURES AT HARVARD UNIVERSITY; ADVISORY
BOARD OF THE PLURALISM PROJECT AT HARVARD UNIVERSITY

"Sumbul Ali-Karamali provides refreshing insight into an impressive range of issues concerning Islam. Her book is the journey of an American Muslim woman struggling with her identity, her tradition, and most importantly, her desire to simultaneously fit in with American culture while preserving her faith. Through the use of both personal anecdotes and extensive evidence from the Islamic tradition, she provides easy-to-read, credible, and thought-provoking analysis."

—IMAM FEISAL ABDUL RAUF, AUTHOR, *WHAT'S RIGHT WITH ISLAM*

"Sumbul Ali-Karamali lives according to her faith, with humor, good grace, and brilliance, so when she shares her insights, they ring true. I was a Catholic nun in my early life, so took particular interest in this modern, savvy woman's faith, which was, to be frank, a little scary to me. This book is fascinating; I couldn't put it down. I recommend it whole-heartedly to people of good will who are grappling with questions about Islam and Muslim in America today."

—ANN MCCORMICK, PH.D., FOUNDER OF THE LEARNING COMPANY

"This is a refreshingly frank and wonderfully accessible account of what it means to be an American Muslim woman today. Sumbul Ali-Karamali speaks from the heart as well as the head and she dispels many misconceptions about Islam today."

—DR. CAROLE HILLENBRAND, PROFESSOR OF
ISLAMIC HISTORY, UNIVERSITY OF EDINBURGH

The Muslim *Next Door*

The Qur'an,
the Media,
and that
Veil Thing

Sumbul Ali-Karamali

The Muslim *Next Door*

The Qur'an,
the Media,
and that
Veil Thing

White Cloud Press
Ashland, Oregon

Copyright © 2008 by Sumbul Ali-Karamali.
All rights reserved. No part of this book may be used or reproduced in
any manner whatsoever without written permission except in the case
of brief quotations embodied in critical articles and reviews.
Inquiries should be addressed to:
White Cloud Press
PO Box 3400
Ashland, Oregon 97520
www.whitecloudpress.com

Cover Photo by Evan Winslow Smith
Cover and interior design by Confluence Book Services

Printed in the United States of America
First edition: 2008

Library of Congress Cataloging-in-Publication Data

Ali-Karamali, Sumbul, The Muslim next door : the Qur'an, the media,
and that veil thing / By Sumbul Ali-Karamali.
p. cm. Includes index.
ISBN 978-0-9745245-6-6 (pbk.)
1. Islam--21st century. 2. Islam--Essence, genius, nature. 3. Muslims-
-Social life and customs--21st century. 4. Islam--Public opinion. I.
Title.
BP161.3.A374 2008
297--dc22
2008019896

For my parents,
with love and gratitude

Contents

A Note on the Qur'an

Muslims use the word "interpretation," and not "translation," when discussing the Qur'an. The reason is the importance, in Muslim tradition, of holding every word of the Qur'an sacred and not allowing it to be changed. A translation can never be 100 percent accurate, and so translations are not accepted as the real Qur'an but rather as aids in understanding it. In this book, I have quoted from primarily two translations (or interpretations): those of Muhammad Asad and A. J. Arberry. I like the former because of its clear and scholarly footnotes, which deeply explain contexts and alternative possible meanings of words. I like the latter because Arberry has tried to capture the poetic cadence of the Qur'an. The numbering of the verses can vary slightly, so sometimes verse 112 in the Asad edition can be more like 106 in the Arberry. That's something to keep in mind, in case you want to follow up on my footnotes.

Acknowledgements

Without my husband, I'm not sure if I ever would have written this book. I had idly considered the idea for years but never started on this path until he urged me to pursue a degree in Islamic law. Whenever I got discouraged, he threatened to finish the book for me and publish it himself. That was usually enough for me to leap back to work. Much of the credit for this book goes to him.

When I needed help, such as when I sprained one hand and sustained heavy burns on the other—from competing with my kids in the long jump and from cooking, respectively—my mother never hesitated to come and stay with me and help me with daily life so I could continue writing. During her absences, my father contrived to make do with frozen meals. So I thank them both for this book, as for everything else.

And more recently, without Michael Aldrich's gentle and irrepressible nagging, this book would have probably continued in limbo, where it had settled when I got sidetracked with other aspects of life. He urged me to join him "on the shelf," where his new history of Beijing resides, and badgered me until I dusted off my manuscript and started working on it again.

There are others to thank, too: my children, for their patience and forgiveness when I needed to work; Sabra Mazzaferro, Katie Hansen, and Shibani Patnaik for tracking down elusive books for my research; Chibli Mallat, Fayeq Oweis, and Abdullahi an-Naim for answering my questions; Carole Hillenbrand and John Esposito for their encouragement; Laila al-Zwaini for her friendship and her views on Islamic law; Laurel Mousseau for her unfailing support; and everyone at White Cloud Press.

And to everyone who ever asked me a well-intentioned question about Islam: this book is a result of your desire to cross cultures.

Introduction

My father tells a story of tea etiquette. In India, he says, if your host offers you tea, you must decline, because to immediately accept a cup of tea would show greed. If your host offers you tea again—as he must, if he is at all hospitable—you must decline a second time, showing your host consideration and a disinclination to be troublesome. But the third time your host offers you tea, as he will, because no host would willingly allow a guest to depart his house bereft of refreshment, *then* you may gratefully accept.

When my father arrived as a graduate student in California, alone and unknown, having left his new wife in India until he could save enough money to send for her—it would be two more years—many people in his university town invited him for meals or coffee. (Tea was relatively mysterious and unknown in 1960s California.) When his hosts offered him food or drink, my father declined, as is only polite. I can imagine how taken aback he must have been when his host acquiesced immediately and my father waited in vain and hungrily for another offer of food!

It was difficult enough adjusting to a strange country and its customs. Like other immigrants, he had no wish to appear more different than he already did. Struggling to assimilate into a new culture, coming from a country in which his religion was in the minority, my father certainly saw no reason to start discussing Islam with his American friends and acquaintances.

When I was a child, my father told me never to discuss religion, mine or anyone else's. He himself never has, because religion, he emphasized, should be a private matter, not a public one. I remember that his hair, still black then, sprouted in vertical peaks all over his head as it always did when he had been tugging at it to facilitate his thought processes. He told me India came to house one of the largest Muslim populations in the world because the indigenous Indians saw that the new Muslim immigrants were worthy people who believed in a humane religion that treated people as equals.

So do not talk about your religion, he said. Be the most worthy person you can be and *show* them, he said. Show them that to be a good Muslim means to be a good person. And that is what I tried to do.

But it didn't work.

Perhaps I was not a good enough person. Or perhaps I—and other Muslims—were too complacent, idealistic, and enmeshed in the daily struggles of balancing Islam and our Indian-Pakistani ethnicity with the culture of an American society that had barely heard of Islam. Above all, we were too silent. We never saw the stereotypes avalanching. We never realized those stereotypes were gradually wrapping themselves around the collective Western psyche with all the insidious menace of a choker vine, until they began to routinely represent a religion so warped and grossly distorted that we could no longer recognize it as our own.

Islam is not encapsulated in the grim, glaring *Newsweek* photograph of Osama bin Laden. Islam is not epitomized by the deeply angry, bearded face of Ayatollah Khomeini. Islam is not apotheosized by the suicide bomber who detonates civilians.

Islam *is* one of many American faiths. Muslims are ordinary people who share the same monotheistic tradition as Jews and Christians. We struggle with the same daily conflicts and challenges as our non-Muslim neighbors.

But the common Western perception of Islam has become a contorted, evil caricature of the real thing, like some reversed portrait of Dorian Gray, where the normal reality hides in the attic and the visible portrait becomes increasingly repulsive. Especially since the end of the Cold War, we in the United States have been bombarded with daily, unchecked, untrue, public denigration of Islam to an irresponsibly defamatory degree. The words of ill-informed fear-mongers, designed to convince us that Muslims are essentially different from the rest of humanity, are accepted by too many people as truth.

Islam is the second-largest and fastest-growing religion in the world, with somewhere between 1.3 and 1.8 billion adherents worldwide. What touches the souls of Muslims, over one-fifth of the world's population, so that they feel compelled to bow their heads to the One God, despite the dangers of hostility and ostracism?

A recent conversation I had with a friend guided the writing of this book. "Why do you live inside your religion?" she asked. "Why is an educated, thoughtful woman like you as committed to your religion as you are?"

This book attempts to answer these questions. It is my attempt to do differently what my father thought could be done so easily: to show what it means to be Muslim. It is an introduction, in anecdotes, of mainstream Islam from the viewpoint of a South-Asian American Muslim woman who grew up in a middle-class suburb of Los Angeles.

There exists no single Islam, no absolute interpretation of it—just as there is no single, absolute interpretation of Christianity or Judaism or any other religion. This book describes the basic beliefs and practices of mainstream Muslims throughout the world, illustrated with vignettes of life as an American Muslim.

Throughout the centuries, followers of every religion have interpreted their religions in myriad ways. Theological debates have raged since, well, Adam. And because it is difficult to know exactly what happened hundreds of years ago, historical debates surrounding religion have always raged, too. I do not explore those debates in this book. When faced with a plurality of views, I try to choose the majority view or, simply, my own view. My goal is to describe what is common to all Muslims and what is open to various interpretations.

At times, my interpretations may seem apologetic or far-fetched. I urge you to remember that Western notions of Islam have been received, for fourteen centuries, through the lenses of a Western culture that viewed Islam variously as an enemy, adversary, threat, and obstacle. This book endeavors to present an explanation of Islam that rarely got transmitted to the West.

I remember a *Star Trek* episode in which Captain Kirk (my first crush) landed on a planet whose people had been warring with another planet for centuries because of habit and a lack of incentive to stop, especially since they had managed to reduce the bloody, messy part of war to a deadly, but easy, computer game. The aliens explained that human beings were brutal and killed each other by nature. Warfare was more humane when conducted on the computer, and the victims simply walked into vaporizing machines to die.

I understand, replied Captain Kirk. Humans were barbaric, yes; they were brutal. But they were *capable* of getting up in the morning and saying to themselves, "You know, I don't think I'll kill anyone today. No, not today."

We humans may be barbaric and brutal, but we can get up every morning and strive for peace. And the first step in striving for peace is understanding the Other. In twenty-first-century America, the Other is Muslim.

Everyday Islam:
How Muslims Practice Their Religion

The adolescent dread of humiliating, nonconforming differences has fueled books and movies for decades. As a Muslim teenager in Southern California, I *personified* nonconformity. For years, I cringed whenever I recalled a high school telephone conversation that terminated shortly after the young man on the other end demanded, "What do you mean you can't go to the prom because of your *religion*?!"

My adolescent life never marched in rhythm with those of my non-Muslim friends. Balancing Muslim practices successfully with teenage life in Los Angeles was no easy feat. As a Muslim girl, I never dated and could not be alone with boys. I rarely attended parties and never attended dances, so I never learned to dance when all my peers did. Even now, the lurking prospect of encountering dancing at parties or corporate functions, even with my husband, never fails to incite, deep within my soul, the irrepressible urge to flee.

Leaving my non-Muslim friends in order to perform my prayers several times a day was uncomfortable. Abstaining from food and water during the fasting month of Ramadan evoked frankly incredulous stares. Those of my Muslim acquaintances who wore a head scarf, a *hijab*, wore daily visible evidence of their differences. Even for those of us not wearing a *hijab*, the common showers after gym class did not exactly facilitate adherence to the Muslim strictures on modesty. And those regulation bloomers we had to wear—! Well.

Although South-Asian Muslims populate many elementary schools in America now, this was not the case three decades ago. I was usually the only one in my school until my second year of law school. Until then, only once did I ever encounter another ethnically South-Asian Muslim student at school, and *he* was a lower life form as far as my fifteen-year-old self was concerned. Throughout my childhood, my parents endeavored to meet other Muslim families, and so I did come to have some Muslim friends near my age, but they all lived over thirty miles away.

My Muslim friends and I continually struggled to maintain both the traditionally Muslim and traditionally American aspects of our lives. It was difficult. Some of my Muslim acquaintances simply began leaning toward one culture, either totally assimilating into the Southern California scene and forgetting they were Muslim or retreating from California teenage life and socializing only with other Muslims. Some simply found it easier to associate with people like themselves, those who did not continually misunderstand them and their Muslim lifestyle and did not regard them as freaky. The retreat from California teenage culture did not constitute a rejection of American society. We were all American Muslims, but the perpetual tension involved in balancing the Indian Muslim identity with the American identity was exhausting.

Islam is a religion of orthopraxy, practice-oriented rather than doctrine-oriented. The practice of Islam, therefore, cannot be kept totally secret, much to adolescent dismay. Islam is often called a way of life rather than a religion. The Qur'an hardly differentiates between practical life and spiritual life. Muhammad,** the Prophet of Islam, led his community practically as well as spiritually.

The five basic tenets of Islam are the guidelines for how Muslims conduct their daily lives. These tenets, called the "five pillars" of Islam, are common in some form to many religions:

- The declaration of faith
- Prayer
- Fasting
- Pilgrimage
- Donation to charity

The only requirement for becoming a Muslim is the first pillar: the declaration of faith, or *shahada*. To declare faith in Islam, the words, "There is no god but God and Muhammad is the messenger of God" must be recited and wholeheartedly believed. That is all that is necessary to become a Muslim: pronouncement of and belief in this one statement. The remaining pillars have more to do with being a good Muslim once faith has been declared.

**When Muslims mention the Prophet Muhammad's name, they always utter the words "peace be upon him" immediately afterward, usually in Arabic. Since it would become cumbersome to repeat that continually in the text, I have omitted it. I mean no disrespect; if you are Muslim, consider it said between the lines.

The practices of Islam, mostly exemplified in the five pillars, may at first seem stranger than they actually are. (They certainly seemed strange to my junior high school peers.) Islamic practices are simply slightly different manifestations of the same basic tenets that frame many religions.

For example, nearly all religions require or advocate prayer in some form, as evidenced by churches, temples, synagogues, and other places of worship. Fasting in some form exists in both Judaism and Christianity, as well as other religions: Jews fast for Yom Kippur, and Catholics fast for Lent. Pilgrimage to a holy place is a familiar concept, too. Thousands of people annually flock to Jerusalem, a city holy to Islam, Christianity, and Judaism.

Prayer in Islam

"Now what would you do," asked my Sunday school teacher at the mosque, "if you were working and it was time to pray? Would you pray in your office or forego your prayers?"

We squirmed silently, not because we had no opinions, but because we were terrified of our teacher.

"What you would do," he continued austerely, "is pray when it was time to pray. I pray in my office, and if any of my colleagues come in, they see that I am praying and come back later."

We dubiously returned his severe regard. As students in junior high, we lived in trepidation of exposing ourselves to ridicule, and prayer in Islam is not exactly inconspicuous. It involves bowing, kneeling, standing upright, and reciting to oneself in Arabic. Interpreting something different as "bad" seems to be a universal human failing, and that is without even taking into account the mysterious thought processes of junior high school students.

Despite our apprehensions, when we did have to pray within sight of non-Muslims, in our dormitory rooms or at home when we had guests, we were encouraged at the lack of ridicule directed toward us. Generally, we encountered polite acceptance, perhaps because of sheer perplexity on the part of those observing, but more likely because prayer in some form is common to nearly all religions and most people respect and understand the concept, whatever the form it assumes and whether they pray or not.

In Islam, prayer takes a very structured form. As a Muslim, I must pray five times a day: dawn, early afternoon, late afternoon, sunset, and evening. These five prayers are mandatory, but I may perform extra prayers whenever I wish. Prayer times are not specific to the minute; rather, the day is divided into sections of time, and each prayer can be performed within a window of time. Prayers consist of certain passages from the Qur'an, recited in Arabic.

Muslims praying together execute actions and words of prayer at the same time, in response to the same words. That is why Muslims bend and straighten and kneel and touch their foreheads to the ground during prayer, all in synchrony. The prayer is concluded by looking to the right and reciting "*Assalamu Alaikum Varhamatullah*" ("Peace and the mercy of God be upon you") and then looking to the left and reciting it again. When Muslims look first right and then left, it is said, we greet each of our two recording angels.

This structured form may seem artificial to those who think of praying as asking God for protection or mercy, for example. But in Islam, worship and supplication are separate. The Muslim prayer is the ritual worship of God, spoken in Arabic. The supplication comes at the end of the prayer, when Muslims lift their hands and individually address God in any language, in a private communication that can include thankfulness and personal appeals.

In my family, we have a story about the strength of faith. My father was born in India just after his uncle died. My father's grandfather always said God had given him my father, his first grandson, to replace his own son. My father's mother had died in childbirth and, although his father lived, it was his grandparents who adored him most and raised him.

But when my father was a year old, he became very ill and feverish. The unanimous diagnosis was that the illness, whatever it was, would kill him. My great-grandfather spent the entire day in the neighborhood mosque, praying the ritual prayers and, at the end of each, kneeling with his hands uplifted and pleading, tremblingly, around the ache in his throat: "Please God, please. I know you can take him, and it's your right. I know that. But if you don't need him, then spare him, please God, and let me keep him . . . ."

As the sunlight darkened and the shadows gathered substance, my great-grandfather entreated God for the life of his baby grandson. His eyes wet and unfocused, he heard a voice at his shoulder.

"Leave it," said the voice. "Leave it! Leave him. Leave the child."

My great-grandfather turned and saw no one. But after sitting still and wonderingly on the quiet floor for many minutes, he looked through the arched opening in the wall to see his wife outside, walking toward the mosque along the rooftops of the huddled houses. She caught his eye, waved, and called, "For heaven's sake, are you going to spend all night there, then, in the mosque? He's all right! Come home! He's *playing!*"

My great-grandfather raised my father. He died in India while my father was a student in California, before he could save up enough money to return to India and visit him. The last words my great-grandfather had said to him were, "Come back soon."

Muslims must show great deference to God while praying, because we are speaking directly to God in God's presence during this ritual of worship. To that end, we wash our hands, face, and feet before praying. A clean place to pray and clean clothes in which to pray are required. Both men and women must be covered; no shorts are allowed for anyone. Women cover their hair during the prayer, even if they do not at other times of the day. Men also may wear caps.

My supervisor at my first full-time job after college rolled her eyes when I told her why women cover their hair while praying. She said sarcastically, "Because hair is so *indecent!*"

No, not indecent. Head covering is simply a way of showing respect and has been throughout the world, among various races and religions, for millennia. One of my Catholic friends told me that when she was young, she and other women always covered their hair in church. Similarly, most of my acquaintances would not attend church or temple wearing a bikini top and hot pants. It is the same concept with different parameters.

When praying, all Muslims face Mecca, Muhammad's birthplace in modern-day Saudi Arabia. It is possible to buy prayer rugs with tiny compasses embedded in the decorative borders. Once we have begun our prayer, we may not look anywhere but at the ground until the prayer has ended. We must ignore all other stimuli and may not talk (other than speaking the words of the prayer), laugh, leave, or otherwise "break" the prayer.

Emergencies are the exception. "Like if a cobra leaps onto your prayer rug and rears its head back so it can sink its fangs into you?" my eight-year-old self asked my mother, who sighed and replied, "Yes, or if you see a child about to fall or hurt itself." The cobra seemed to be a greater probability to me.

All prayers may be performed at home, individually, but also may be prayed in the mosque. Even those who rarely go to the mosque to pray often attend to perform the Friday midday prayer there.

When I was young, I worried about Friday the thirteenth. I felt I had become an authority, having read several children's books on the subject of curses. Once my mother understood my apprehension, she told me this: God gave us every day as a gift. If anything, she said, Fridays were days particularly close to God, whether or not they fell on the thirteenth of the month.

Because Muslims gather at the mosque for the Friday midday prayer, Friday tends to be a holiday from work in some Muslim countries. Fridays have been referred to as the "Muslim Sabbath," but that is really more of an attempt to equate aspects of Islam to the familiarity of Christianity. Rather, the Friday midday prayer is simply a traditional time to gather at the mosque to pray.

In the mosque, prayers are led by the *imam*, who recites portions of the prayer aloud and keeps everyone synchronized. During the prayer, the *imam* functions somewhat like the conductor of an orchestra; it is not uncommon for thousands of people to participate in a single prayer. The *imam* may simply be someone who can recite enough verses to lead the prayer, or he may be someone who is learned in Islamic jurisprudence. It is not always possible to discern which kind of *imam* you have. Certainly, the goal is to find someone learned, as well as capable of leading the prayer. Whenever Muslims pray in a group, anyone may assume the role of prayer leader.

Although it is rare, women have historically led prayers and continue to do so today. The Prophet Muhammad, far back in the seventh century, appointed at least one woman as the *imam* over her household, even though her household included men.[1] Amina Wadud, professor of Islamic Studies at Virginia Commonwealth University, has led prayers as an *imam*. I will define *imam* further in chapter six.

My friends often asked me, and still ask, whether I attend a "church." Attending a mosque, the nearest equivalent to a church in Islam, is not one of the five pillars of Islam. Mosques are really only gathering places, not innately holy buildings. They have no real structural or program requirements, except that prayers are always held there. Although Muslims hold group prayers in mosques, these are just the individual prayers that Muslims must perform five times a day, except that everyone prays them at the same time in the mosque. Praying at home is no less valid a religious act.

Attending prayers at the mosque does not incur any religious credit in Islam. A mosque does not even necessarily have a religious authority in charge of it, given that an *imam* is sometimes simply one who leads the prayer (although he can be more than that, as we'll discuss in chapter six).

A friend visited a mosque once and asked me whether every mosque included stained glass in its decor. A mosque can be someone's garage (the one I attended as a child was a *two*-car garage), or it can be the spectacular mosque of Suleiman the Magnificent in Turkey, whose delicate, yet massive, soaring architecture and intricate mosaic artistry I sought vainly to capture on film. My friend, still troubled by her imprecise mental picture, asked me whether every mosque offered donuts after prayers.

Whatever takes place at the mosque besides prayer just depends upon the people attending. No particular decoration is required. Wedding ceremonies may be held, but need not be held, there. My own wedding took place at a hotel. During Ramadan, many Muslims go to the mosque daily to break their fasts, pray special Ramadan prayers, and (in some places) distribute food to the poor. The mosque itself has no innate religious significance, except as a symbol of Muslim belief or as an historical landmark.

In fact, before we progressed to the two-car garage, my family would meet with other Muslim families in the living room of whichever family had a house large enough to accommodate even our admittedly sparse numbers. The adults discussed religious issues. At least I assume they did. As one of the children running around playing games, I never really knew what they talked about. I just thought of it as a time to meet with my one Muslim friend, who lived forty-five minutes away.

Although our two-car garage fulfilled basic requirements for a mosque, a garage obviously is not the limit of what a mosque can be. As Muslims have become more numerous in the United States, mosques have been built to accommodate their traditional function as the hub of Muslim society, as they are still in other parts of the world. The great mosques of the Middle East traditionally housed hospitals, libraries, and schools, as well as prayer rooms. They were arenas for political discussion and the airing of public affairs.

All mosques do look very different from churches, at least on the inside. Because Islamic tradition prohibits any visual depiction of Muhammad, angels, or other religious figures (the next chapter elaborates upon this), the only adornments allowed in mosques are unrepresentative, such as geometric and arabesque patterns painted or set in mosaics or perhaps delicately complex Arabic calligraphy of Qur'anic verses. We had nothing so grand in the mosque I attended; décor may just barely have extended to travel posters. In fact, I never saw a mosque that was built specifically to *be* a mosque until I visited Istanbul in my twenties.

Nicer mosques have carpets on which prayers are held. In our two-car garage, we had old sheets. The important thing was that we had a clean place to stand, which is why our shoes were always left at the doorstep. Some mosques also have an enclosure of some kind with running water, like a fountain (or, more prosaically, a bathroom), where worshipers can wash their hands, face, and feet before coming into the mosque. At home, I and my family members now have prayer rugs on which to pray. When I was young and it was difficult to find Muslims, much less prayer rugs, in the United States, we used a twin sheet folded twice into a rectangle.

Women cover their heads when praying; but we are sometimes asked to cover our heads before entering the mosque, as well. When I visited the Blue Mosque in Istanbul, a smiling oak tree of a man stood on the doorstep of the main entrance, his arm tucked around a straw laundry basket from which he affably pulled brightly colored scarves and handed them to women who, like me, did not have their heads covered. I did not mind—every culture shows respect in different ways.

On that same trip to Istanbul, my husband and I shared a bus one day with a Saudi couple. *She* was very nice. *He* informed me arrogantly that if I would only read the Qur'an (I had) I would know that only Muslims are allowed in mosques. I argued for a while and then lapsed into a fulminating silence while my husband patted my hand. It is not true that only Muslims can enter mosques. Every mosque I have ever heard of in America or any other country I have visited has been open to all religions and races. My own mosque invites non-Muslims to visit and break fast during Ramadan.

I must say, though, that my husband bumped into the strangely twisted exception when he visited the West African country of Mali. Though Muslim, he was disallowed entry into a mosque because he was not black. Not *black*? I was outraged. Muhammad, the Prophet of Islam, was not black, either, but he had followers of all colors, black and white and in between. In fact, the Qur'an specifically states that we are none of us better than others because of race or ancestry.

In every mosque, the women stand in lines to pray; the men form separate lines. The reason is modesty. Since Muslims stand very close to one another while praying—"Stand shoulder to shoulder!" is the common entreaty—it is considered immodest for men to stand so close to women. So women pray in different lines, in a different area, or sometimes in a different room entirely.

In the mosque I attended as a child, men usually sat on one side of the room to listen to the "sermon," and women sat on the other. The women's prayer lines were behind the men's lines. Where women stand exactly, whether they go to the mosque at all, and whether they are totally covered are all matters of local custom and not religion. The status of women in Islam is discussed in more detail in chapter seven, but I want to stress from the outset that the treatment of women in Islam is usually a cultural issue and not a religious one.

I understand the idea that men and women should not be touching each other while praying, because I can see how that might be distracting. But I see no reason for women to be treated unfairly because of this concept of modesty. Standing on two sides of the room with the *imam* at the front seems equitable to me, but standing behind the men is insulting because the men *never* stand behind the women. (If they took turns, that would be different.) And I do resent being shut away in a different room entirely, in which the *imam*'s sermon brokenly crackles on an inevitably malfunctioning public address system.

Besides, the historical record shows that women in the Prophet's time prayed unsegregated from men.[2] If the Prophet didn't mind, I don't see why the local *imam* should.

Despite the choreographic imperfections at mosques, I do go when I can, because I am so rarely in the presence of other Muslims in my life. It is difficult to feel isolated in one's beliefs, whether they relate to politics, religion, child-raising, or anything else. I find solace, especially in these divisive times, in hearing the familiar sing-song chanting of the Arabic verses of the Qur'an.

In the grand variety of mosque, the *muezzin* calls the faithful to prayer from the minaret, or tower in the mosque. This "call to prayer," or *azan*, is always proclaimed before every prayer in every mosque in every Muslim country.

Our two-car garage lacked a minaret. Even so, someone always came forward and declared the *azan* in Arabic. Especially when someone with a beautiful voice proclaims it in the elongated, ornamental chanting of Qur'anic recitation, the *azan* is compelling to hear:

> God is most great. (*Allahu Akbar!*)
> God is most great. (*Allahu Akbar!*)
> I testify that there is no god but God.
> (*Ash-haduan la illaha il-Allah!*)

> I testify that Muhammad is the Prophet of God.
> (*Ash-haduana Muhammad-ur-Rasulullah!*)
> Arise and pray. (*Haya alas-Salah!*)
> Arise and flourish. (*Haya alal-Falah!*)
> God is most great. (*Allahu Akbar!*)
> God is most great. (*Allahu Akbar!*)
> There is no god but God. (*La illaha il-Allah.*)

As the *muezzin* in his neighborhood mosque in northern India, my great-grandfather called everyone to prayer five times a day. Such was the strength of his voice that Muslims who lived nearly two miles away routinely came to the mosque in answer to his call to prayer. It was an accepted truth that sometimes at dawn, when the air was still, even those sleeping in their beds three miles away from the mosque would awaken to the clear sound of my great-grandfather calling to them to arise and pray, arise and flourish.

A colleague of my husband's complained that when he traveled to Muslim countries on business, the call to prayer awakened him before every dawn. "And it's not," he said, "a pretty sound, I assure you."

Now that depends upon your point of view. Granted, my view might be more jaundiced if my sleep were daily extinguished by someone shouting "Allahu Akbar!" for the sole purpose of waking me and the whole city at 5 a.m., especially if I did not blearily agree with the message. But I have always thought the call to prayer was beautiful. Next time you hear the *muezzin* calling the faithful to prayer from a minaret (or lack of one), you might judge for yourself.

God first informed Muhammad that his followers must pray fifty times a day, or so one of my favorite stories is related. This occurred during Muhammad's mystical night journey from Mecca to Jerusalem, an inconceivable distance by camel and thus a miracle in itself. The night journey was followed by an ascension to heaven (the *miraj*), during which Muhammad traversed the seven heavens and traveled even further, to Paradise, to tremble awestruck in the presence of God. The Dome of the Rock in Jerusalem, built by Muslims in the seventh century, is said to cover the very place from which Muhammad departed to the heavens. That is why Jerusalem is one of the holiest places in Islam. Muhammad met many prophets on this journey to heaven, Moses among them.

When Moses heard that God had required prayer to be performed fifty times a day, he shook his head incredulously and advised Muhammad that his followers would never be able to pray that often.

"Ask for a reduction," Moses urged.

Muhammad did as Moses suggested, and God reduced the requirement to forty prayers a day.

When Muhammad returned with this new result, Moses clutched his hair and said (the equivalent of), "Are you out of your *mind*? I *know* these people. I used to *live* with them. They'll *never* pray forty times a day. Go back and ask again."

So God reduced the required number of prayers to thirty.

Moses probably flung up his hands in frustration. He sent Muhammad back. God reduced the requirement to twenty prayers a day. Moses lost patience. The number was reduced to ten and then, finally, five so that Muhammad might have a chance of succeeding.

Moses remained skeptical, but Muhammad, ashamed, refused to plead further. The requirement since then has been five prayers a day and has been, probably to everyone's surprise, relatively successful. (I cannot help thinking that God must have been teasing.)

Muhammad encountered other prophets, too, as he traversed the seven heavens. He watched various souls meted rewards or punishments according to their deeds and shielded his eyes against the glare of the fires of hell. In the highest of the heavens, he met Abraham, who sat near the gate to Paradise. And in Paradise he bowed before God, who gave him the duty of prayer.

It is generally accepted that Dante based his *Divine Comedy* on the story of Muhammad's night ascension to heaven.[3] I read the *Divine Comedy* in my first few months of college, never realizing this. It is clear, though, that the general plan and also many details of the *Divine Comedy* come from an embellished version of Muhammad's night ascension that was translated from Arabic to Latin.[4] How ironic that Dante filched the story of Muhammad's experience and then consigned him to one of the lowest levels of hell in his *Divine Comedy*!

The frequency of prayer was established, then, after Muhammad's night journey. In junior high, a friend in my algebra class asked me if I ever recited the words without really meaning them, without pouring my soul into them, especially since I prayed so many times a day.

"Doesn't praying so much," my friend asked, "diminish the value of the prayer?"

I must confess that sometimes I do rush through my prayer because I am running late. Sometimes I do mumble the words with insufficient clarity because I am too exhausted to move my lips after fourteen hours of chasing my small children. Sometimes I do pray with less attention on the words I am reciting and more attention on whether my toddler is contemplating danger on the other side of the room. I can only hope that I am forgiven.

But I must also say that even when my prayer is rushed and not properly pious, the very act of stopping whatever I am doing and praying the ritual prayer, for the simple reason that it is time to pray, is itself a reminder of God and an act of piety. The average preschooler imposes three demands per minute on his primary care provider—that would be me—which means that any thoughts unrelated to meeting those demands with patience, including thoughts of God, are banished. It is not always easy to remember prayers and halt the continuing onrush of life in order to perform them. The goal, of course, is to focus on the words of the prayer as a real communication with God and to worship with the utmost concentrated sincerity. But I hope that even when I fall pitifully short of that standard, I receive some credit from my recording angels when I greet them at my right shoulder and at my left.

Prayer in Islam has a number of functions. Its frequency means it is a constant reminder of God. When prayer is held in congregation, it coalesces the Muslim community. It is a very powerful feeling to pray alongside and in synchrony with thousands of people, all focused on the same soul-deep activity. Prayer in Islam is always a direct, personal communication to God from every individual, whatever his or her class, race, status, or gender, without the need for an intermediary.

Fasting and Holidays

Many religions prescribe some form of fasting. Islam requires fasting only during the lunar month of Ramadan, though anyone can fast anytime as an optional personal devotion to God. During Ramadan, Muslims fast every day from dawn, which is approximately ninety minutes before sunrise, to sunset. During the fast, Muslims abstain from food, water, sex, and smoking.

Ramadan tests everyone. Fasting for thirty days is—forgive me—no picnic. No food or water until sunset? When I was growing up, most reactions from non-Muslim acquaintances concerning fasting fell into two categories. The majority opinion was that fasting was too dangerous (it wasn't); the minority opinion was that fasting was really just like missing lunch (it wasn't). Both camps unanimously viewed it as pointless.

Islam requires fasting for several reasons. The Qur'an says, "God desires your well-being, not your discomfort. He desires you to fast the whole month so that you may magnify Him and render thanks to Him for giving you his guidance."[5] The connection between fasting and prayer has long been acknowledged in many religions; somehow, one enhances the other. Fasting teaches self-control, introspection, and discipline, all emphasized in Islam. And finally, no better way exists to experience even a fraction of what it must be like to starve. Believe me, we do not take food or water for granted during Ramadan.

The most common question I am asked is, "But do children fast?" Fasting in Islam is meant for healthy adults. Fasting is not required of children or those who are ill, pregnant, elderly, nursing a baby, menstruating, or traveling. The fast is meant to be difficult but not dangerous. To that end, most Muslims awake before the fast starts (in the summer months, this can be at an uncivilized 3 a.m.) in order to eat and drink. It can be centuries until sunset.

Though fasting may be undertaken at different times of the year, fasting during Ramadan has special significance and is mandatory for those who are able. It was during Ramadan that God first revealed the Qur'an to Muhammad. Ramadan also commemorates the Prophet and his followers, who were laid under siege and deprived of food and water.

Muslims participate in special traditions during Ramadan. For example, we pray extra prayers at nighttime. In Egypt, artisans painstakingly craft glittering confections from old tin cans and colored glass and place candles inside; children swing the glowing "Ramadan lanterns" along the dusky streets, singing the obscure but traditional words of a song thousands of years old. Those whom they pass bestow upon them nuts and sweets. Feeding others during Ramadan is approved of by God (though not required), so I and my family always attended many dinner parties during Ramadan. In some countries, neighbors send dishes of food to each other in time for the breaking of the fast.

The most special night of the month is the Night of Power (*Lailat al-Qadr*), usually said to occur on the twenty-seventh day of Ramadan. The Night of Power commemorates the evening Muhammad received the first revelation from God. Prayers on the Night of Power, it is said, reach God with more strength and clarity than on any other night. Nature is infused with a heightened awareness. On this night, devout Muslims stay awake as late as possible at home and at the mosque, praying, eating, and socializing.

Breaking a fast intentionally is very, very sinful, unless the fasting person becomes ill or needs medication, in which case the fast should be broken. But the idea of "cheating a little" is totally alien to the practice of fasting in Islam and a shocking concept; once a Muslim has begun a fast, she may not intentionally eat or drink—even a little!—until sunset. Accidentally eating or drinking while fasting is rare but not unheard of. Stomachs growl and throats get parched, and it is easy to forget that we cannot eat or drink until sunset. Mistakenly eating or drinking does not break the fast.

I remember making lemonade for a party, once, while fasting. I was about fifteen. I added the sugar, stirred, and unthinkingly tasted a spoonful. My mother found me standing perfectly still in the kitchen, the pitcher of lemonade clutched in one hand, the slow-dripping spoon in the other, consternation on my face. She smiled and told me that accidentally eating during a fast was a gift from God, because God made me forget that I was fasting.

During the Ramadan that fell during December of 2001, the Pope called upon Catholics to fast for a day to show solidarity with Muslims. More than one Christian church (Catholic and otherwise) in Southern California rallied its members to fast during the whole month or part of it. The Christians who fasted during Ramadan did not necessarily follow the strict rules of the Islamic fast—rather, they all fasted in various ways, according to what they could do. The sole fact that anyone would wish to fast at *all*, just to show such generous solidarity, indescribably moved me.

I cannot help comparing the Christian "solidarity fast" with a high school experience, in which I futilely tried to hide the fact that I was fasting. I remember running a mile, having had no food or water, for a physical fitness test. I clearly should not have done this, but my physical education teacher would have stared blankly if I had interrupted his coaching to explain that I could not participate because my religion did not allow me any food or water until sunset. Most people I knew had barely heard of Islam, except in connection with Khomeini, and knew very little of Islamic practices. Imagine being the P.E. teacher and skeptically listening to a fourteen-year-old trying to squirm out of running because (she said) she could not eat or drink because of her religion!

"Why go without water?" asked another teacher I could not avoid telling. "Okay, a lot of people don't have enough to eat, but everyone has water."

But not everyone does. In parts of the world where the desert is endless and the heat oppressive, water is much more precious than it is in first-world countries. In Iraq, for example, as in Africa, people are dying for lack of drinkable water. In California, we have years of drought, it is true, but the faucet always emits water when I turn it. Certainly, during Muhammad's time, water was cherished and scarce in the sands of Arabia. The Arabic word for the Islamic guidelines of life is *Shari'a*, which means "the road to the watering place." That is a poetic image if you live in the desert.

Fasting Muslims are enjoined to turn their thoughts to matters more spiritual than bodily. We must donate extra charity during Ramadan, in addition to our regular charity. Special care must be taken not to become angry or impatient or nasty; that is always the goal, of course, but especially true during Ramadan. Having stated the goal of conduct during Ramadan, I must say that most of us do get unbearably grumpy and extremely tired. Most of us find the exhaustion and inability to concentrate more debilitating than the hunger and thirst. It is difficult to deal with everyday life when hungry and thirsty. Every year, Muslims fast precisely to remember first-hand this sometimes forgettable truth and to experience the circumstances of people for whom every day is like a fasting day.

My husband and I renovated our house one year, fully expecting to live in it during the whole process; but one unexpected construction crisis after another necessitated our moving from friends to hotels to parents nine times in three months. We had two small children, the weather was freezing, rats had nested all over our unheated and partially constructed house, and we were fasting because of Ramadan.

I regularly reminded myself how paltry these difficulties were in the grand scheme of things, but not eating or drinking makes everything seem insurmountable. Tempers cannot be much stemmed. My husband's strategy in coping with Ramadan was to awaken for the pre-dawn meal, drink a quart of the strongest coffee available to humankind, and go straight to work at 4:30 a.m., since he could not give up his caffeine and still function. We searched unflaggingly for hotels with coffee facilities.

As for me, not only had I sacrificed my caffeine addiction so I could go without tea during Ramadan, I was the parent our toddler called for at night, traumatized without her own bed, own bathroom, own kitchen, and so on. I failed to reconcile gracefully the sleep-caffeine-food-water deprivation very well with the exhortation to patience and cheerfulness of demeanor. The moral of the story: never renovate your house during Ramadan. Oh yes, and aspire to good conduct.

Eid ul-Fitr

The day after the last day of Ramadan is the most celebrated Muslim holiday of the year, *Eid ul-Fitr,* which means the "Festival of Fast-Breaking."
A special Eid prayer is held in the mosque and followed by feasting (what
else but feasting after a month of fasting?), visiting, and gift-giving. We
traditionally wear fancy, brand-new clothes on Eid, if possible, but always
combined with at least one old piece of clothing to keep us humble.

The importance of food after a month of fasting cannot be overstated.
In India and Pakistan, the traditional food on Eid is called *sheer khurma,*
a creamy pudding made of milk, vermicelli noodles, golden raisins, and
pistachios. Were we to betake ourselves on Eid visits and not taste *sheer
khurma* at every house, we would risk incurring life-long umbrage;
everyone concocts their own special version that must be savored and
complimented. Muslims of all ethnic backgrounds came to the mosque
I attended as a child, and I always thought the best part was tasting all
the different kinds of traditional food.

Whereas Indians and Pakistanis make *sheer khurma,* Egyptians bake
kahk, powdered-sugar dusted cookies with nuts nestled in the middle.
Another Eid dessert, *Umm Ali* ("mother of Ali"), consists of thin pastry
sheets cooked in cream, nuts, and fruits. Muslims in other Middle Eastern
countries, such as Jordan, bake cookies that hide sweet date mixtures
within their centers. During Ramadan, Palestinians make *qatayef,* pancakes
with a variety of sweet fillings.

The Turks serve *konafeh al-id,* layers of pastry, soaked in syrup and filled
with sweet custard-like cheese and nuts. During Ramadan evenings, they
eat rose-scented *gullac* wafers in cream sauce; according to tradition, the
cook must recite prayers over the *gullac* mixture or it will not attain the
correct consistency. (It must be particularly chancy to confect.)

The varied, colorful, shiny new clothes were the second best part of
Eid. We were all different: Indians and Pakistanis wore shimmery, flowing
silky clothes often embroidered with gold or beads. Our Egyptian and
Turkish friends wore blouses and long skirts and sometimes long, elegant
tailored coats over them. Some men wore suits and some wore traditional
long tunics or coats over loose trousers. Many men and little boys wore
crisp white shirts, black caps, and vests embroidered with dense patterns
of gold thread.

These days, my husband and I host an annual Eid dinner party for
fifty of our friends, Muslim and non-Muslim alike. We greet them at the
door and offer them scent for their wrists. We sprinkle rose water on their

shoulders to welcome them to the house. We burn incense and bestow gifts on all the children. I paint henna in intricate floral designs on the palms of adventuresome guests; the henna leaves a rich, dark-red stain that adorns their hands for a few weeks before it fades away.

At our house, Eid dinner must include, at the very least, *samosas* (triangular pastries filled with spicy potatoes) and *biriyani* (saffron rice with spices, nuts, and chicken). These dishes constitute holiday food in North India, which means "comfort food" to me. We serve *sheer khurma* for dessert, along with a platter piled high with sticky Indian sweets, spherical and flat, rectangular and pretzel-shaped, orange and white and green and pink. Upon leaving the party, our guests receive a pouch of bright cloth tied with a ribbon, containing dates for remembrance and sugared almonds for luck.

In many countries, Muslims celebrate Eid for three days. But here in the United States, even getting a day off for Eid is difficult for many. In fact, when I was a child, Eid was never as much fun as I annually hoped, although my mother did all she could.

She stayed up all night sewing Indian clothes, which I loved, for my brother and me. She always made *sheer khurma* for breakfast, though she must have been exhausted. We attended the Eid prayer at the mosque, and we received gifts of money. But my father usually had to teach and all the Muslims we knew lived so far away that visiting was difficult. We had no relatives in the United States, either. In those days, we did not have nearby Indian restaurants or sweet shops or clothing stores. We never saw Eid decorations in stores, never heard Eid songs in shopping malls, and never encountered any indication from the outside world that Eid was special, in the way Christmas, Easter, and Hanukkah were. My mother did her best, but Eid always seemed bereft of any festive atmosphere.

My husband and I are establishing our own traditions for our children, since we never had that many, growing up. They know to expect a treasure hunt for presents, a visit to the Indian sweet shop, and a huge party. I take food to their classrooms to share, too. We keep the old traditions, so we don new clothes (with an old piece inside for humility), attend the Eid prayer at the mosque, visit anyone who is home, breakfast on *sheer khurma*, and give the kids a holiday from school.

Eid ul-Adha

Eid ul-Adha, or the "Festival of the Sacrifice," arrives sixty-nine days after Eid ul-Fitr and commemorates God's test of Abraham's faith, an event described in the Old Testament, as well as the Qur'an. God sent Abraham a dream in which he was told to sacrifice his son to God. Agonized, Abraham consulted his son, who composedly told his father that if God required the sacrifice, then obviously it was necessary and please get on with it. Just as Abraham drew his knife, God sent down a lamb in the boy's place.

The Old Testament story is different from the Qur'anic version in one respect: in the Old Testament, Isaac was the son Abraham nearly sacrificed to God. In the Qur'an, it was Ismail, Isaac's elder half-brother. Abraham's story and its significance in Islam is discussed further in the next chapter.

Eid ul-Adha is celebrated in much the same way as Eid ul-Fitr, except that on Eid ul-Adha, a lamb is traditionally sacrificed and the meat is given to the poor. Eid ul-Adha is sometimes called the "Little Eid" because it is not celebrated with as much enthusiasm as Eid ul-Fitr. While important, Eid ul-Adha always seems to catch everyone by surprise, especially in the United States, where it does not appear on calendars and usually falls on a working day.

Other Holidays

Muslims commemorate a few more occasions during the year, although in my family and my particular Muslim community we did not celebrate any except for Eid. *Milad al-Nabi* celebrates the birthday of the Prophet Muhammad. *Ashura* commemorates the death of al-Husayn, the Prophet's grandson, at Karbala. Shi'i Muslims, whom we discuss in chapter five, mark it particularly sorrowfully. The Night Journey and ascension to heaven of the Prophet is another holiday and is called *Isra wal miraj*.

The only other kind of Muslim party we attended besides Eid was when someone gave a party for a child who had memorized for the first time (usually around age four) some verses of the Qur'an.

Muslims may celebrate any holiday that does not conflict with Islamic principles. Easter definitely does. Christmas, viewed narrowly as Jesus' birthday, does not, although some of the surrounding Christian traditions do conflict with Islam, such as the depiction of angels, of Jesus, and of the manner of his death. Despite that, I often give Christmas presents to neighbors, friends, my children's teachers, or anyone inviting me to celebrate Christmas with them. My husband's mother is Christian, so we usually help her celebrate Christmas. My Lebanese advisor in gradu-ate school told me that in his home town of Beirut, all the Christians celebrated Eid with the Muslims and all the Muslims celebrated Christmas with the Christians. I always thought that was the right attitude.

My favorite childhood holiday was Thanksgiving. It was the only holiday my family celebrated in common with the rest of America, and it was nice to fit in for once. It was a relief to be able to answer the question, "What did you have for Thanksgiving?" when I could never give a simple answer to "What did you get for Christmas?" or "What did you do for Easter?" Anybody can give thanks.

The Islamic Calendar

Living in a country and world that follow the solar calendar can be frustrating if your holidays fall according to the lunar calendar. The Islamic calendar is based on the lunar cycle and contains 354 days in a year, divided into twelve months, of which Ramadan is the ninth. Because the lunar year is shorter than the solar year, Ramadan occurs ten or eleven days earlier every year than it did the previous solar year.

The Islamic calendar is never adjusted by the addition of extra days. Currently, Ramadan falls in the winter months, but when I was in college, it arrived in early summer. In a little over thirty-six years, Ramadan will be back where it started.

That aspect of the lunar calendar does not bother me. What does cause me ongoing frustration is that we Muslims can never be sure exactly when our holidays will fall until the day before they are upon us. The reason for this relates to the new moon.

When the new moon appears, the following day is the first day of the next lunar month. Every lunar month is twenty-nine or thirty days, and whether the next month starts on the thirtieth or thirty-first day depends on whether someone sights the new moon. Eid ul-Fitr falls on the first day of the month of *Shawwaal*. That means the moon must be sighted the night before to determine whether the following day is Eid or whether the day following that one is Eid.

We live in the same time zone as my parents. But sometimes, their local mosque reports a sighting of the moon and my local mosque does not. That means Eid falls on different days for us.

Why, you may reasonably ask, cannot we simply look at a calendar to see when the new moon will be? Are we not advanced in astronomy? Can we not calculate the presence of the new moon?

Yes, we can. We have the technology. We could predict the new moon and put the date of Eid on the calendar. Everyone could celebrate on the same day and be spared ongoing frustration. But, the Prophet said that when we *see* the new moon, the next day will be the first day of the next lunar month. Many people, bound to tradition, insist that the moon must actually be seen with the naked eye. Traditions are hard to abolish, especially when based on the words of the Prophet from almost fourteen centuries ago.

This was one reason Eid was boring when I was growing up. Not knowing the exact day of our holiday meant Muslim parents could not take the day, whichever it was, off. It was hard to be festive when everyone headed for their offices after 7 a.m. prayers at the mosque.

In recent years, many mosques have taken a middle view. They announce somewhat beforehand the day on which Eid prayers will be held, basing their announcement on the date the new moon ought to appear, the weather conditions that might affect visibility, and whether the moonrise will occur at a time when the daylight or the sun would obscure the moon. This way, at least we can be informed a week ahead when Eid will be.

In my opinion, it is still not good enough. I believe if the Prophet could have calculated the new moon months ahead, he would have done so. The pursuit of knowledge is sacrosanct in Islam, and we would know for certain when to take the day off and plan a celebration.

Pilgrimage

Pilgrimage, or *Hajj* (meaning "effort"), in Islam is another of the five pillars. A Muslim must pilgrimage to Mecca once in his or her lifetime, if it can be managed without hardship. The Ka'ba has been the focus of pilgrimage since before Muhammad and, Muslims believe, since the beginning of humankind.

Muslims believe God gave Adam a special stone, called the Black Stone, when he was expelled from heaven. Adam built the first house in which to worship God. This house was destroyed in Noah's flood. But later, Abraham and Ismail rebuilt the house of God, the Ka'ba, in Mecca, incorporating into it the original Black Stone.

Abraham left Mecca, but Ismail settled there. Over the centuries, Ismail's descendants forgot the purpose of the Ka'ba and converted it into a shrine for paganism. One of Muhammad's duties was to restore the Ka'ba to its original purpose, the worship of the One God.

The Ka'ba is now the most important Muslim holy place and the site of the *Hajj*. Muslims pray facing toward the Ka'ba. The pilgrimage lasts up to seven days. Male pilgrims wear two sheets of unstitched, wrapped white cloth to equalize them. Women may wear anything as long as they leave only the hands and face uncovered. The pilgrims all leave worldly possessions behind.

I have not yet made my pilgrimage to Mecca, so I cannot discuss it firsthand. But I have known several people and have heard tales of many whose spirituality has been sparked or solidified by it. To be one of millions of pilgrims can be, I understand, a powerfully gripping experience.

Certain rituals are performed in connection with the pilgrimage, such as: circumambulating the Ka'ba seven times, starting at the Black Stone; running (well, walking) between two nearby hills; and stoning a pillar representing Satan. Running between the two hills symbolizes Ismail's mother's frantic search for water in the desert. Stoning the pillar recreates Abraham's throwing of stones at the devil in rejection of his insinuating whispers.

It is at the end of the *Hajj* that Eid ul-Adha takes place.

Charity

Every adult Muslim of sound mind must annually donate a percentage of his or her total wealth to charity, unless debts are owed. This is called *zakat*. During Ramadan, extra charity is due in addition to the *zakat*. The Qur'an requires charity and approves of anonymity:

> If you do deeds of charity openly, it is well; but if you bestow it upon the needy in secret, it will be even better for you, and it will atone for some of your sins. And God is aware of all that you do.[6]

In the past, sometimes the charity was levied as a tax and distributed by the state. Otherwise, it is a personal requirement.

Other Islamic Practices

Dietary Restrictions

The two dietary restrictions that Muslims most often come up against in the Western world are the prohibitions against pork and alcohol (as part of the prohibition against anything that intoxicates). Other items Muslims cannot eat are carrion, blood, and animals with fangs. ("Do eels have fangs?" I once asked my husband hopefully, peering doubtfully into the plate of wriggly sushi he had brought home.) Anything not forbidden in Islam is allowed, such as seafood (without fangs).

Abstaining from alcohol has become increasingly common in the United States, and nobody stares at me in shock when I order a mineral water with dinner. (Student culture made avoiding alcohol less easy in college and law school.) Sometimes alcohol in desserts and sauces is difficult to detect. I am often told by waiters, "There's only a *little* bit of alcohol in it" or "It's all cooked out, so you can eat it." But I cannot know whether the sauce was cooked enough to evaporate all the alcohol, and I would rather order something else. Nearly all extracts, such as vanilla and almond, contain up to 40 percent alcohol.

More than one person over the years has patronizingly informed me that I will not get drunk on something that contains vanilla extract. But even a little bit is against my religion. Alcohol, even in an extract, is forbidden food, so I would simply rather not eat it. I respect that other people may have different self-limitations.

Avoiding pork, which appears in the most unexpected places, gives me more difficulties than avoiding alcohol. When I was eleven, a student's mother brought wontons into our class. I was chewing on a mouthful when I heard two students behind me mention the filling contained pork. I stopped chewing and sat still, my mouth full and my eyes filling with tears, completely at a loss for what to do. How could I spit it out before all those people? I finally swallowed and was wretched with guilt and self-doubt for the rest of the day, until that evening when my parents told me God would forgive me.

People who have not had to be hypersensitive regarding their food intake may not recognize the various incarnations of pork. But it is my soul that is endangered when I ask a waiter, "The spinach salad has no pork in it, does it?" and he or she does not realize that my question includes "bacon bits."

The meat Muslims do eat must be *halal*; that is, the animal must be killed by cutting the jugular vein in the neck, outside the presence of other animals, and after saying a prayer over it, which evinces the intention of eating it and not killing it for any other purpose. After the slaughter, the blood must be allowed to drain from the animal's body. Kosher meat satisfies the requirements for *halal*.

Recently, my family has decided to buy meat only from farms that guarantee the animals have been humanely raised and slaughtered. Torturing an animal renders it no longer *halal*. In our family, we have decided that the way animals are treated in many factory farms and processing plants constitutes torture. This was a personal family decision, though there is some religious literature supporting this view, as well.

To my amusement, I recently came across something that cheerfully proclaimed on its cellophane packaging, "Halal Krispy Treat!" The manufacturers meant to provide an alternative for Rice Krispy treats, which are made with marshmallows, which in turn contain gelatin that comes from pork or non-*halal* meat. The "Halal Krispy Treat" used *halal* marshmallows. Admirable, I suppose, to help Muslim children conform to the universal urge to eat junk food, but what an unexpected food product to focus on reforming!

Dating and Romance

"Your *religion* prevents you from dating?"

Admittedly not a weighty question except to those parties immediately involved, it was still difficult to answer convincingly to my high school contemporaries. Strictly speaking, Islam does not prohibit *dating*, depending upon how "dating" is defined. Islam does not precisely prohibit men and women from talking or having coffee together or going out with chaperones. However, Islam does prohibit any physical intimacy between males and females outside marriage.

Most people would agree it is much easier not to date at all than to date and abstain from all physically intimate activity. As one Catholic friend ruminated, "Yup, that first kiss just about annihilates all further thought processes . . . ." Even if overcoming one's own hormones is not a problem, the reluctance to cause offense or hurt feelings (excruciating during adolescence) may be one. Add to that the difficulty of being assertive enough to say no, and the proverbial slippery slope appears underfoot. In Islam, sex is reserved for wedlock; therefore, the prudent view is to avoid unchaperoned (even chaperoned, some people say) dating. Of course, the parameters of what constitutes "dating" and what constitutes permitted social interaction is interpreted differently by different Muslims (and by different parents of adolescents of whatever religion) all over the world.

Is this dating prohibition sexist? The extra-marital intimacy prohibitions apply to men as well as women. The same Qur'anic verses that urge women to be modest urge men to be modest, too. If an unfortunate tendency exists on the part of parents to not worry as much about their boys as their girls, that is not a religious sexism, but a cultural one.

I find this double standard in Western cultures, too. A friend from Paris strongly disapproved of not dating for boys and said, "Well it's okay for your daughter, but your son has to live and fall in *love* and be with *women*."

Well, who are those boys dating but girls, anyway? The idea of "sowing wild oats" has always applied to men, not women, in some Eastern *and* Western cultures. It was perfectly acceptable for even married men to have mistresses until the last century or so. Sex has always been a different proposition (or pitfall) for men than for women, but Muslim men are expected to conform to the same dating restraints as women.

During college, I spent afternoons working in an office. The staff, consisting of two kind, motherly women, routinely asked if I had a boyfriend. Finally, I reluctantly produced the dreaded explanation of dating in Islam and, predictably, my supervisor responded wonderingly, "Really! In this day and age!"

They did not understand that my lack of romantic life did not spring from a function of time or lack of modernity. They automatically associated "different" with "backward." But different value systems do not necessarily amount to backward value systems.

Perhaps they thought my not dating constituted some sort of oppression. Then Muslim men are, if they follow religious dictates, similarly oppressed. How do they marry, then?

A Lebanese friend told me that in Lebanon, Muslim men and women socialize in groups and find someone they want to marry that way. Many Muslims meet and then continue to get to know one another by talking on the telephone. Email is a great new innovation for finding a life companion; no risk of immodesty and no possibility of getting carried away by physical attraction.

"Arranged" marriages are looked upon with abhorrence by many Western people, I have found; my friends were, without exception, shocked whenever the subject arose. Most of the marriages in my parents' generation were not "love matches," but neither were they arranged in the sense that the bride and groom met one another for the first time at the altar. Usually, a marriage was settled upon because the families had known each other for years, the bride and groom grew up in the same community, or the families had acquaintances in common. They may not have been "in love," in the movie sense or even in the tortured, introspective, soul-searching Henry James sense; but they were not strangers, either. My mother's brother was my father's best friend; it seemed only natural that they would marry.

Observing the relationships around me, it seemed that the admittedly unquantifiable level of happiness in the marriages that had been somewhat arranged (most of our Indian Muslim friends) approximately equaled the level of happiness in "love" marriages, or those that had not been arranged (all our non-Muslim friends). Certainly, expectations were different. Muslim cultures tend to emphasize finding compatible life companions rather than movie-style romance.

Where my American Muslim friends and I were concerned, many of our parents were stymied as to the correct approach to marriage. Although our parents hesitated to arrange marriages in the strict sense, there were hardly any Muslims around for us to meet on our own. If the few Muslim boys I knew were any sort of accurate statistical sample, I would have embraced life-long spinsterhood with heartfelt joy.

I resignedly understood that being introduced to someone via many chain-links of mutual acquaintances might be necessary, but I hoped that I would at least be able to meet him in a natural setting and not in a stiff, formal visit engineered by a matchmaker, official or unofficial. I admit to a vague, bubbling panic whenever my parents were approached by the families of prospective suitors. As it happens, I met my husband myself, while we were both working at the same law firm. My mother always told me Muslims believe pairs are made in heaven, and I think it must be so.

I find that many people of various backgrounds agree it is easier for two people to become genuinely acquainted with one another when they are not dating. The physical aspect of dating—How do I look? Will I have to resist his advances? Will I want to? How does he look?—can be confounding and distracting. A happily married Methodist friend described how she and her husband had been friends for years before they became romantically inclined. "It's a good thing we got to know each other as friends first," she said dryly, "because once the physical side kicks in, forget about everything else."

She did not know it, but that is the Muslim view on dating, too.

No Drinking, No Drugs, No Sex, and …
No Gambling, Either?

Many of my parents' Muslim friends love to go to Las Vegas. Some gamble, despite the Islamic prohibition on gambling. Some go just to revel in close proximity to all that sin.

The prohibition on gambling in Islam is not one of the five pillars, but I was always taught that I would go straight to hell for gambling, along with drinking alcohol, engaging in unlawful sex, and committing homicide. The purpose of prohibiting gambling is humanitarian and similar in purpose to the prohibition on drinking. Both are potentially addictive and destructive, so Islam forbids them altogether.

Precisely which activities constitute gambling is not always entirely clear. Casino games and slot machines are clearly prohibited. But so are some financial activities, such as futures contracts, which may constitute gambling because they are essentially games of chance and not skill. Again, the Islamic purpose prohibits a practice that is seen as potentially destructive and addictive.

A Note on Islamic Finance

One of the most unexpected places in which Muslims in non-Muslim countries bump into Islamic regulations is in the world of finance. Giving or taking interest on loans, buying a house, buying insurance, options and futures contracts, partnerships—routine building blocks of the Western economy—are all impacted by Islamic guidelines. These are all issues that I and my family must consider from time to time.

Islamic finance is primarily concerned with the two concepts of *riba* and *gharar*. The meanings are not unanimously agreed upon, since the Qur'an is nearly 1,400 years old, but *riba* is often translated as "usury" and *gharar* as "risk." The purpose of Islam was to uplift the downtrodden and spread equality. *Riba* and *gharar* were used in pre-Islamic Arabia for the opposite purpose of taking advantage of the downtrodden and enabling the rich to get richer.

In pre-Islamic Arabia, when a loan became due, the lender would commonly ask, "Do you pay or do you double?" If the borrower could not pay, he owed double the amount of the original loan. The Qur'an fiercely prohibits this practice, which is clearly *riba*.

The issue for me, as an American Muslim, is whether *riba* constitutes only this "doubling and redoubling" or something wider. Most scholars agree that *riba* has a wider meaning that can include any kind of profit not earned or received in exchange for something else. Because Islamic law does not regard the time value of money as sufficient consideration for the increase in capital, interest on a loan can be one example of *riba*.

This is not a unique attitude. Aristotle condemned interest, too. But as a Muslim living in the West, I and my family have very little choice in the matter of whether to pay interest, given that the entire economy runs on interest rates. Most people would never be able to buy a house, for instance, if they refused to enter into loan contracts that required interest payments. Increasingly, however, alternatives are becoming available to

Muslims, as Islamic banking options and financing schemes become less rare even in the United States.

Where Islamic banking is offered, it usually works to the advantage of those who are not so affluent. Islamic investment schemes, which emphasize profit-sharing, are generally more accessible to the masses. They usually do not require qualifying for and paying subsequent interest on a loan or having enough up-front capital to finance a business venture. For example, stock market investment and venture-capital financing are approved, because they emphasize profit-sharing.

Gharar, or "risk," means that none of the terms in a contract may be speculative or solely dependent upon chance rather than skill. Insurance contracts are a type of gambling, because it is impossible to know when the insured person will die, fall ill, or be victimized by theft. Futures contracts are also forbidden because they are speculative, essentially gambling on whether the value of the stock will increase.

My husband and I do have insurance and we do pay interest on our loans. We do not gamble at casinos. For us, the troublesome question is whether, by paying interest and contracting life insurance, we are compromising our values in order to fit into the society in which we are citizens, or whether Islam allows us to disregard some of its strictures in certain situations.

Since American banking is so regulated (compared to sixth-century pre-Islamic Arabia, anyway) and it is not so easy these days for lenders to take advantage of borrowers simply by virtue of taking or paying interest, perhaps we are not committing a sin. On the other hand, it could be argued that abuses still occur that would not have occurred had we eliminated interest. Savings-and-loan bailouts and insurmountable credit card debt are two examples.

Again, the question continually reappears in financial matters and others: are we compromising our religion to be Americans? Or is Islam flexible enough to reconcile to American society?

A Soul-Risking Balancing Act

This is an issue we and other American Muslims collide with all the time. Where do we draw the line? In a society that has been relatively tolerant to Muslims but sometimes extremely removed from day-to-day Islam, how do we reconcile culture and religion? As a parent, this question is never far from my mind. How will I convince my children to abstain from extra-marital sex? It's there in movies, on television, in advertisements, at parties, in everyday conversation. I shielded my small daughter's eyes the other day from a six-foot-tall Guess jeans advertisement displayed in the shopping mall because it was so suggestive it made me blush.

How will I teach my children never to drink alcohol when so many high school and college students do? How do I swim at the pool when wearing a swimsuit causes me acute embarrassment? I was raised to always dress modestly. So, while I do not impose my personal dress restrictions on anyone else, Muslim or non-Muslim, shorts and miniskirts have never been included in my wardrobe, except as uniforms when I was in school. That is how I draw my line, at least on clothing.

Everyone draws their own lines. American Muslims, constituting less than 3 percent of the American population, perforce constantly balance their religion with a culture that has Christian roots. Balance is necessary and continual, because we are American as well as Muslim, Muslim as well as American.

Just recently I received a shipment from Amazon.com. I opened the box, which contained the book *Toward Understanding Islam*. On the shrink-wrapped book within the sealed box was penned a large "X" with the words "GO HOME" lettered crudely below it.

As I write, the opened box and the hatred within sit heavily on my desk, like some sort of loathsome evidence I cannot destroy, like a gargoyle I am determined to ignore, wishing to obliterate but reluctant to touch.

This *is* my home. I *am* American. I just happen to be Muslim, too.

2

Some Basic Islamic Concepts and How Islam Fits in to the Judeo-Christian Tradition

An explanation of terminology may seem, at first, too elementary and more appropriate for a glossary than a chapter. But most of the questions my friends and acquaintances ask me relate to the basic concepts of Islam, those which are neglected in the surge to understand suicide bombers and jihad and the miniscule percentage of extremists that populate every religion at the expense of the overwhelming mainstream majority. This chapter is not elementary; it is *crucial* because sometimes an entire worldview can shift on the axis of a basic truth.

Some Basic Concepts and Terminology

Labels can alienate entire cultures and engender misunderstandings and even hatred if used carelessly. In the winter of 2001, when President George W. Bush described his campaign against Osama bin Laden as a "crusade," Muslims all over the world flinched. Anxiously optimistic, I pointed out to a friend in the Netherlands that "crusade" was merely a word and did not necessarily mean President Bush intended to revisit the Christian Crusades on the Islamic world. She replied impatiently that "mere" words had started wars. It is important to get the labels right.

Islam has two meanings in Arabic: "submission" and "peace." The religion of Islam is not named after a person, but after the central concept it embodies: gaining peace in your soul through submission to God, to the will of God and to His laws. The standard greeting of Muslims worldwide is "As-salamu alaykum," which means, "Peace be upon you."

For about 1,300 years, until well into the twentieth century, non-Muslims in the West, including scholars, erroneously called Islam "Mohammedanism." Initially, they made this mistake because of a natural assumption: early Western scholars assumed that as Christ was to Christianity, Muhammad was to Mohammedanism. They realized their mistake early, but the label persisted. A current online Catholic encyclopedia still consistently refers to Muslims as "Mohammedans."[1] My husband's college course on Islam, offered in the 1980s, used a textbook called *Mohammedanism*. The author even admitted in the introduction of the book that he knew Muslims found the term offensive.

Calling Islam "Mohammedanism" is offensive for a few reasons. First, it is a bit like someone calling Peter "Bob" when he knows Peter's real name, knows that Peter hates the name "Bob," but keeps calling him Bob anyway. Peter would get tired of this after a few centuries.

"Mohammedanism" is also inaccurate for a theological reason that has to do with the position of Muhammad in Islam. Muslims believe God chose Muhammad as His messenger, the man through whom God's word would be revealed to others. Although Muslims revere Muhammad as the embodiment of goodness and human perfection, we have always resisted deifying him or attributing to him any superhuman characteristics. Therefore, calling Islam "Mohammedanism" offends Muslims because it implies that we worship Muhammad or, at the very least, that Islam was named after Muhammad.

Huston Smith analogizes the non-Muslim use of "Mohammedanism" to a labeling of Christianity as "St. Paulism."[2] Christianity is not centered around St. Paul, even though St. Paul was important to the development of Christianity. Similarly, Islam is not centered around Muhammad, but named after the central theological concept embodied in the religion that Muhammad preached: submission to the will of God and the resulting peace in the soul.

Although it may seem obvious, many people still ask me about the difference between "Islam" and "Muslim." Islam is the name of the religion. Muslims are those people who follow the religion of Islam. An equivalent example would be Christianity and Christian. "Muslim" can also be used as an adjective, as in "Muslim views" or "Muslim tradition." Linguistically speaking, the words "Islam" and "Muslim" may not sound as similar to the Western ear as "Christianity" and "Christian," but they actually come from the same Arabic root.

One of my favorite nurses at my medical clinic told me once that her "husband was Islam." She had been married to her Muslim husband for five years. This was analogous to my saying my college roommates were Christianity.

On a similar note, "Arab" is not the same thing as "Muslim." Arabs are the Semitic people indigenous to the Arabian peninsula. They can be of any or no religion. Muslims can be Arab or any other ethnic group. The word "Arab" is now often extended to people who speak Arabic as their mother tongue. But that is not necessarily correct, either. Moroccans speak Arabic and French but usually do not refer to themselves as either Arab or French.

Linguistic differences can be crucial, because they can convey an erroneous impression of ideological differences. The most common example is the confusion about what exactly *Allah* means. In 2002, when the Ninth Circuit Court of Appeals ruled unconstitutional the federal statute that inserted the words "one nation under God" into the pledge of allegiance in 1954, a woman interviewed on the radio said, "I think it was the right decision, because I couldn't help thinking of all those Muslims out there."

This was a very kind thing to say, and I appreciated her sentiment. It was refreshing to be thought of so benevolently. Muslims in the West appreciate any effort to be understood, believe me! But a Muslim friend of mine could not keep from bursting out laughing when she heard the interview. She said, "But we worship God, too!"

Allah is simply the Arabic word for God. God is the English word for Allah. Arabic-speaking Christians call their God "Allah," not because they worship a different being than English-speaking Christians, but because Allah means God. This is no different from *Dieu* being the French word for "God," or *hola* being the Spanish word for "hello."

So the "one nation under God" language actually does not offend my religious beliefs. As it happens, it does offend my belief in religious freedom; I think an atheist or a non-monotheist should not be required to declare that her country is "one nation under God" in order to pledge allegiance and loyalty to it.

The confusion about God and Allah is compounded by some of the ways in which these two words are used, both by Muslims and non-Muslims. For example, because Muslims pray in Arabic, they sometimes refer to Allah rather than God even when they speak English. I heard an American comedian once say that his surname, "Obeidallah," meant "Servant of Allah." Since he was speaking English, he should have defined it as "Servant of God."

The media also exacerbates confusion about "God" vs. "Allah." Newspapers and television reports often use "Allah" instead of "God" when speaking of Islam, as if Allah were an entirely different being, or as if no English equivalent existed for Allah. This leads to the impression that Allah exists only in Islam. But the Muslim God is the God of Moses and Jesus and Abraham and is called Allah because Muhammad, the Prophet of Islam, happened to speak Arabic. It is a difference of language, not ideology.

Islam's meaning of "submission" also seems to confuse people. Shortly after the 2001 September 11th attacks, I read a *New York Times* article in which the journalist defined the idea of submission ominously, implying that it meant the submission of non-Muslims to Muslims. This assumption was not only foundationless and erroneous, it was divisive. I have also heard the nonsensical implication that "submission" in Islam means the submission of women. Submission in Islam means submission to the will of *God*, not submission to Khomeini or Saddam Hussein or the submission of women to men or the submission of non-Muslims to Muslims.

This concept of God's will is not uncommon and appears in other religions, as well. In fourth grade, I read *The Witch of Blackbird Pond*, and I distinctly remember Uncle Matthew, a Puritan, saying wearily of his family's illness, "It is God's will . . . ." That is the same general idea of submission to God's will as in Islam.

During my wedding ceremony, I found an alternative way to think of this concept of submission, preoccupied as I was with getting married. The *imam* who performed the ceremony described Islam as "God-centeredness." Submission, or *Islam*, can be thought of as "God-centeredness."

I mentioned in the last chapter that belief in the *shahada* is the sole formal requirement for being a Muslim. In Arabic, the declaration of faith is pronounced, *La illaha il-Allah Muhammad ur Rasulullah*. This means, "There is no god but God and Muhammad is the messenger of God." Sometimes it is translated as, "There is no god but Allah, and Muhammad is His messenger."

The phrase, "no god but God," may sound strange to the Western ear. But the wording and capitalization both intend to clarify that no other gods exist. Only *the* God. And it is a better translation than, "no god but Allah," because that implies Allah is something other than God. I also prefer the first version because, in Islam, God is neither male nor female.

The reason for this declaration is largely the rejection of polytheism. As Islam was revealed in an idol-worshipping, polytheistic society, Muslims have a particularly strong abhorrence of polytheism and anything that could lead to polytheism. Because of the uncompromising monotheistic nature of Islam, Muslim tradition prohibits the visual portrayal and depiction of Muhammad and other religious figures. Other figures, as well as animals, may be portrayed. In the Muslim view, it would be too easy to begin worshipping the human figures who brought the message of God rather than God Himself.

During my teenage years, I saw a movie called *Muhammad, Messenger of God*, starring Anthony Quinn. (The movie's video version is entitled *The Message*.) The movie was about Muhammad, but no one could assume the role of Muhammad without offending Muslims, because Islamic tradition does not allow Muhammad to be visually portrayed. The movie was fascinatingly directed. The actors would speak to "Muhammad" offscreen as if he were just out of sight of the camera and then respond as if he had spoken. Sometimes the camera itself would be "Muhammad" and Anthony Quinn would argue with it as if it were the Prophet of Islam.

My son's teacher called me last year to see if I would be offended if one of the children in the school dressed up as Muhammad for Halloween. At my son's school, the children choose historical characters to dress up as at Halloween and write reports on them. They must choose people who did more good things than bad things. My first impulse was gratitude that this teacher had thought to call me. My second impulse was the urge to laugh at the thought of a little Halloween Prophet of Islam.

I told her I would not be offended and that I was actually pleased a child would even know about Muhammad, much less want to dress up as him and portray him positively. I did tell the teacher, reluctantly, about the religious prohibition on visually portraying the angels and religious figures. This prohibition meant that dressing up as Muhammad would be contrary to Islamic principles. She understood immediately.

People can get carried away in their efforts to be devout. I went to a Muslim wedding recently in which we were disallowed from taking photographs. This is the most extreme and expansive interpretation of this fear of idol-worship (photograph-worship in this case) that I have ever come across. Nearly all the guests at the wedding, mostly Muslim, did not agree with this view. A Muslim friend of mine said in disgust, "Are we so weak? Are we Muslims so weak that we cannot have pictures of our memories without worshiping them?"

It is the movie example, not the wedding example, that illustrates what most Muslims believe about visual depiction. Though it applies only to the angels and religious figures, some people extend the message further. Every American Muslim household I have ever set foot in has as many graduation portraits, wedding pictures, and family group photos displayed as any non-Muslim household. But even the movie example illustrates how very strictly Muslims adhere to their definition of monotheism. In Islam, God exists without predecessor, progeny, or associates. Everyone besides God is human (except for the angels, the devil, and the *jinn*, which we'll talk about later).

In the last chapter, I touched on how some characters from the Judeo-Christian tradition figured in Islamic tradition. I want to explain further how Islam fits into the Judeo-Christian tradition, because so many people I have spoken to express such surprise that Islam does fit squarely there.

How Islam Fits into the Judeo-Christian Tradition

A friend whom I have known since I was six years old—more interim years than is quite comfortable for me to remember—recently expressed surprise to hear that Islam belongs to and follows much of the Judeo-Christian historical and ideological tradition. In Islam, Jews, Christians, and Muslims (but arguably other religious groups, as well) are all the "People of the Book" or, more accurately, "Followers of an Earlier Revelation," because they each received a scripture or revelation from God.

As a Muslim, I believe that Muhammad received verses of the Qur'an from the angel Gabriel, who brought them from God. During a conversation with a Catholic friend about the Muslim worldview, I mentioned the angel Gabriel and then had to work very hard to convince her the same angels inhabited Muslim tradition as Christian tradition. She would not believe we were talking about the same Gabriel.

Muslims view Islam as continuing on where Judaism and Christianity left off. Islam accepts much of the Jewish and Christian traditions, sometimes with variations, but then adds its own chapter beginning with Muhammad. This verse from the Qur'an illustrates the respect with which Muslims must treat Jews and Christians:

> And do not argue with the Followers of Earlier Revelation,
>   otherwise than in a most kindly manner,
>   unless it be such of them as are bent on evildoing
>   [and are therefore not accessible to friendly argument]
> and say, 'We believe in what has been bestowed from upon high upon us,
>   as well as that which has been bestowed upon you:
>   for our God and your God is one and the same,
>   and it is unto Him that we [all] surrender ourselves.[3]

I want to clarify the Qur'an's attitude toward Jews and Christians because Islam is so frequently portrayed in America as adversative to both Judaism and Christianity. "Islam versus the West" is a commonly used phrase that completely ignores the Islam *in* the West. This polarizing attitude means the questions I am asked, the newscasts I hear, the books I read—from airport fiction to academic nonfiction—more often than not start from a contentious "Islam versus the West" presumption. Yet, one of the proofs that Islam is not hostile to Judaism and Christianity is here, in this verse of the Qur'an.

Islam recognizes numerous other prophets besides Muhammad, many of whom are common to the Judeo-Christian tradition. The especially important prophets in Islam are Adam, Abraham (whom Islam considers the first Muslim), Moses, Jesus, Noah, and David. Muslims believe Jews, Muslims, and Christians are all descended from Abraham, who had two sons, Isaac and Ismail. Isaac's descendants became Jews and Christians. Ismail's descendants became Muslims.

The Muslim version of Abraham's story goes as follows: Abraham's first wife, Sarah, was afraid Abraham would prefer Ismail—his firstborn son by his second wife, Hagar—to Isaac, her own son. Sarah persuaded Abraham to reject Ismail and Hagar; Abraham did so, abandoning Hagar and Ismail in the isolated desert near Mecca, Saudi Arabia.

After her stores of food and water were depleted, Hagar ran frantically between the two hills Safa and Marwa, searching for water for her small son. When she gave up, the angel Gabriel appeared and reminded her to trust in God, at which point the boy Ismail struck his heel into the ground and a spring gushed forth. Abraham later returned and, with Ismail, built the Ka'ba as the House of the One God. Ismail's descendants settled there in Arabia near the Ka'ba and eventually became Muslims.

As I discussed in chapter one, Muslim tradition contains the same story of the sacrifice as the Old Testament: God instructed Abraham to sacrifice his son, but before he could do it, God substituted a lamb in the child's place. The only difference is that in Muslim tradition the child to be sacrificed was Ismail. In Judeo-Christian tradition the boy was Isaac, Sarah's son. Muslims understand the Qur'an to say that God gave Abraham his second son, Isaac, as a reward for being willing to sacrifice Ismail, his elder son.

In addition to ancestry, Muslims, Jews, and Christians have the same God in common. As the above Qur'anic verse illustrates, Muslims believe the God who appeared to Muhammad is the same God who appeared to

Adam, Noah, Moses, Abraham, Jesus, and all the other prophets of Islam.

In the Muslim view, God's message was revealed to all these prophets but was not accepted in its true form until Muhammad conveyed it. Muslims believe, for example, that God entrusted Jesus with the same message as Muhammad, but that Jesus's message went a little awry and his followers began worshipping him instead of Allah. This awareness of human fallibility is why it is very important to Muslims that the Qur'an remain unchanged and uncorrupted as the literal word of God.

The Muslim perception of Jesus may sound like a huge and troubling difference between Christianity and Islam, but the rest of the story is nearly the same and Muslims think of Jesus *always* with tremendous, unfailing respect. The only real issue of debate is whether his was a divine nature.

When I lived in London, one of my devout Muslim friends celebrated Christmas. "It's Jesus's birthday, isn't it?" he demanded, "And we believe in Jesus, don't we? So what's wrong with celebrating his birthday?"

Muslims believe that the message entrusted to Jesus was the same message entrusted to Muhammad and, indeed, Moses. When Islam was revealed to him, Muhammad first counted on support from the Christians and Jews, whom he regarded as "religious brethren," for this very reason. The Qur'an allows Muslims to marry Jews and Christians, which was extremely open-minded for a religious document of the seventh century.

Muslims do believe in the virgin birth of Jesus. The Qur'an describes how a messenger from God, probably the angel Gabriel, appeared to the virgin Mary, chosen by God, to tell her she would birth a son. She skeptically demanded how she could possibly have a son when no man had touched her. The angel must have smiled indulgently before he said,

> "Even so thy Lord has said:
> 'Easy that is for Me; and that We
> may appoint him a sign unto men
> and a mercy from Us; it is
> a thing decreed.'"[4]

God does not beget a son, according to the Qur'an. God is all-powerful and simply says, "Be." And Mary's baby *is*, in order that he may be a Sign unto men and a Mercy from God.

As for Jesus's death, the Qur'an says the Jews neither killed Jesus nor crucified him.[5] Nevertheless, the cross is important in Islam because it symbolizes the rejection of Christ, a prophet of God, and therefore the rejection of God's message.[6] According to the Qur'an, God informed Jesus his term was coming to an end.[7] God then raised Jesus up to Him and made Jesus's followers superior to those who denied the truth of God's message.[8] How exactly Jesus was taken to heaven is not clear, though many have theorized. It *is* clear in the Qur'an that Jesus was a human, albeit extremely respected, messenger of God.

It follows that, in the Islamic view, Jesus did not die for the sins of humanity or atone for anyone else's sins. In Islam, only the sinner can atone for his or her own sins. There is no original sin, and a person is held accountable only for the sins he himself commits.

The story of Noah's Ark is also in the Qur'an. Almost every child of any or no religion in the United States knows about Noah's Ark, the subject of many picture books and birth announcements. In the Qur'an, God sent Noah to give his people the message of God, which was: worship God alone, you people, and stop sinning. Noah's people did not believe him, so God told him to build an Ark.[9]

Noah built the Ark while his people ridiculed him and then received another command from God. This one instructed him to board the yacht with a male and female of each kind of animal, along with those people who believed his message.[10] God invoked the Great Flood, drowned the evil-doers, and then told Noah to come down from the Ark in safety.[11]

Islam also recognizes Moses as a prophet, one to whom God spoke directly, and one who is especially important because he was given a scripture. The Qur'an describes how God spoke to Moses:

> "Moses, I am God, the Lord of all Being.
> Cast down your staff."
> Then when he saw it quivering like a serpent;
> he turned about retreating, and turned not back.
> "Moses, come forward, and fear not; for surely thou art in security."[12]

I have always thought of Islam as ideologically encompassing both Judaism and Christianity, or perhaps as ideologically somewhat halfway in between the two. Muslims believe Jesus was a true prophet but do not believe in his divinity, and Muslims have great respect for Moses and the other prophets in the Judeo-Christian tradition.

The Islamic concept of mankind's place in the universe belongs in the Judeo-Christian tradition, too. In Islam, people who believe in one God and do good things go to heaven. People who do bad things go to hell. However, one difference is that Muslims are spared universal guilt and original sin because the Adam and Eve story, integral to three religions, ends slightly differently in the Qur'an than in the Bible.

In the traditional Judaic and Christian views, Eve eats the apple and gets both herself and Adam evicted from Eden. God banishes them both and informs them their sin will taint all their future descendants. Eve is the culprit and she and Adam are both punished. She gets pain in childbirth, the ground under him is cursed, and he gets thorns and thistles.[13] The doctrine of original sin comes from this story.

In Islam, sin is not a state of being but a specific forbidden act. Adam and Eve both fall from the Garden, just like in the Bible. But in the Qur'an, Eve does not cause the banishment. God forbids Adam and Eve to go near the tree, but Satan arrives to tempt Adam, not Eve. I cannot help thinking of a bumper sticker I saw just the other day, insisting, "Eve was *framed*."

To me, the Islamic version of the Adam and Eve story is the paradigm for the way in which men and women are treated in Islam: as equals. If I had one response to all the accusations of "sexist!" that are frequently leveled at my religion, I would point to this story. It illustrates an absolutely unequivocal, deliberate departure from all the old views—spanning many centuries and cultures—that hold Woman as responsible for all the evil in the world (remember Pandora?).[14]

The Qur'anic creation story, then, rejects the traditional view and chooses instead to illustrate that, from the very beginning of humankind, men and women have been equally responsible. As a Muslim woman, this has a profound, validating importance.

In Islam, Adam and Eve both eat the forbidden fruit and incur God's anger. But they repent, and God forgives them. Their sin is their own and does not taint future generations. However, God does expel them from heaven. God tells them He will give them guidance, which, if they follow it, will enable them to return to heaven.

One scholar comments, "The [Biblical story] views the Fall as the cause of man's flawed nature and existence; the [Qur'anic story] finds here the story of sin, God's mercy, and repentance."[15] The Adam and Eve story in the Qur'an is representative of the treatment of sin in the Qur'an generally. In Islam, if someone sins but repents and mends his or her ways, then God is merciful. Heaven is the ultimate reward after death.

Islam does not reserve heaven for Muslims only. I remember a story a Sunday school teacher told us once about a prostitute who went to some personal trouble to compassionately bring water to a dog dying of thirst.

Prostitution is antithetical to Islamic doctrine, which regards extra-marital sex as a sin. Despite this, I was told, the prostitute was destined for heaven because of her kindness to a dog. I do not know where the story comes from, who decided the result, or how authentic it is, but it illustrates that Islam allows people to go to heaven if they have undertaken enough good works, even if they are not perfect, even if they are not Muslim. And here it is, in the Qur'an's own words:

> Yea, indeed: everyone who surrenders his whole being unto God, and is a doer of good withal, shall have his reward with his Sustainer; and all such need have no fear, and neither shall they grieve.[16]

To achieve heaven, though, we must first bypass Satan, the tempter. When God created Adam, God commanded all the angels to bow down before Adam. Satan, named *Iblis* originally, became absolutely disgusted and wildly offended at this command. With more arrogance than good sense, he refused to bow. He announced that Adam was no better—but in fact, worse—than he, because Satan was made from crimson sheets of fire and Adam from clumps of the lowliest, grayest clay. Angry at this insolence, God banished Satan from heaven. He allowed him to slink amidst humans until Judgment Day trying to seduce those, like Faust, who might be enticed from the straight path, the path of goodness and righteousness.

Those who follow Satan's sultry whispers, warns the Qur'an, will follow him to hell, as well, on Judgment Day. On this day, the world will end and all souls will rise up and answer for their earthly deeds. The good souls will go to heaven, the nasty to hell. I remember watching a science fiction show when I was a child—the old *Battlestar Galactica,* I think—and noticing that one of the aliens bore the name Iblis. It scared me to my toes.

God made *jinn,* as well as the angels, from fire. *Jinn* were elemental spirits abounding in pre-Islamic Arabia. The Qur'an confirms their existence and states that *jinn* will also be judged on the Day of Judgment. However, the Qur'an says little of them otherwise.

I grew up watching reruns of *I Dream of Jeannie,* which featured a genie named (what else?) Jeannie. The term and related concept of "genie" comes from "jinn," but not the concept of *jinn* in the Qur'an. Rather, "genie" is derived from the depictions of *jinn* in Arabic folk tales like *The Thousand and One Nights,* in which the story of Aladdin also originates. These folk tales contain an embellished concept of *jinn* and give them powers to grant wishes and change shape. No one I know, Muslim or otherwise, has ever seen a *jinn*, if you do not count Barbara Eden.

The Qur'anic concept of *jinn* is not as colorful as the folk version. *Jinn* has several meanings in the Qur'an. Muhammad Asad describes them as follows. First, *jinn* refers to spiritual forces which are concealed from human senses, and this definition might include angels as well as satanic forces. Second, *jinn* encompasses other, sentient organisms that our senses cannot discern because they have a physiological composition completely unlike our own and "are not accessible to our sense-perception."[17] *Jinn* may also refer to certain "forces of nature" or represent unseen forces. [18]

The popular notion of *jinn* is that of Arabic folklore, but that is not really the Qur'anic definition. It makes sense to me that the Qur'an was apprising Muhammad and his contemporaries of knowledge that was yet beyond them and warning them of truths upon which humankind had not yet stumbled, rather than merely referring to genies.

The Muslim concept of heaven and hell is slightly different from the Christian one. Islam does not give the "spiritual" much superiority over the "bodily." No nuns or monks exist in Islam because sex is a gift from God to be enjoyed in wedlock and is irrelevant to the worship of God. In Islam, theologically speaking, an unwedded state has no religious advantages over a wedded state. The attitude of the Qur'an celebrates life and all aspects of it.

In the same way, the Qur'an's description of heaven is not an exclusively spiritual, sober one. It contains many earthly pleasures, such as beautiful gardens, fruits and water more pure than imaginable, and even immortal dark-eyed beings or *houri* to serve these things. I realize this picture of heaven may shock some Western sensibilities. The Qur'anic picture of heaven would shock *me* if I were not aware that the Qur'an was addressing an ancient, patriarchal, polygynous society and conveying concepts in the terms people (*men*, actually) nearly fourteen centuries ago would have understood.

The concept of *houri* has, predictably, been seized upon by Western literature, in which it is usually translated as "dark-eyed female virgins." I cannot remember how many times I have come across this term—usually in an offensive context—in unexpected places, where it is used as a whipping post for Islamic culture. This frustrates me. At the same time, it is difficult, as a woman and a Muslim, to understand why the Qur'anic picture of paradise includes it. Given that the rest of the Qur'anic description of paradise conveys visions of gardens and fruits and environmental splendor, interpreting *houri* to mean dark-eyed virgins and veiled promises of sexual favors seems jarringly incongruous.

Apparently, said a Muslim friend of my parents, shaking his head, those patriarchal seventh-century Arabs simply could not conceive of a heaven without sexual favors.

"And anyway," another Muslim friend of mine said, laughing, "where have we women been provided for in heaven, if men get the dark-eyed female virgins?"

This interpretation of *houri* is not the unanimous one. I prefer another Muslim linguist's explanation: he states that *houri* means "pure beings" or "pure companions," and believes the female connotation of the word is a more modern one than it was originally.[19]

Many passages in the Bible that do not conform with modern notions of society are shrugged off as "historical" and a result of long-ago, irrelevant worldviews. Some interpretations of the Qur'an, such as the male view of heaven, must be considered in the same way. Certainly, all the modern Muslims I know regard that verse as one example of the Qur'an speaking to a primitive, male-dominated society in a language to which they would have related. It is not to be taken literally, just as many verses in the Bible are not to be taken literally.

You may ask: the Bible is older, but it is not so earthly in its concepts, so why is the Qur'an? I think two responses legitimately answer this valid question. First, I think the Bible *is* as earthly. Those familiar with the Bible automatically know which parts are metaphorical and which are to be taken literally but may not know which parts of the Qur'an are meant to be taken metaphorically. For example, the Song of Songs is replete with erotic imagery but is understood to be a metaphor. The Qur'anic view of heaven is metaphorical, too. Whereas most Americans are familiar with the Bible at some level—it was required reading for me in college—we are not, as a culture, familiar with the Qur'an, which was not required reading. Second, even if we set aside the issue of literal versus metaphorical, the Qur'an and the Bible come from different starting points. They were received and understood in different circumstances amidst different perspectives regarding what was "pure" and "spiritual." That is not to say that one is right and the other wrong; it is simply a different way of looking at things.

Whatever the Qur'anic concept of heaven, the Qur'anic concept of God is completely the opposite of earthly. God is omniscient, omnipresent, and too altogether grand an entity for us to comprehend. In Islam, no attempt may be made to depict or represent God in any way except through His words, the words of the Qur'an. That is why mosques are often adorned with verses from the Qur'an, inlaid in jewels or lapis or painted in Arabic calligraphy. The Qur'an is the only attempted representation of God that is permitted.

The Qur'an conveys God as strict but forgiving. The beginning of every *surah* (chapter) of the Qur'an begins with a phrase traditionally translated as, "In the name of God, the most Merciful, the most Compassionate." One scholar translates this phrase as "In the name of God, the Compassionate, the Caring,"[20] which I think conveys the tone of the Qur'an more accurately to us modern English speakers.

When Muslims undertake a task, begin a meal, or embark on a journey, they say, "In the name of God, the Compassionate, the Caring." In Islam, God has ninety-nine names. The majority of those have to do with compassion, forgiveness, and mercy. Very few have to do with punishment and fear.

My husband and I wanted to name our son Azeem when he was born. My father hedged when we asked him what he thought of the name. He finally admitted he would pick another name if he were us, because Azeem is one of the ninety-nine names of God. As a word, it means "great." But as a name, it means "Great One." Therefore, naming our son Azeem would have been the equivalent of naming him "God." To avoid naming him "God," we would have had to name him Abdul-Azeem, which means "servant of the Great One." It did not have the same ring and, besides, it would eventually have been shortened to "Abdul," which means "servant." Not the same thing at all. My husband was particularly disappointed because he wanted to be able to call our son Azeem-the-Dream. We wanted to spare our son constant explanations of why he had been named "God," so we found another name for him.

In the 1991 *Robin Hood* movie starring Kevin Costner, Morgan Freeman played Robin Hood's Moorish Muslim friend, Azeem. He was a good guy but only waveringly loyal. He prayed incorrectly and was apparently also misnamed. At least he was one of the few Muslim good guys to ever appear in a Hollywood movie. Despite being a good guy and any sympathy we might have felt for him, his character remained impenetrable and alien. Azeem in the Costner movie was emblematic of how Islam and Muslims have been perceived in the United States: at best, good guys, some of them, but with alien values and an incomprehensible worldview.

Muslims do not believe in some mythical, mysterious God and accompanying religious worldview completely different from that of Christians and Jews. Despite the differences between these three religions, they are far closer than most people realize. After all, when Muslims say, "Thank God!" they pretty much mean what Jews and Christians mean by it. And although not everybody belongs to the Judeo–Christian tradition, most of us in the Western world are at least familiar with it. Islam, too, is part of this familiar tradition.

The Story of an Arab, an Angel, and the God of Abraham: Muhammad and the Birth of Islam

For as long as I can remember, stories of Muhammad, the Prophet of Islam, have formed part of life's lessons. During my childhood, I often heard sentences begin with the familiar phrase, "Well, the Prophet told us . . ." When I hated school in fifth grade and wanted to stay home, my parents said to my mutinous face, "The Prophet told us that we must seek knowledge even if we have to travel to China to do it."

For Muhammad, living in sixth-century Arabia, China was so distant it may as well have been the moon. And yet he told us to pursue knowledge as far as China. I sighed and trudged off to school.

When I procrastinated finishing my homework, my parents said, "Remember the first word that God ever said to the Prophet? It was *read*."

When I was eight and argued with my brother, my mother admonished me, "The Prophet said that smiling at your brother counts as a charity." I cannot remember if I could bring myself to smile at him; I doubt I even stopped fighting with him, but I did remember what she said.

For Muslims, the Prophet Muhammad is not a mythical or divine figure. Rather, we regard him as an ordinary man who, late in life, was given the difficult mission of religious and social reform. Just as Christianity cannot be understood without some knowledge of Jesus, Islam cannot be understood without some knowledge of Muhammad and the society from which he sprang. Everything he taught must be examined with pre-Islamic Arabia in mind, because much of what he preached had to do with overturning the particular society in which he lived.

The Suggested Reading List in the back offers some longer biographies of Muhammad for those who wish to delve further into his life. What I attempt in this chapter is a short description of Muhammad's society and his story, primarily as narrated by Muslim traditional sources.

It all started in the sixth century, in the western Arabian peninsula, in what is now Saudi Arabia. The two superpowers fighting it out from Europe to Asia were the Roman, or *Byzantine*, Empire and the Persian, or *Sassanian*, Empire. I still remember having to shade in the ancient Persian Empire on a map I drew in my sixth-grade class. It, too, may as well have been on the moon for all the relevance it had to my eleven-year-old life. (I didn't comprehend where "Persia" fit into today's world until much later.)

The Romans were champions of Christianity, and the Persians mostly practiced Zoroastrianism. Neither empire had taken over the Hijaz, a stretch of desert in the Arabian peninsula encompassing what are now the towns of Mecca and Medina—the two cities that are important in this story—in Saudi Arabia.

Before Islam, Mecca was a minor regional trading center and Medina was primarily agricultural. Those in the desert who did not live in settlements like Mecca and Medina were parts of nomadic tribes or clans, which were formed around a central ancestor of that tribe. No central government existed in the Hijaz, in cities or otherwise. The clans had autonomous power.

Without a central government or police force, the tribes wielded justice themselves. (Police forces were not really developed in many countries until several centuries later; England got one in 1830, for example.[1]) If a member of a tribe were murdered, the fellow tribesmen, and not any central authority, exacted revenge on the tribe of the murderer. Revenge commonly took the form of many lives for one life. Blood feuds sometimes dragged on for decades.

The pre-Islamic Arabs admired revenge and regarded it as a sign of virility. In addition, they considered revenge to be necessary in such a society; to neglect immediate revenge would have been a show of weakness, because they had no other recourse or protection. At least we Americans get to sue.

As for wealth, pre-Islamic Arabs considered stealing from another tribe to be perfectly legitimate. Tribal raiding was part of the economy; that is where the jobs were. Safety of person and property lay in protection of the tribe. Anything that was not adequately protected was fair game.

The predominant religion in the Hijaz was paganism. The Ka'ba had become a shrine for pagan idols. Not everyone in the Hijaz was a polytheist, however, and Jews and Christians resided there, too.

Women did not fare too well in pre-Islamic Arabia. A man was entitled to as many wives as he wanted and could terminate the marriage unilaterally at any time. Women were not even parties to the marriage contract but objects of sale, and a father could sell his daughter to the highest bidder. Actually, this was the case in the Western world, too, until only a few centuries ago. (You may have come a long way, baby, but it took awhile.) As for inheritance, it was totally inapplicable to women, who did not inherit at all. In fact, even males could not inherit if their connection to the deceased was through a female relative.

It was into this society, which Muslims call the *Jahiliya*, or Age of Ignorance, that Muhammad, the Prophet of Islam, was born.

Muhammad was born in Mecca in approximately 570 CE★★ into a poor but respectable family of the Quraysh tribe. Orphaned at the age of six, Muhammad's paternal grandfather, the head of his clan, assumed guardianship. He died when the boy was eight, and Muhammad's paternal uncle became his guardian. Muhammad had no formal schooling and was, indeed, illiterate, a relatively common state and not a bar to success at that time.

Muhammad embarked on a career in commerce and soon made a reputation for himself because of his honesty and trustworthiness. Because of this reputation, Muhammad obtained a position as business manager for a widow, Khadija, who had interests in the camel-caravan trade. Impressed with Muhammad's honesty and integrity, Khadija proposed marriage to him when he was twenty-five years old and in the prime of life. She was forty and, according to tradition, beautiful.

He accepted her proposal and they were married for the next quarter-century. They were companions and partners until her death in 619. He never took another wife while she was alive, though polygamy—*polygyny*, more accurately, which is one husband married to more than one wife—was standard practice in pre-Islamic Mecca, both among the pagan Arabs and the Jews. They had six children together, though the two boys did not survive.

Muhammad had been married for fifteen years when he experienced the extraordinary revelation that was to launch one of the world's largest religions.

He was forty years old. One night, later to be called the Night of Power, he traveled to a nearby mountain cave retreat to meditate. Social injustice and inequity had always concerned him, and he periodically

---

★★"CE" stands for "common era" and is used because it is more universal than "AD," which refers to the Christian calendar. All dates in this book are CE unless specified otherwise.

escaped to the mountain to contemplate these problems in peace. On the Night of Power, as Muhammad meditated in the isolated darkness, a sudden reverberating voice shattered the air around him.

"Read!" the voice commanded.

Unseen arms pressed suffocatingly on him from every side, as if to elicit a response. Muhammad, heart pounding, replied to the charged darkness that he did not know how to read. Once more the ringing voice erupted from the depths of the cave.

"Read!"

Again he replied that he was illiterate. And again his lungs were squeezed, his body pinioned, his gasping breaths resounding in the cave.

After the third such command, Muhammad desperately asked the voice what exactly he was meant to read, or "recite," as the word is sometimes translated. From the waiting darkness, he received this answer, which would become part of Surah 96, the first to be revealed, of the Qur'an:

> Recite! In the name of your Lord who created,
> Created man from a clot of blood!
> Recite! Your Lord is the Most Generous,
> Who taught by the Pen
> Taught man what he knew not.[2]

Understandably, Muhammad shook with terror, shock, and doubt. Whose was the voice? A demon's? An *angel's*. The angel Gabriel would act as God's messenger to Muhammad and relay to him God's words and instructions for the remainder of his life.

But Muhammad could not have apprehended all this yet and, after this first encounter, he stumbled home, shaken and shivering. He confided to his wife all that had transpired. The second miracle of the night was that Khadija believed him (they must have had trust as well as love in their marriage). She believed he had received the word of God, and she became his first convert to Islam. She arranged for Muhammad to consult her Christian cousin, Waraqa, who listened to the fantastical story Muhammad had to tell him and then reassured him that surely he was a true prophet of God.

Every year, on the anniversary of the Night of Power, Muslims stay awake all night praying and meditating. It is said that God's presence fills the earth particularly intensely this night and that it is possible to hear the speech of the animals and the whispering of the trees.

My mother vividly remembers one particular Night of Power when she was a child of nine in India. She had remained awake long past her bedtime, praying with the rest of her family. Throughout the night, one particular wish had stayed uppermost in her mind. My mother hoped this night, of all nights, God might grant her prayer. When she knew she was unobserved, my mother secretly penciled her prayer onto a scrap of paper. With a child's agile fingers, she folded the scrap numerous times into a tiny wad and knotted it securely in her long, blue gauzy scarf. No one saw her secret prayer, which was a wish for a doll just like the one her friend had. Her wish hidden, she returned to pray with everyone else.

As soon as she awakened the next morning, she ran to retrieve her scarf. The knot was still tied, exactly as she had left it. But the paper was gone. She looked all over the house for it, for days. She never found it.

At the age of nine, my mother understood that God or the angels must have caused the paper to vanish. God is everywhere always, Muslims believe, but particularly omnipresent on the Night of Power. Even as a child, she accepted that God had given her a fragment of wisdom: wishes for dolls are not the kind of heartfelt, soul-flooding prayers that one asks from God.

Thirteen centuries before my mother's childhood epiphany was the history-making, very first Night of Power, the one that launched the world's second-largest religion. After Muhammad recovered from his shock on that night, he began preaching the glory of the One God. The first surahs he received from Gabriel, such as Surah 112 below, were short and powerful, stressing the magnificence of God:

> Say: He is God,
> The One and Only
> God the Eternal, the Absolute
> He begets not,
> Nor is he begotten
> And there is none Like unto him.[3]

Because Muhammad could neither read nor write, his followers recorded these verses as they were revealed, on whatever materials came to hand. Each revelation would later become one of the 114 surahs that comprise the Qur'an. It was not a new religion Muhammad preached, but a return to the religion of Abraham, the worship of the One True God.

At first, Muhammad did not succeed terribly well at preaching Islam. His first converts were those who knew him, such as his wife, cousin, and uncle. But as Muhammad became more successful, he became increasingly resented by the people of Mecca.

The Meccans opposed his religious preaching, but they also resented his advocating social reform. He denounced the injustice he saw in his society, which was brutal, violent, oppressive of women, encouraging of slavery, heavy on gambling, exploitative of orphans, and usurious. The Meccans feared that Muhammad, if allowed to succeed, would change not only the religion of the area but the entire social structure of their society.

Muhammad did threaten the very tribal infrastructure of Meccan society, because people converted to Islam individually, rather than as clans. As Islam stressed equality among people, many of the converts to Islam were of the lower classes rather than the landed wealthy. This democratic aspect, by the way, has always been one of the appeals of Islam. Historically, many of those converting to Islam, such as those of the "untouchable" class in India, did so to convert to a better life.

Because Islam has no real religious hierarchy, nobody has any more religious clout than anyone else. Everyone is equally close to God. Therefore, those without connections and without the protection of a clan stood to gain more by allying themselves with Islam than those already prospering under the tribal system.

The simple message of Islam appealed particularly to the poor, isolated, and disadvantaged: Believe in the One God. Believe that Muhammad is His messenger. And be equal in the eyes of God.

Many of the early believers were of African descent. One of the first Muslims was a former slave, an East African named Bilal, whom Muhammad had bought solely to set free. It was Bilal who became the first *muezzin*, he who had the honor of first proclaiming the *azan*, the call to prayer. Zaid, also a freed slave and Muhammad's adopted son, was another of the first Muslims. All this democracy and free thinking, at a time when equality amongst people was not considered a virtue, made the wealthy, elitist, leading powers in Mecca very, very nervous. (Free thinking *today* makes some political powers very, very nervous.)

Muhammad's new religion also threatened the Meccan polytheistic religion. Mecca's religious society was symbolized by the Ka'ba, Abraham's House of God, which had become populated with idols by Muhammad's time. Pilgrims came to worship the idols in the Ka'ba, and Mecca enjoyed the elevated local status.

Because of the visitors to the Ka'ba and resulting large gatherings, trade flourished in the Meccan marketplace. Mecca benefited from the increased commerce around the Ka'ba. Therefore, Muhammad, with his one God, was a threat not only to the local religion and social norms, but also to Mecca's social and financial status as home of the Ka'ba.

As Muhammad became more successful, the Meccans increased their persecution of the new Muslims. Muhammad and his followers were harassed and tortured; some Muslims migrated to Ethiopia, where they were free to practice their new religion under the Christian (Coptic) ruler. Muhammad stayed in Mecca, under the protection of Abu Talib, his uncle, who headed the Hashim clan. Protection from persecution depended upon bloodlines and the clan. For the time being, Muhammad was protected.

But in 619, Muhammad's beloved wife and uncle both died. The new head of the clan was not prepared to defend Muhammad from persecution, and life became seriously dangerous for him and his followers. He faced inevitable assassination.

It was at this critical time that leaders from the neighboring city of Medina approached Muhammad. Medina contained two large feuding tribes who needed an impartial outsider to lead and arbitrate. The Medinans had heard of Muhammad's trustworthiness (his nickname had long been "al-Amin," the trustworthy). They invited him to emigrate to their city, not because of his religious message, but because of his integrity.

After ensuring he would be welcomed by all factions in Medina, Muhammad and his followers, in danger of their lives, secretly trickled out of Mecca in small groups. Muhammad and his best friend, Abu Bakr, stayed behind until the rest had emigrated. The Muslim calendar begins on the date of this journey, which is called the *hijra*. The year was 622.

My daughter's picture book of Muhammad's escape to Medina tells the story of how he and Abu Bakr hid in a cave to avoid being murdered by the pursuing Meccans. God commanded the spiders to weave a web across the mouth of the cave and the doves to build their nest at the cave entrance, all with supernatural haste. When the assassins came, they saw the web and the nesting doves and concluded that no one could have disturbed the mouth of the cave to enter. They departed and Muhammad was spared.

Whatever the details, Muhammad and his followers did escape to Medina and settled there. They and the Medinans entered into an agreement called the "Constitution of Medina," which named Muhammad as the arbiter or judge for every Medinan citizen. For the Muslims, though not for the non-Muslims, Muhammad functioned as the religious and community leader. The Arabs in Medina who had previously converted to Judaism became political allies of the Muslims but followed their own religious and cultural laws.

Muslims consider the Constitution of Medina to be the first charter of religious freedom in the world. Non-Muslims had equal rights with the Muslims and were free to practice their religions in a truly pluralistic society, whose vision was to influence the later multireligious states of the Islamic Empire. Not too bad for 622.

Despite the *hijra*, the Meccans who had exiled them still threatened Muhammad and his followers, who continued to grow in number. A state of war existed between the two cities, and several skirmishes and battles took place between them during the following seven years. In addition, internal strife and even treachery between the various factions in Medina itself began to ferment. Tensions grew daily, internally and externally, and the new Muslims struggled simply to survive.

Muhammad did fight. He fought against those who attacked him and those who broke their treaties with him. He fought those who militarily conspired to betray him. He and his thousands of followers fought to defend themselves and the practice of their religion. But Muhammad never entered into a war that was not defensive and never used military operations if he could use diplomacy instead.[4] He followed the rules of war and politics that were standard at the time and in the region, those practiced by Jews and other Arabs.[5]

During these years in Medina, Muhammad aimed to win Mecca to his cause without bloodshed. Several reasons made this goal crucial. First, Mecca was the religious center of the area. The Quraysh had considerable connections. If the powerful Meccan tribes could be persuaded to join Muhammad, their influence would help develop Islam into more than just a temporary religious phenomenon.

Second, the Ka'ba was in Mecca. And the Ka'ba was very important to Muhammad. The Qur'an had named the Ka'ba as the direction that Muslims should face while praying. It was also designated as the Muslim place of pilgrimage. The Ka'ba was the holy shrine in Mecca and a powerful symbol; the Qur'an had named it as the original house of the One God. Part of Muhammad's duty, therefore, was to restore the Ka'ba to its rightful role.

Note that Muhammad did not plan to attack Mecca and convert it at sword-point. He said, "Will you then force men to believe when belief can come only from God?"[6] He worked and waited until he could go back and incorporate Mecca not as "a beaten and resentful enemy, but as a willing, if not enthusiastic partner."[7]

In 628, Muhammad and his followers traveled to Mecca to make the pilgrimage. The Meccans denied them admittance. Muhammad and his followers then negotiated a peace treaty with the Meccans, the "Treaty of Hudaibiyah," which allowed Muhammad to return the following year to make the pilgrimage. The Muslims went home.

During the following year, the Meccans broke the peace treaty. Muhammad and his followers—10,000 of them now—traveled again to Mecca and surrounded the city with their own campfires and extra campfires to exaggerate their numbers. The Meccans saw their city illuminated by thousands of surrounding campfires and surrendered. Without bloodshed. The year was 630 CE.

According to the standards and rules of war of the time, Muhammad had the right to execute the men and take the women and children as slaves. In Mecca, he destroyed nothing except the pagan idols in the Ka'ba, which was rededicated to the One God.

Muhammad died not long after Mecca surrendered. It was 632, and he was sixty-three years old. He had lived to see the Ka'ba restored to the One God. Indeed, centuries later, the Ka'ba is still the holiest site in Islam and is the destination of the pilgrimage undertaken by Muslims every year.

In his lifetime, Muhammad managed to accomplish significant social reforms. For example, he opposed the common practice of wife-beating, raised the status of women to revolutionary new heights by limiting polygyny, and required that women inherit from their relatives. He allowed women to divorce their husbands, obtain custody of their children, contract their own marriages and keep their property upon marriage. He forbade men to sell into marriage their daughters, sisters, and other relations. In case this does not sound like much, remember this was seventh-century Arabia. Women in England and other parts of Europe did not have as many rights until centuries later.

Muhammad's other social reforms are still in place today. Instead of tribal rules, Muhammad established an entirely new set of rules of conflict so that blood feuds could not endure for endless decades, with tribes murdering each other in an ongoing cycle. He required sharing of wealth with the poor. He and the Qur'an set down rules prohibiting gambling, flaunting of wealth, intoxication, murder, theft, female infanticide, eating of pork, adultery, usury, cheating, and fraudulent contracts. Muhammad condemned exploitation of widows and orphans, who had previously lacked status in the tribal society based on bloodlines and protection of the clan.

Muhammad also strengthened the concept of the *umma*, a community of believers that supported one another and adhered to specific rules. Muslims still refer to one another as "Brother So-and-so" and "Sister So-and-so." The formation of an *umma* meant that anyone, whatever their bloodlines, whatever their tribe or clan, could be part of the Muslim community. This community of believers in turn negated the tribal system, in which people were protected only by their tribe and were subject to the whim of the tribe. In other words, the Prophet of Islam had not only established the religion of Islam, he had managed to establish an entirely new social system in Arabia, as well.

Nothing was more important to Muhammad than social justice. The Qur'an and the recorded quotations of the Prophet make this absolutely clear. He wanted to change the entire social and moral fabric of Arabia, but he knew that to turn the world of his fellow Arabs upside down would backfire and do no good at all.

Therefore, Islam sometimes does not prohibit outright undesirable, pre-Islamic practices. Rather, it retains them but fences safeguards around them and strongly encourages a gradual progression toward their elimination. For instance, the Qur'an does not ban polygyny but restricts it to four wives and contains several verses encouraging monogamy. And although the Qur'an accepts slavery as the *status quo*, it dictates rules for their welfare and urges people to free their slaves. The Prophet bought slaves in order to free them.

Stories have arisen around the life of the Prophet, such as how two angels came to him when he was a boy and opened up his chest to purify his heart. But Muslims have resisted raising Muhammad to anything above human status. When my parents spoke of the Prophet, they, like other Muslims we knew, spoke of him with affection and great respect. We allow him his foibles—his *humanity*—but strive to emulate his goodness.

Muhammad is portrayed by historic literature as someone who had unfailing patience, a contemplative and gentle personality, an abhorrence of violence, a loving relationship with his family, honest and trustworthy even before his prophethood, a shyness of demeanor, and an active sense of humor. According to H.A.R. Gibb, some of these personality traits would have been considered so strange for a man in the Prophet's time and place that they *must* be reflections of the real man![8]

I realize it is difficult for those who think of Jesus or Buddha as the epitome of a prophet to reconcile Muhammad's dual function of both spiritual prophet and pragmatic political leader of a community. Muslims consider Jesus to be one of the greatest prophets—not divine, we believe, but one of the best human beings who has ever lived on earth. We admire his message of love and forgiveness.

But Jesus and Muhammad were born in different times and places and were faced with different challenges. Each was guided by God, Muslims believe, and each made the right decisions and behaved as well as humanly possible within his circumstances. Jesus's message worked for his situation and his world. Muhammad lived in a different time in a particularly brutal society in which violence was taken for granted and considered a legitimate course of action. He had to struggle for the safety of thousands of men, women, and children in his care. When the Meccans attacked, they attacked not only Muhammad but the thousands in his community. In the Qur'an, God gave Muhammad the right to defend those other, innocent lives.

It has been said that Muslims do not become as upset about differing opinions on God, theology, and (to them) blasphemy as they do about insults to the Prophet. In addition to this being human nature, there are two reasons for this.

First, when Islam was a fledgling religion, Christians of the time attacked it more by insulting Muhammad than by faulting the tenets of the religion itself (which they were confused about anyway).[9] Because Muslims revered Jesus, Moses, and a host of other Judeo-Christian prophets, they could not reply in kind. The result was an entire host of Christian polemic battering on the figure of Muhammad.

That attitude has never disappeared. The political cartoons of 2006, depicting Muhammad in various derogatory guises, is but a recent illustration. In that case, although the ensuing violence was completely unjustified, the cartoons were supremely disrespectful and inflammatory, implying that Muhammad would have condoned the terrorism that is now taking place in the world. I believe that freedom of speech should always be encouraged, and yet I found this entire episode to be deeply saddening. I revere the Prophet and I view terrorism as criminal behavior outside the realm of Islam. To equate the two was hitting below the belt.

In addition, it is still possible to find academics nonsensically referring to him as a "false prophet" and a "self-proclaimed prophet" (but which prophet has not been both of these things to those who disbelieved him?).[10]

The media frequently indulges all sorts of spectacularly ill-informed and defamatory attacks on Muhammad in the blissful confidence that ratings will remain unblemished by any accusations of racism that might be forthcoming.

CBS's *60 Minutes* interviewed Jerry Falwell in the fall of 2002. In a display of xenophobia and staggering ignorance of history and comparative religion, Falwell called Muhammad a "terrorist,"[11] never mind that the rules of terrorism in classical Islam were so strict as to cast some of our modern ones in the shade[12] and that Muhammad never conducted a war except to defend himself and his people. It should be no wonder that attacking Muhammad is still a sore spot with Muslims. It is part of a thirteen-century-old tradition of hatred that is still flourishing.

Today, as I read the news and explore the internet (even sites unrelated to religion, like chess clubs and bookstores), I come across tirades of the same sort as Jerry Falwell's. So many more voices are trying to convince themselves and others that *this* is the reason for all their woes, this Islam, this religion preached by Muhammad. Any contrasting views are summarily dismissed. As Karen Armstrong states:

> It is still common for Western people to take it for granted that Muhammad had simply 'used' religion as a way of achieving world conquest or to assert that Islam is a violent religion of the sword, even though there are many scholarly and objective studies of Islam and its Prophet that disprove this myth ...[13]

The second reason Muslims feel offended when the Prophet Muhammad is attacked is that vilifying the Prophet is denigrating the person whose behavior every Muslim strives to emulate. An attack on Muhammad is an attack on every individual Muslim's goals of good conduct and morality.

And that is the important thing, anyway, is it not? If Muslims believe Muhammad was the epitome of kindness and goodness and they strive to be kind and good, like him, then that must be commended. Ongoing calculated attempts to portray Muhammad sinisterly achieve only the propagation of hatred, prejudice, and dichotomizing medieval attitudes. Whatever I may believe about Moses or Jesus or Muhammad or Buddha (and I happen to respect them all), it is more important to stop arguing about unprovable specific details of their lives and to try instead to understand the religions they preached.

The most valuable question, then, is, "What is it you believe and how does that affect your behavior?" If you are a good person because you believe Jesus or Moses or Muhammad or Buddha or Ganesh (or something else) requires you to be a good person, then I must admire your goodness and the reason for it, whatever my own beliefs.

Given Muslim reverence for the Prophet of Islam, it should surprise no one that his death, shortly after his return to Mecca, left the new Muslims at a bit of a loss. No one else had ever led them. Who would lead them now? What were they duty-bound to do? The answers to these questions would change the face of the world forever.

The Prophet had not left any instructions for the succession or selection of a new community leader. A tribal society had no precedents for selecting a central community leader. Some followers maintained that the Prophet's cousin and son-in-law, Ali, should be his successor, but the majority settled on Abu Bakr as the new *caliph,* or leader, of the Muslim community.

When Abu Bakr died, the Muslims elected Umar as caliph. The most vivid and vocal of the Prophet's companions, Umar had adamantly opposed Islam at first. In fact, Umar had actually been on his way to assassinate Muhammad when he happened upon his own sister and her husband secretly reading verses from the Qur'an. He exploded angrily, but when he snatched their papers and started to furiously read them, he became so moved by the words that he converted to Islam in their living room. He continued on his way to find Muhammad, not to murder him, but to join him.

Even after converting, Umar argued with many of the social reforms the Prophet struggled to implement. He represented the part of Muslim society that could not bear to give up all the pre-Islamic traditions because they were so ingrained and long-standing. I remember a story portraying Umar as quiveringly, hands-on-hips indignant because the Prophet Muhammad told him men could not beat their wives. After all, it was the custom!

After Umar, Uthman became the caliph. It was he who gathered the scraps upon which the Muslims had been writing down verses from the Qur'an and who compiled them into one volume. Ali succeeded Uthman and led the community for five years. Sunni Muslims call these four the *Rashidun,* or "rightly guided caliphs."

I do not discuss the history of the Islamic empire from Muhammad's death to the present day, as it would fill several volumes in its own right. That part of history is crucial in understanding the present-day world, and I urge further reading on the subject (the Suggested Reading List contains wonderful books by respected scholars). Rather, in this text, I describe and periodically refer to the society that provided the backdrop for the Islamic reforms of the seventh century. To understand the message of Islam today, it is crucial to understand the world in which the message was received and understood in the first place.

4

The Qur'an: What It Is and
Why Quoting It Can Be Problematic

When I was twelve, a friend of my mother's gave me a volume of Shakespeare's plays. It was nearly a hundred years old, its leather binding romantically crumbling to the touch, its pages yellowed, and its few illustrations faded. I loved it.

I took it with me to read at the next Indian dinner party I had to attend. Indian dinner parties were enormous, with fifty to one hundred guests all crammed into someone's house. Dinner was always a buffet that took many days of anxious preparation. Despite wearing formal clothes, we all ate sitting on a floor spread with enough sheets to accommodate so many diners. I tended toward long-suffering boredom at dinner parties unless the family of my one Muslim friend had been invited, too. So I arrived armed with my newly acquired volume of Shakespeare, settled myself into a corner, and began reading *A Midsummer Night's Dream*.

I understood almost none of it. At twelve, I was an enthusiastic reader, but the text had no footnotes and no summaries of the plays. I had not seen any Shakespeare plays yet, in theatre, on television, or elsewhere. I had not encountered any lines clichéd by common usage (like "to be or not to be"), owned no books that condensed the plays for children, and had no clue what the words would have meant in Shakespeare's time and part of the world. I doubt I even realized that familiarity with Shakespeare's historical England was important to reading *A Midsummer Night's Dream* in the first place. I came from a completely different culture that did not study Shakespeare, any more than Americans study the Indian poet Ghalib, so we had no Shakespearean paraphernalia around the house. I had barely heard of Shakespeare himself.

I console myself somewhat by remembering that anyone in my very same situation, even an adult, would likely have encountered the same difficulties in understanding *A Midsummer Night's Dream*. As I look back on my struggles to understand Puck and his machinations, I wonder how many English-speaking people in the world could read a Shakespeare play—without any background, footnotes, historical familiarity, experience with the play, instruction on the play, or cultural knowledge relating to it—and accurately comprehend the meaning of every line. I would guess zero. Or as close to zero as to be negligible.

Shakespeare lived less than 500 years ago and wrote in English. The Qur'an was compiled over *1,300* years ago in Arabic. I cannot help but wonder how many English-speaking people today can pick up a copy of the Qur'an, even an English translation—without any previous experience, historical familiarity, knowledge, background, footnotes, or instruction—and accurately understand the meaning of every line. I would guess, oh, zero. Or certainly fewer than those who could pick up a Shakespeare play and comprehend it.

Yet, a few months after the September 11th attacks on the World Trade Towers, Andy Rooney swaggered onto his television show, *60 Minutes*, and announced, "I don't know whether the president has read the Koran or not. I've been reading it for the past six weeks now and I'm so pleased with myself." Unsurprisingly, Mr. Rooney continued to discuss the Qur'an and make about every mistake imaginable in his self-described "analysis" of it. First of all, the camera filmed him sitting at his desk with a pile of books beside him, saying, "These are all versions of the Koran—all a little different . . . like the difference between these versions of the Bible."

Mr. Rooney did not have different versions of the Qur'an, because only one version exists in the world, and that is in Arabic. Muslims do not accept that the Qur'an can be translated because a translation would never be able to convey the Qur'an's exact meaning; they certainly cannot imagine new versions, new editions, or new rewordings of Qur'anic text. The Qur'an contains just the words that first went into it over 1,300 years before Andy Rooney was born.

As I mentioned in the note at the beginning of this book, Muslims do not consider translations to be the Qur'an itself, but rather aids in understanding the meanings imparted by God. Qur'anic "translations" or renderings of the meaning of the Qur'an are often called "interpretations." These are what Andy Rooney probably had piled on his desk—not different versions of the Qur'an but different attempts at translating its meaning from Arabic to English.

Shakespeare's plays have been translated into many languages. They have even been simplified for children's books, some of which my children own. But the plays themselves have not been changed. The Qur'an has not been changed, either.

The confidence that allows Mr. Rooney to make invalid statements about the Qur'an on national television seems to have pervaded the soul of many a journalist and commentator. Verses are selectively taken from the Qur'an at face value and used as "proof" of the commentator's arguments. These commentators pontificate on English translations of the Qur'an with less knowledge of how to interpret the verses than if they were to expound on Shakespeare's plays without any previous background or instruction.

For one thing, they read the English interpretations, which are by definition imperfect, some more than others. For another, they have not consulted the books of Islamic jurisprudence, which interpret the Qur'anic verses and sometimes come up with results that do not seem to follow from the face value of the verses. These commentators cannot know the idioms of thirteen-century-old Arabic. They remove words from their historical, temporal, and cultural contexts. They would not know, unless they did further research, which verses of the Qur'an have been superseded by other verses or by other sources of Islamic law. Even native Arabic speakers cannot just pick up a copy of the Qur'an and understand its meaning.

Only a small percentage of people in the United States know enough about the Qur'an and Islam to denounce an ignorant analysis of either. And we do not have voice enough in this country to do it. We do not have a large, organized public relations force. We are disproportionately underrepresented in the media to the point of being non-existent, and obstacles are thrown our way when we do attempt to voice our views.[1]★★ That is what this chapter must be, then: my attempt to explain the Qur'an and try to set the record straight.

The Nature of the Qur'an and Problems of Translation

The word "Qur'an" means "recitation" or "reading." It is a compilation of the words revealed by God to Muhammad, transmitted by the angel Gabriel, and written down by Muhammad's followers as he recited them.

★★For example, in 1999, the first Muslim American, Salam al-Marayati, was appointed to a federal panel. Several Zionist groups put so much pressure on Gephardt that he rescinded the appointment, though many people of all faiths, Christian, Jewish, Muslim, and other, had defended it.

Muslims believe the Qur'an is the very literal word of God, written in first-person narrative, and containing nothing but the words actually spoken by God and relayed to Muhammad. Not just divinely inspired words, but divine words.

The Qur'an addresses Muhammad himself at times and all humanity at others. The Qur'an sometimes criticizes Muhammad. The Prophet perceived the revelations in different ways, but the effects upon him were discernible to his observers. His voice and speech altered, he seemed to fall into a trance, and he is documented as saying he never experienced a revelation without feeling as if his soul were being torn from him.

Since Muslims believe the Qur'an to be the literal word of God, they have steadfastly refused to change a word of it. Translations would introduce different meanings and human error into the text, and the words of a translation would no longer be God's words. Muslims are afraid of losing accuracy. Moreover, since God spoke in Arabic, the Qur'an itself can exist only in Arabic. For this reason, prayers, which involve recitations of the Qur'an, must be in Arabic.

When I was in junior high, much of my absolute belief in Islam turned on this simple fact: The Qur'an was written down as it was revealed, compiled within a few years of Muhammad's death, and never subsequently altered.** The Arabs of Muhammad's time wrote his words down while he lived, though they considered the oral tradition to be completely reliable. Not everyone would have found this so convincing, of course, but how can faith be explained, anyway? You believe or you do not believe. Or, perhaps you choose to believe.

In high school, student members of Campus Crusade routinely cornered me with their flyers promoting Christianity and my born-again Christian friends copied pages of the Bible for me to read. I felt unwillingly polite and unfairly besieged. I had never tried to convert them to Islam, after all, and I respected their different faiths. Though I respect Christianity and consider it to be a part of my own tradition, one of the reasons I never wavered in my faith was that the Qur'an was written down at the time it was revealed. For one of my close Christian friends, this fact has no significance at all. That's okay. We all have different reasons for faith, different reasons that resonate with each of us, and we must acknowledge that.

** Just as there are theories suggesting Jesus never existed, there are theories suggesting the Qur'an was not written until much later. These are not the majority view, though, and are certainly not the Muslim view.

For me and all Muslims, the Qur'an is the embodiment of God on earth. For Christians, it is not the Bible but Christ who is the embodiment of God on earth. One scholar explains it this way:

> The Word of God in Islam is the Qur'an; in Christianity it is Christ. The vehicle of the Divine Message in Christianity is the Virgin Mary; in Islam it is the soul of the Prophet. The Blessed Prophet must be unlettered for the same reason that the Virgin Mary must be virgin. The human vehicle of a Divine Message must be pure and untainted.[2]

Because Muhammad was illiterate, or "unlettered," the task of recording the Qur'anic verses fell to his followers, who had partial collections of Qur'anic verses, which they used in private prayers and devotions. An official, complete collection was compiled by the third caliph, Uthman, within twenty years of the Prophet's death.[3]

The Qur'an is divided into 114 chapters, or *surahs*, each of which contains a varying number of *ayahs*. The word "ayah" is usually translated as "verse," though its real meaning is "sign" or—when referring to the Qur'an—a "statement in the speech of God."[4] The sequence of surahs and number of total ayahs varies with different editions, although the actual Arabic words of the Qur'an do not change. The variations are simply differences in numbering. Surahs vary in length, depending upon the particular system of numbering. The Qur'an contains about 6,236 total ayahs.

With the exception of Surah *Fatiha*, which is always first, the surahs are arranged by length. The longest is second (after Fatiha), the shortest last. Some scholars have tried to arrange them chronologically but have had trouble doing so without splitting apart some of the surahs.

The Qur'an is also not structured according to subject matter. The surahs themselves each often cover a variety of topics and do not limit themselves to one subject per surah. In fact, sometimes one historical occurrence or story will be mentioned many times throughout the Qur'an, in many surahs, piecemeal and in passing.

The result of the ordering of the surahs and the lack of "subject-oriented" chapters make the Qur'an look very different from what we are accustomed to in the West. I remember how incomprehensible it was to me when I first tried to read it and how difficult it still is for me and even for native Arabic speakers. To those of us in the West, the Qur'an seems fragmentary and fractured, and therefore confusing.

In fact, I never really understood the Qur'an until I started reading *about* the Qur'an. The key in reading the Qur'an is remembering that it is not really a book in the same way we think of novels or textbooks or chapter books, but rather like a long poem or song. It means, after all, "recitation." It has been described as "a vibrant, powerful outpouring of divine messages."[5] A long poem or song does not necessarily adhere to a narrative organized by subject.

Scholars have espoused various theories for why the surahs cover so many subjects and, conversely, why the same subject is sometimes covered by so many surahs. Professor Arthur J. Arberry impatiently observed this pedestrian analysis simply misses the entire point of the Qur'an, because "everlasting truth is not held within the confines of time and space, but every moment reveals itself wholly and completely."[6]

Although not Muslim himself, Professor Arberry understood the need to read the Qur'an as a divine document in order to understand its mystery and power. He did not mean that someone reading the Qur'an must believe in Muhammad's revelation or the entire message of Islam—he himself did not. Rather, Arberry meant that, in order to understand why the Qur'an is a powerful and influential piece of literature, it must be read *as though* it were revelation.

The Qur'an, then, catches us unawares if we think of it as a book rather than a poem. Like poetry, the Qur'an is not written in prose but unmetered verse. It even rhymes. Originally, the Qur'an was recited, just as poetry is.

Even today, in fact, recitation of the Qur'an is still an art form. In many countries, people gather in auditoriums to hear contests of Qur'anic recitation. It has been shown, interestingly, that Qur'anic chanting actually affects the breathing patterns of those listening to it, slowing and deepening their breaths.[7]

I remember lying in bed as a child and falling asleep to the sounds of my father chanting the Qur'an from where he sat in the living room, the sing-song cadences flowing into my very breaths. I drifted on the sounds and patterns, comforted, even without knowing what the words meant. I never thought to ask him why he chanted Qur'anic poetry at night, any more than I thought to ask why my husband recited *Casey at the Bat* to our baby son every night.

Consistent with poetry and music rather than prose, the Qur'an is not narrative, but allusive. That is, it alludes to certain historical events and episodes, often without specifying names and places. Partly, this is because the Qur'an assumes a certain knowledge of the Judeo-Christian tradition.

But, the Qur'an simply does not consider names and places to be so terribly important. The stories are merely vehicles for specific points and morals that need to be stressed, not necessarily noteworthy in themselves. The story of Moses, for example, is scattered over several surahs. This is not because the Qur'an continually forgets things about Moses that it remembers to add later, but because various parts of Moses' story become relevant at various times and with respect to various points to be illustrated.

Poems and songs are allusive, too, and not given to detailed explanations of all the concepts they embody. For instance, in musical terms, parts of the Qur'an operate as choruses, leitmotifs, or refrains in Arabic; when translated into English, however, they sound merely repetitive.[8]

The poetic character of the Qur'an makes it difficult to translate. *Any* text so old and poetic would be difficult to translate well. But the Qur'an is especially problematic. Arberry discusses some of the reasons why:

> [T]he rhetoric and rhythm of the Arabic of the Koran are so characteristic, so powerful, so highly emotive, that any version whatsoever is bound in the nature of things to be but a poor copy of the glittering splendour of the original... .[9]

In the preface to his translation, Arberry tries to explain the rhythm that pulses throughout the Qur'an and how difficult it is to reproduce this rhythm in a translation. He writes:

> [It] is to the rhythm that I constantly return as I grope for a clue to the arresting, the hypnotic power of the Muslim scriptures... . [An Arab friend] expressed exactly what was in my mind. 'Whenever I hear the Koran chanted, it is as though I am listening to music; underneath the flowing melody there is sounding all the time the insistent beat of a drum... . It is like the beating of my heart.'[10]

The Qur'anic voice gets lost in translation. In English, God's voice in the Qur'an sounds angry. Yet, in Arabic, it is a sense of sadness, not anger, that permeates the tone of the Qur'an. That is an enormous difference.

When I first read the Qur'an in English, my reaction was fear of hellfire because God sounded angry. But my father laughed and said, no, that was because I was reading it in English. The Qur'an is tender and compassionate and all about forgiveness, he told me. Why else would every surah start with the phrase, "In the name of God, most Merciful, most Compassionate"? And why else, he asked me, would the Qur'an follow every injunction for punishment with the qualification that forgiveness is always better, that mercy is *always* better?

In addition to the difficulties of translating poetry, the Arabic language presents specific problems of translation because of its nature, grammar, and style. According to one view, a modern non-Arab cannot perfectly understand Qur'anic diction without two things: an academic expertise in classical Arabic, which is very different from modern Arabic, and an intimate knowledge of the speech of the Bedouin desert Arabs, because this is closest to the Arabic of the Qur'an.[11]

These two factors are crucial, because after so many centuries, not every word of the Qur'an is entirely clear in its meaning. A word may have had several original meanings. In addition, many words may have originally meant something different from what they eventually *came* to mean in light of later Islamic doctrine.

I realize this discussion of linguistics may seem irrelevant or overly academic, but it is vital, even to daily life as a Muslim. The impression that an English speaker (Muslim or not) gets from a translation of the Qur'an does depend upon all these linguistic issues, because countless words in an English translation may not be the right ones. And sometimes a single disputed word of text can mean the crucial difference between veiling or not veiling, inheriting nothing or everything, polygamy or monogamy, equality or sexism.

Let me illustrate how a translation could totally change the meaning. An aspect that gets lost in translation is an Arabic linguistic pattern (called *ijaz*) that is characterized by elliptical phrases representing sequences of mental associations, or particular thoughts.[12] These are elliptical in that they deliberately omit intermediate phrases to make a powerful leap toward the final idea to be expressed.[13]

Those unfamiliar with this pattern of elliptical phrases may not understand the underlying meaning of a phrase even if they understand the Arabic words. When translated, these elliptical patterns become disrupted, meaningless jumbles.[14] And those meaningless jumbles, before they were "translated," were earth-shatteringly important to Islam, as part of its holy scripture.

The very construction of Arabic also makes translation difficult. Arabic is "built up upon mathematical principles—a phenomenon not paralleled by any other language."[15] Its structure allows religious and psychological ideas to be centered around one grammatical stem. This results in an intense concentration of language that allows one word to convey many different concepts.[16] When translated, a many-layered Arabic word might lose many meanings in the new language. That's why at least one translator considers the linguistic notes to his translation of the Qur'an to be an intrinsic part of the translation itself.[17] What I find to be a particularly interesting consequence about this feature of Arabic is that the Qur'an, read in English, probably seems more repetitious than it does in the original Arabic.

Why should I really care about all this? Because sometimes translation of a single word can have effects as far-reaching as women's rights.

For example, Arabic has a gender dynamic that is difficult to convey properly into English. What could be translated as "her" or "it" or neither is instead, at times, translated as "him."[18] Translation erases the multiple dimensions of the Arabic gender dynamic:

> The loss of the Qur'anic gender dynamic in translations reinforces one of the most misleading stereotypes about Islam and the Qur'an—that the Qur'an is based on rigid, male-centered language. Yet this stereo-type of a language of "he-God and he-man" is at odds not only with Islamic theology (which denies that God is male or female) but also with the intricate and beautiful gender dynamic that is a fundamental part of Qur'anic language.[19]

The Qur'an contains much more of a female presence than translations demonstrate. In other words, the Qur'an does not use male-centered language but includes women in its worldview. The Qur'an does not address men only but women, as well; the proof is there in the grammar. I cannot overstate how monumentally important this is to me. As a Muslim woman who is constantly fighting to overturn the stereotypes and the notion that Islam equals sexism, the fact that the Qur'an is *not* male-centered is critical.

If the fact that the Qur'an speaks to women as well as men does not seem remarkable, compare other equally ancient texts: not many address women. The words in our own Constitution, only a few hundred years old, decree "all men are created equal," but non-white men and women were not originally included in that phrase.

Another aspect of the feminine that gets lost in translation has to do with something Michael Sells calls "sound figures." These are patterns of language that actually provide undertones of meaning and implicit "partial personifications," which are mental and emotional images that reside between the lines of the literal text.[20]

Remember the term *onomatopoeia* from (probably) junior high school English class? Onomatopoeia describes a word whose very sound suggests its meaning, like "swish" or "crunch." The sound figures in the Qur'an function along the same lines, in that they give rise to implicit means—but in a far more complex manner:

> These [sound figure] patterns create partial personifications—of a woman giving birth, conceiving, suffering, experiencing peace, or grieving at the loss of her only child. The sound figures that create the implicit personifications also have the impact of interjections—that is, expressions of feeling, wonder, contentment, and sorrow—in which the sound itself is intertwined completely with the meaning.[21]

All this is lost when the Qur'an is translated, though the proof is there in the grammar. Because English is gender-neutral (nouns, for example, are not assigned masculine and feminine forms), the gender subtleties in the Qur'an cannot be translated. And that, Sells points out, is "particularly damaging because of the way Islam has been perceived in stereotypes about gender and the role of women in society." [22]

The sound figures also tie together various parts of the Qur'an. Someone hearing the recitation of one passage will hear, because of a specific sound pattern, echoes of *another* passage, undertones of a secondary meaning.[23] In this way, passages achieve interweaving connections, combining to produce more complex meanings.

These sound figures, as well as other linguistic aspects of the Qur'an, contribute to a narrative voice that Sells says is a very distinctive combination of absolute majesty and tender intimacy.[24] But as the sound figures cannot be translated, that unique melding of awesome grandeur and personal compassion totally disappears, as does the feminine presence.

Arabic and English are stylistically very different, too, and this causes translation difficulties. Arabic is very poetic in style. The Qur'an is in unmetered verse and it rhymes; but the entire Arabic language and culture, not just the Qur'an, emphasizes the poetic.

For example, imagine a campfire, men in white robes, the endlessly black desert night waiting quietly just beyond the flickering light. They sit listening to the traveling bard with them, the man who brings them the latest news, rumors, stories of heroism, and politics, all couched in poetic phrases. For thousands of years, since long before Islam, stories and tales have been communicated through Arabic poetry. Even today, poetry is an integral part of everyday language, not just something trudged through reluctantly in school.

Poetry and storytelling are the highest art forms in Arabic-speaking cultures. In Marrakech, my husband and I bought dates and cloth in the bustling public square called *Djemaa el-fna*, or "The Gathering of the Dead." It is a fascinating place, bursting with sounds and colors and smells. On any given weekend, a storyteller in a robe striped in red, purple, and blue might travel down from the hills to the square. He might enter the square, carefully sidestepping the python charmers, as we did, and find a sun-baked piece of ground on which to spread his carpet. He might release his white pigeon into the sky and watch it, smiling, as it drops down onto his outstretched hand, bearing a story. The gathering crowd might grow silent with anticipation. Time might stop and tasks remain undone until the storyteller finishes, because time is unimportant beside poetry.

My husband and I thought of naming our daughter *Sameera*, which means "storyteller." When I mentioned this to a friend, she was shocked I would give my child a name that meant "liar."

"No," I explained, caught between amusement and surprised dismay, "it doesn't mean teller of lies. It means teller of stories—someone who can tell a good story, you know, like around a campfire."

My family speaks Urdu, not Arabic. But the linguistic traditions are similar, including the poetic inclinations. For example, I am not uncomfortable mixing metaphors. Occasionally, during my formative years, my parents' Indian and Pakistani friends would arrange a "poetry party." The requisite hundred guests would dine and then sit listening for hours to poetry and sometimes songs accompanied by a *tabla*, a small Indian drum. My husband, a very literal person, still has difficulty understanding my tendency toward metaphorical turns of phrase.

But even to me sometimes, and certainly to others in the West, the linguistic style of Arabic sometimes seems excessively flowery. During the Gulf War of the early 1990s, Saddam Hussein sounded silly to Americans because his speeches were bursting with stylistically exaggerated phrases like "the mother of all battles." Poetry does not translate well. The Qur'an is no exception.

Perhaps the only solution is to hear the language yourself. In Damascus, if you sit on a rooftop at night, you will likely hear the sing-song chanting of Arabic love poems floating in the air, drifting toward you from all directions, from other rooftops. In Egypt, to sit in the evening air on the front porch after dinner is to hear snatches of chanted poetry wafting through the night. And sometimes, the chanting of the Qur'an.

Qur'anic Content

While attending college and taking a human biology class under duress (my parents wanted me to be a doctor), I studied evolutionary theory along with the rest of the class. My best friend asked me how I could psychologically cope with evolutionary theory. As a Muslim, I was supposed to believe God made everything. (She was not Muslim.) I told her I did believe God made everything. She gazed at me incredulously and asked, "So you think everything they're talking about in class is just *made up?*"

I found it difficult to articulate why exactly I did not perceive a conflict between the Qur'an and evolutionary theory. The answer that came to me later, too late to redeem my self-esteem, was simply this: I believe God made everything. *How* exactly God made it, I do not know. Darwin may very well have gotten it right. As Akbar Ahmed explains:

> While stating that creation took six days (Surah 7: verse 54), the Quran explains that one of God's days may be like a thousand years (Surah 22: verse 47) or even fifty thousand years (Surah 70: verse 4) of ours; clearly, Darwin may be accommodated.[25]

The Qur'an is not meant to be a story, set of laws, or sequence of academic arguments, although it contains elements of all these things. The content of the Qur'an covers everything from specific rules of inheritance to general injunctions of kindness and justice. The Qur'an calls itself a "guidance for mankind."[26] The Qur'an most concerns itself with these themes: God, human beings as individuals, human society, women's rights, the Qur'anic worldview, nature, prophets, Satan and evil, and the Muslim community.[27]

The following verse is the "Throne Verse." Lyrical and powerful, it illustrates the first theme, God:

> God! There is no god but He, the
> Living, the Everlasting.
> Slumber seizes Him not, neither sleep;
> To Him belongs
> All that is in the heavens and the earth.
> Who is there that shall intercede with Him
> Save by His leave?
> He knows all that lies open before men

And all that is hidden from them,
And they comprehend not anything of His knowledge
Save such as He wills.
His Throne comprises the heavens and the earth;
The preserving of them oppresses Him not;
He is the All-High, the All-Glorious.[28]

Although worshiping anything other than God is adversative to Islamic principles, many verses in the Qur'an instruct Muslims to be tolerant of people who do not believe in Islam or God. The following verse instructs Muslims to never revile anything that other people hold sacred, even if Islamic principles are contravened: "Do not insult those beings whom they invoke instead of God."[29]

The word "insult" in this verse has also been translated as "revile" or "abuse." Clearly, hurting someone's feelings because they do not follow Islam is prohibited. Similarly, the Qur'an forbids Muslims from disputing with the People of an Earlier Revelation (definitely referring to Jews and Christians, but arguably including other groups), as we discussed in chapter two. The following surah also urges religious tolerance:

Say: "O you who deny the truth!
I do not worship that which you worship,
And neither do you worship that which I worship... .
Unto you, your religion, and unto me, mine!"[30]

Not only that, the Qur'an commands belief in all revealed scriptures of God:

Say: "I believe in whatever revelation God has bestowed from on high;
And I am bidden to bring about equity in your mutual views....
Let there be no contention between us and you..."[31]

The words "bring about equity in your mutual views" mean to encourage tolerance between various views and reduce contention and sectarianism. For a centuries-old religious text, this attitude of tolerance is remarkable.

But the media, as well as the person on the street, cannot seem to stop talking about violence in the Qur'an. Understandably, people seem to be struggling to comprehend why the September 11th attacks occurred. I and other Muslims have sought to puzzle out the very same thing. Unfortunately, however, I encounter increasing numbers of those who have begun to read the Qur'an in order to prove to themselves and others that Islam is a violent religion. Not only is this hostile approach simplistically self-fulfilling, it leads to incorrect results.

Consider the verse of the Qur'an that has been quoted *ad nauseum*, the one that reads, "And slay them wherever you may come upon them, and drive them away from wherever they drove you away… ."[32] I have heard this quoted many times in news pieces. But usually, those quoting this verse omit the end of the sentence, which reads, "for oppression is even worse than killing."[33] This, of course, means that the permission to slay is in response to being oppressed.

Even more significantly, I have not heard any of the journalists quote the verse that comes immediately before the "slaying" verse and is a condition upon it, the one that says:

> But do not attack them if they do not attack you first.
> Allah loves not the aggressor.[34]

Nor have I heard quoted the verse that comes right after this one, which reads, "but if they desist [fighting], then all hostility shall cease."[35]

Puts a whole different spin on it, doesn't it? These verses allow war in self-defense.

It makes me wonder how every single person quoting those verses could have failed to see the rest of the sentences and the verses immediately preceding and following. Perhaps they simply did not think them worth mentioning. It is convenient to insist the Qur'an is violent because that provides a nice, tidy reason for the terrorism carried out in the name of Islam and a nice, tidy group of people to hate.

But in almost every case that the Qur'an mentions fighting, it also commands in some form or another that if the enemy desists fighting, then you must desist fighting (Surah 2, verse 192). The Qur'an insists if the enemy asks for peace, you must agree to peace (Surah 4, verse 86). Do not attack them unless they attack you first (Surah 2, verse 190). You may not treat noncombatants as the enemy, says the Qur'an, even if they are hostile to you and Islam (Surah 4, verse 94). And if the enemy repents, let them go their way (Surah 9, verse 5).

Not only is reading the entire passage crucial in reading the verse, reading the entire Qur'an is crucial because all Qur'anic verses interact with each other.

In addition, historical context is crucial, too. Many of the last twenty-three years of Muhammad's life were spent resisting persecution and torture, to protect himself and his followers. Muhammad did fight to defend himself and the thousands of people under his protection. Many verses sanctioning warfare and killing were revealed in the context of either an ongoing battle when the other side had begun hostilities, cases of self-defense, or when the other side had broken their treaties. All such "fighting" verses★★ must be interpreted in the context of a struggle against oppression and persecution.[36]

Of the approximately 6,236 verses of the Qur'an, only fifty-nine mention fighting or warfare in any context. (Again, the number may vary slightly depending on the way the text is numbered.) Of these fifty-nine verses, at least ten contain injunctions *not* to fight. A few more mention fighting only in passing and in the context of historical stories of past prophets. That leaves only about forty-seven verses—of the 6,236 total verses of the Qur'an—that urge warfare.

It seems to me that only a misguided and unsuccessful manual for murder would spend less than 1 percent of its narrative discussing fighting. Far more of its verses (114) urge peace. The over 6,000 remaining verses have nothing to do with war at all.

Those verses that do sanction fighting do so in the context of a just war and against the backdrop of the verses that command Muslims to practice tolerance, never aggress, make peace when the other side desires it, and never harm noncombatants.[37]

An accusation that is periodically flung at my feet as a sort of medieval gauntlet is the self-righteous, "But Jesus never fought anyone, even in self-defense."

I admire Jesus for that. He is one of Islam's greatest prophets. But in addition to being a prophet, Muhammad lived in a violent society as the political leader of over 10,000 people who were struggling against persecution. In the event of an attack, had Muhammad sat back and allowed thousands of men, women, and children to be massacred, I cannot imagine anyone would have deemed this to be a good and virtuous action.

In the summer of 2002, the University of North Carolina (UNC) was sued for including on its reading list Michael Sells' *Approaching the Qur'an*, which is not even the Qur'an itself, but simply a book on how to read a translation of the Qur'an and understand it. The plaintiffs asserted, among other groping arguments, that the book was one-sided because it did not discuss those passages relating to warfare. (Perhaps that is because less than 1 percent of the Qur'an relates to warfare.)

★★This is my own term and not a religious term or term of art.

As a freshman in college, I was required to read the Bible, not just a book about the Bible. But we read mostly Genesis and did not read the Biblical passages involving violence. No one complained that we were not assigned any other religious texts to read. No one complained of getting a non-representative or one-sided view of Christianity.

The trial court and federal appeals court dismissed the lawsuit against UNC. My daughter's babysitter, a recent college graduate, actually defended this lawsuit to me. She said, "But I heard that they didn't like the book because it wasn't representative of Islam."

"Because it didn't include the fighting verses?" I asked.

"Yes," she nodded.

That assumes the forty-seven fighting verses (never mind the over 6,000 verses covering other subjects or the 114 verses urging peace) are representative of Islam.

"Yes, but," said my daughter's babysitter, "the violent verses are representative of Islam because there are Muslim fundamentalists who still believe in them."

All Muslims believe in them, because they are part of the Qur'an, which is God's word in Islam. All Muslims do not believe in violence, however. The vast majority of Muslims believe the fighting verses were revealed in a specific, historical context to permit the use of force in self-defense; the vast majority of Muslims believe that war according to Islam is justifiable only in self-defense; the vast majority of Qur'anic verses have nothing to do with warfare. It is faulty logic to conclude that the fighting verses in the Qur'an are representative either of Islam or Muslims.

Besides, every religion has people who justify violence on the basis of religious scripture. Groups who blow up abortion clinics do so because of religion. The Ku Klux Klan justified killing Jews and blacks on the basis of the Bible. Timothy McVeigh believed that blowing up federal buildings was necessary to preserving Christian identity. Some Muslims justify their violence on the Qur'an. But that does not make violent Qur'anic verses representative of Islam any more than the violent verses in the Bible form the sum total of Christianity.

Universities should indeed teach the entire Qur'an, as some people opposed to *Approaching the Qur'an* have sarcastically challenged them to do. It would then be patently obvious that the Qur'an has many more passages urging peace and tolerance than it has passages sanctioning fighting.

My husband traveled to Seattle on a business trip recently and over-heard two men sitting at the table next to his in a restaurant. One of them said, "Well, the Bible says that a false prophet shall not be allowed to live, and that's why we should kill Osama bin Laden and his followers."

No one ever claimed bin Laden (or any follower of his) was a prophet, not even bin Laden himself. But more importantly, would every Christian agree with that statement? The man at the table held a Bible in his hands and used it to justify killing. Does that mean that verse is representative of Christianity? No. His statement should not allow me, for instance, to start generalizing about Jews or Christians.

Over 99.2 percent of the Qur'an discusses subjects other than warfare. For instance, the Qur'an laid down many rules for the reform of pre-Islamic Arabian culture. This is the "humankind in society" theme. The Qur'an gives us specific directions on how to implement social and moral justice in verses touching on everything from family law to commercial law.

The Qur'an teaches us how to behave as individuals, as well as a society. Humans differ from angels because we possess the ability to think creatively, a positive aspect that balances (somewhat) our wreaking havoc and creating chaos.[38] The Qur'an instructs us to use that ability to cling to the straight path and reject pettiness and sin. This struggle, incidentally, is called *jihad*. And if we indeed struggle with the utmost effort and are virtuous, we can even resist Satan, who slithers among us to insinuate his shadowy whispers into our hearts.

When I was young and scared of the dark, my mother would pat my head and counsel me to recite one surah in particular that would help me find peace and sleep. It was this one:

> Say: I seek refuge with the Sustainer of humankind
> Sovereign of humankind
> God of humankind
> From the evil of the whispering slinker,
> Who whispers in the breasts of humankind;
> From all invisible forces as well as humankind.[39]

Long after I should have been afraid of the dark, I saw an unnerving play on the London stage that was so well-acted and convincing that I could not sleep. I kept listening for creaky footsteps and watching for lifeless faces floating above my bed. Finally, to my embarrassment, I had to recite this surah to myself, barely, furtively whispering so that my softly snoring husband would not hear. I was relieved to find that it still worked.

The Qur'anic worldview does not allow for ghosts, anyway, as I should have remembered. The exact and ordered universe with its smoothly functioning machinery is the prime sign of God. The Qur'an describes nature, the Islamic worldview, the multiple heavens, the prescribed paths for the celestial bodies, heaven, hell, and the Day of Judgment. Because the Qur'an does not overtly distinguish between natural causes and religious causes (winds and clouds do *cause* rains, but it is God who *brings* rains and Who is working within the natural causes[40]), it can absorb many layers of knowledge and meaning. Without difficulty the Qur'an can accommodate science, religion, daily earthly existence, secular knowledge, heaven, and holy knowledge.

Perhaps the one surah that most captures the spirit and essence of Islam in a few short lines is the first one. I and other Muslims recite it many times a day as a prayer and an entreaty:

The Opening

In the Name of God, the Compassionate, the Caring
Praise belongs to God,
Lord sustainer of the worlds
The Compassionate, the Caring
Master of the Day of Reckoning
To you we turn to worship
And to you we turn in time of need
Guide us along the road straight,
The road of those to whom you are giving,
Not those with anger upon them
Not those who have lost the way.[41]

Muslims recite this surah when they pray in public or in private. This is the surah that comes to mind when extra guidance or confidence is needed and it is not the time for a full, formal prayer. It's been called The Lord's Prayer for Muslims. I do not remember ever taking any sort of exam without muttering Surah Fatiha hurriedly under my breath first.

I think this desperate appeal to the Deity was in keeping with the spirit of the Qur'an, not because the Qur'an contains advice on exam-taking, but because it is a practical, contemporary document. That is, the verses revealed in the Qur'an were often in direct response to a crisis or question arising among the followers of the new religion. Therefore, the context and historical background of the verses remain crucial to understanding them. But historical context is only one reason a Qur'anic verse may not mean what you think it means.

Why Quoting Qur'anic Verses Out of Context Is Particularly Misleading

Quoting isolated verses from the Qur'an is dangerous because too many factors affect the meaning, and none of these are obvious from a face-value reading. The problems with translation, already discussed, is one factor.

Other factors are crucial, too. For instance, some verses were revealed in response to specific seventh-century circumstances, and some applied only to specific seventh-century institutions. It is difficult to know whether verses are metaphorical or symbolic. Still other verses are superseded by later Qur'anic verses or by *hadith* (sayings of the Prophet). Sometimes, a Qur'anic verse carves out an exception to a rule in another verse. All Qur'anic verses are interpreted and sometimes expanded by the massive body of interpretive literature developed by early Islamic scholars.

Moreover, words that appear in Arabic today may not mean what they meant fourteen centuries ago. The Qur'an has not been "modernized." Many verses have multiple possible meanings and it is impossible for anyone to know, simply by reading the Qur'an, which one was accepted by Islamic scholars. In fact, sometimes the early scholars disagreed on meanings of terms.

Most importantly, the Qur'an and the *Sunnah* (the words and deeds of the Prophet) cannot be perfectly understood without the massive body of religious jurisprudence (called *fiqh*) that was developed to interpret them. The early Muslims began to develop a set of guidelines based on and derived from the Qur'an and *Sunnah*, and this analysis and interpretation continued over centuries. Generally, these guidelines, when taken together with the Qur'an and *Sunnah*, are collectively called the *Shari'a*.

My guess is that most journalists had not read the books of Islamic jurisprudence (or even basic primers on Islam, for that matter) before they started opining about the Qur'an.

A friend recently asked me what *Shari'a* meant, because he had read a reference to it in the newspaper. I was surprised that newspapers were discussing it, because not even Islamic scholars agree on exactly what constitutes *Shari'a*. Basically, *Shari'a* means "the road to the watering place," or "the clear path to be followed." It means the path of goodness as specified by God. Loosely, it can simply mean, "Islam." The divine, abstract *Shari'a* is the path God wants us to follow. The concrete *Shari'a* is usually considered to comprise the Qur'an, the *Sunnah*, and the books of jurisprudence. Some modern scholars have distinguished between the man-made jurisprudence and the divine law of the Qur'an and *Sunnah*. Shi'i and Sunni scholars differ on some points, as well. The concrete, man-made part of the *Shari'a* is fallible because it was developed by fallible human beings in an attempt to understand and record what God meant for us to do—that is, what God's *Shari'a* required of us.

Sometimes *Shari'a* is translated as "God's law" or "Islamic law." This term is misleading because "law" is something that is usually made by a state or ruler. *Shari'a*, on the other hand, was never made by the state and remained traditionally separate from the state. It was the divine law of the Qur'an and *Sunnah*, developed and interpreted by religious scholars to form a body of religious guidelines. Islamic law is law in the way the Ten Commandments are law. One scholar defines it this way: "*Shari'ah* as conceived by God is flawless, but as understood by human beings *Shari'ah* is imperfect and contingent."[42]

All this goes to show that quoting the Qur'an out of context and without the interpretive literature is misleading. The actual meaning may be completely unrelated to what it seems to mean. Considering the idiosyncrasies of 1,300-year-old Arabic, the obscure historical figures and events the Qur'an refers to without explaining, the enormous difficulties of translation, and the historical context of the verses, it should be obvious why someone knowing nothing about Islam might come up with inaccurate conceptions of what the Qur'an means. Yet, many in the public discourse have felt confident enough in their ability to understand the Qur'an that they have made ludicrous statements in the public domain (some of these are discussed in chapter ten).

But so what? Even all Muslims do not agree on what each verse of the Qur'an means. No particular meaning is absolute, leaping to the eye of whoever (however casually) picks up the Qur'an to prove a point.

Quotes from the Qur'an have lately been so selective as to sometimes even imply the opposite of what the Qur'an means. For example, Mr. Rooney stated on television that Muslims "are not allowed to think that there may be any truth to any other religion."[43] This statement is so belligerently incorrect that it directly contravenes Islamic principles, which not only do not dictate anywhere that only Muslims will go to heaven, they specifically establish that a person need *not* be Muslim to attain paradise.

A primary reason my husband is Muslim is because it is established in Islam that anyone, Muslim or otherwise, may go to heaven. Forgiveness does not apply exclusively to Muslims, and Muslims are not a chosen people. In Islam, if you do good things, you go to heaven.

Every religious scripture, by definition, treats its religion as the correct one; that is the whole purpose of a religious scripture. That is the whole purpose of the Qur'an, too, to educate humankind about the One God and how to live life in surrender to the One God. But the Qur'an not only stresses that good deeds will take you to heaven, it specifically enjoins respect of unbelievers and repeatedly commands tolerance of other religions. It forbids discourtesy to Jews and Christians, forbids insulting those who worship an object other than God, and allows people to be ruled by their own religious laws.

The overwhelming message of the Qur'an is forgiveness, mercy, peace, and freedom to better oneself and worship God. In a nutshell, context and the entirety of the scripture is everything. Most people I have spoken to understand that religious texts were products of ancient societies and need to be read in context, metaphorically, and sometimes homiletically (as deliberate overstatements not meant to be taken literally but as seeking to convey the serious nature of the crime). These texts were received and understood hundreds of years ago. This is true of the Qur'an, as well.

As I discussed earlier, Muslims have been careful to disallow any change in the Qur'an because we consider it to be the word of God and because we are afraid of introducing human error into the text. The Qur'an can never be changed. If the Qur'an is forever, then it can apply equally well to different societies and time frames with different results. Forever does not mean *static*.

The Qur'an is the only miracle Muhammad ever claimed, and not on his own behalf, but God's. As part of the community of believers (*umma*), Muslims worldwide look to the same words for their religion. They recite the same words—those of the Qur'an—when they pray, whatever their culture, whatever their native language.

5

Who's Who in Islam:
From Ayatollahs to Whirling Dervishes

When my parents moved from India to a California university town in the 1960s, the residents were kind and welcoming but the Indian staples of tea and spices and plain yogurt were only sparsely available and little cherished. Pining for rare treasures like mangoes and cilantro, my parents were grateful for any connection that made them feel less alien. They formed an addiction to enchiladas because Mexican food, though not very similar to Indian food, contained the only incendiary flavors in local restaurant cuisine.

Shortly after my father started his graduate program, he encountered an American cafeteria for the first time. A fellow graduate student had persuaded him to join him for lunch in the student union, where behind the counter sat small dishes of optimistically arrayed but unfamiliar foods, wrapped in plastic, wrapped in foil. Pushing his tray along behind his friend, my father peered surreptitiously at the offerings—cheerfully colored gelatinous substances that jiggled at the slightest shake, cellophane-wrapped sandwiches with indecipherable fillings squashed between the bread, tins with baffling names that gave no hint of their contents. He scrutinized them in the hope that inspiration would arrive to assist him and his dignity.

When it did not, he did the next best thing and imitated his friend. If his friend took a bowl of the red jiggly stuff, my father did, too. If his friend took a plate of some meat smothered in a beige sauce and brightened by small orange cubes (carrots?), my father, hoping he was not buying pork, took that, too.

It was only at the cash register that my father's friend glanced back at him and then started in surprise.

"You're going to eat all that?" he exclaimed.

"I only took what you took," my father protested.

His friend stared blankly and then started laughing. "But I'm buying lunch for my mother, too!"

My father still laughs ruefully when he tells the story.

Given all the difficulties of adjusting to an alien culture and language, it was only natural that the rare accidental meeting with other Indians or, rarer still, other Muslims inspired such delight as to forge instant lifelong friendships. Whether the Muslims identified themselves as Sunni, Shi'i, Sufi, or something else never mattered.

Even now, though many more Muslims reside in the United States than when my parents arrived here, we do not consider the various divisions of Islam to be terribly relevant or important. They cannot accurately be called "sects" because Islam has no orthodoxy or central Muslim authority to break away from.

This chapter clarifies some of the confusion with respect to the various divisions of Islam: Sunni, Shi'i, Sufi, Wahhabi and Taliban, and, though it has very little to do with Islam despite its name, the Nation of Islam.

Sunni and Shi'a

The two largest groups of Muslims are *Sunni* and *Shi'a* (or *Shi'i*, depending on the grammatical context). These terms are occasionally Anglicized to *Sunnite* and *Shi'ite*. About 90 percent of Muslims in the world are Sunni and most of the rest are Shi'i. Sunnism and Shi'ism developed roughly side by side. They separated not because of a theological or doctrinal dispute (such as about the nature of God or the identity of the Prophet), but an argument regarding who was entitled to wield religious authority.

While the Prophet was alive, the only authority in the new religion of Islam was, well, the Prophet. He dispensed justice in accordance with the Qur'anic verses that had been revealed to him, although he regularly consulted his companions. After he died, his followers faced the sticky problem of leadership.

As we discussed in chapter three, the new Muslim community lacked precedents to follow because the seventh-century tribal Arabs had never before followed a single leader. Some Muslims believed that leadership of the new Muslim community should be kept within the Prophet's family. These people favored Ali and believed that the Prophet had designated him as the new leader. Another group believed the Prophet had not made such a designation, and these people put forward Abu Bakr as the next leader. The second group prevailed and would later become Sunni

Muslims, as those regarding the *Sunnah* of the Prophet as authoritative. The group that had favored Ali would later become the Shi'a.

Abu Bakr was never considered a prophet, nor was he ever considered a secular king; the caliph was the leader of the Muslim community. His full title was *khalifat rasul Allah*, or "successor to the prophet of God." By contrast, "sultan" designated a ruler more similar to a king and was also not a prophet or religious authority. As the concept of caliph developed, it came to mean someone who preserved the territory of Islam and acted, not unilaterally, but according to the wishes of the Muslim community and the teachings of the Prophet.

After the Prophet's death, differences of opinion regarding leadership and interpretation of Islamic tenets grew. By the time Uthman assumed leadership, the Muslim community had become internally stressed. Ali became the fourth caliph, and he personifies the focus of the split between the Sunni and the Shi'a.

In addition to being caliph, Ali was the Prophet's son-in-law and cousin, married to the Prophet's daughter, Fatima. The first civil war within the Muslim community occurred during his rule. Ali's forces triumphed, but he was assassinated after ruling as caliph for five years. His two sons, Muhammad's grandsons, did not succeed to his office. The elder, Hasan, was persuaded not to try, but Ali's younger son, Husayn, did lead a rebellion that failed spectacularly and resulted in his tragic death.

The death of Husayn, the Prophet's grandson, left a legacy of guilt and sorrow burdening the new Muslim community, particularly those who had been loyal to Ali from the beginning and had advocated retaining leadership in the Prophet's family. These people began to maintain that Ali should have been the Prophet's successor from the first and that, from then on, succession should have continued from father to son in a direct line from the Prophet Muhammad. The Muslims who maintained this view became the *Shi'at 'Ali* ("party of Ali"), shortened to Shi'a.

The Shi'a had a different vision of leadership from the Sunni. They maintained that the leader of the Muslim community, the *Imam*, was divinely selected and descended from the Prophet's family. This Shi'i *Imam* was infallible and, in a way, an heir of the Prophet Muhammad, though the *Imam* was not considered to be a prophet himself. The *Imam* was a divinely-inspired political and religious leader. Shi'i religious authority rested in the *Imam*s.

Note that the *Imam* was different from an *imam*. The *Imam* was an heir of the Prophet and divinely inspired. But an *imam* can simply be someone who has memorized enough surahs to lead the group prayer. Or, an *imam* can be someone who is learned in Islamic teachings and can lead the religious community and answer their questions. Both of these *imams* mean something different from *Imam*.

In contrast, Sunni Muslims did not require that leadership of the Muslim community remain within the Prophet's family, and they rejected the notion of the divinely inspired *Imam*. Sunni Muslims regarded the caliph not as the religious leader, but as the political leader of the religious community. Sunni religious authority eventually settled in the consensus of the religious scholars, or *ulama*.

The majority of the Shi'a are called Twelvers, also called *Imami* Shi'a, as well as *Ithna Ashari* Shi'a. Shi'i Muslims in this group identify twelve *Imams* descended from the line of Ali. The twelfth, the *Mahdi*, disappeared and is said to return one day. They believe the line of descent from the Prophet died out with the *Mahdi*. Until the *Mahdi* returns, Shi'i religious authority by default rests in the hands of the religious scholars, as it does in Sunni Islam.

Practically speaking, majority Shi'i authority in the present day is not all that different from Sunni authority. In both cases, it lies with the consensus of the religious scholars. But the Shi'i scholars claim they exercise authority on behalf of the absent *Imams*, whereas the Sunni scholars exercise authority on their own behalf, as scholars interpreting the *Sunnah*. Religious scholars can be female, by the way, and so can judges.

Aside from the Twelvers, there are two other main branches of the Shi'a: the *Zaydis* and the *Ismailis*. They constitute only a fraction of a percent of the total population of Muslims. *Zaydis* are the closest to Sunni Muslims. They believe that *Imams* must be descended from the Prophet and Fatima but do not believe they are divinely guided.

The *Ismaili* Shi'a do not believe the line of descent from Ali has died out. Since the nineteenth century, the authoritative head of the *Ismaili* Shi'a has been the Aga Khan, who is believed to be directly descended from Ali and Fatima. Rita Hayworth, the glamorous actress who costarred with Gene Kelly (my hero after I recovered from my crush on Captain Kirk) in the 1944 romantic comedy *Cover Girl*, married one of the Aga Khans. The Aga Khan is now the spiritual and cultural head of the *Ismaili* community and interprets Islamic law in light of modern society.[1] Therefore, in the *Ismaili* community, in contrast to other Muslim communities, an authoritative figure does exist. The current Aga Khan (the fourth) was educated at Harvard and lives in France.

Beyond the idea of the rightly guided *Imams*, no real doctrinal differ-ence exists between Sunni and Shi'i Muslims. All Muslims believe in the five pillars of Islam. The Shi'a have separate books of jurisprudence from the Sunni, and their interpretation of some Qur'anic verses, such as the inheritance verses, is somewhat different. The Shi'a celebrate additional holidays that relate to the Prophet's descendants, such as Ashura.

Aside from such minor differences, Sunnism and Shi'ism are very similar. It seems to me they are unnecessarily made to look more different than they are because both Muslims and non-Muslims try to apply to them the concept of "sect" in the way the word applies to Christianity. But Islam considers minor differences in interpretation as normal and valid and does not insist on one particular meticulous model as the correct one. That is why the four Sunni schools of thought, as well as the Shi'i school, are all considered valid.

I find this encompassing worldview appealing because it sends the message that arguing about little things is not only petty, it is un-Islamic. If you believe in one God and the Prophet, in taking care of orphans and widows, tolerating other religions and races, and practicing the five pillars, then you're a good Muslim, whatever your views on authority or other minor issues.

The Sufis

Before I had ever heard of the various divisions within Islam, I had heard of whirling dervishes. I did not know they belonged to my own religion. I only knew they whirled. I later learned that whirling dervishes were Sufis and that Sufis were Muslim. In America, Sufis are probably the most famous affiliation of Islam. In my parents' local Borders bookstore, most of the books on Islam have to do with Sufism.

Sufism is not a separate division within Islam like Sunnism and Shi'ism, but a *way to God*. A Muslim can be a Sunni Sufi or a Shi'i Sufi. The Sufis are sometimes called the mystics of Islam, but that unfairly stereotypes them as "impractical" and "unrealistic." More accurately, Sufism is a concentration on the interior, inner dimension of Islam:

> In general, Sufis have looked upon themselves as Muslims who take seriously God's call to perceive his presence both in the world and in the self. They tend to stress inwardness over outwardness, contempla-tion over action, spiritual development over legalism, and cultivation of the soul over interaction.[2]

Traditional Sufi masters sometimes describe Sufism in terms of geometry.[3] Imagine a circle with a center point and an infinite number of radii from the circumference to the center. The circumference represents the *Shari'a*, the divine guidelines of Islam. The center represents God. The radii are the infinite pathways that lead to God, the Center.

Only after one accepts the *Shari'a*—that is, stands on the circle—can one discover a path (a radius) that leads to God, the Center. [4] God is the only Reality and everything else is relative to Him; the *tariqah* is the way to unite with the Reality.[5] How in practical terms one goes about uniting with the Reality—which practices Sufism entails and what the radius involves in practical terms—is difficult to define because of the huge variety of diverse practices and theories within Sufism.

Sufism began in the prosperous time of the Umayyad dynasty (661–750), when a particular group of people became disgusted with the pursuit of wealth and overly legalistic religious perspectives. Seeing these as antithetical to the true message of Islam, they based their views on the example of the Prophet, who was a frugal and humble person, and on the Qur'an, which emphasizes God's mercy, compassion, beauty, and beneficence much more than it does God's wrath and punishment. The word *sufi* means "wool," a coarse weave of which these people began wearing as part of their practice of shunning wealth.

The Qur'an says, "God's is the east and the west; and wherever you turn, there is God's countenance."[6] Sufis seek to find God everywhere and distance themselves from worldly luxuries and distractions so they may discover the nearness of God, even in their own selves. One method the Sufis use to embrace the nearness of God is a concentrated, repetitive chanting (called *dhikr*) of the names of God or the *shahada* ("There is no god but God"). This chanting brings the focus away from the distracting outside world and onto God's name.

And so does whirling. Sufis use music and dancing to achieve a state of "ecstasy" that can be viewed as intoxication or "drunkenness" with the nearness of God. Whirling dervishes exemplify the dancing attempts to reach God. The whirling dance represents the whirling of celestial bodies in the universe.

In order to become intoxicated with the nearness of God, Sufis sing songs of adoration to God, the Prophet Muhammad, and various other "friends" of God. They often assume a frugal and simple lifestyle in order to distance themselves from the materialistic aspects of life that prove obstructive to oneness with God.

Sufism is not a single practice and doctrine but contains within itself many forms. Two extremes of Sufism have been referred to as "sober" Sufism and "drunken" Sufism. (This is metaphor!) Sober Sufism emphasizes the *Shari'a* and the importance of reason. Drunken Sufism emphasizes ecstatic union with or nearness to God and de-emphasizes strict Islamic doctrine.

Historically, drunken Sufism gave rise to a rich tradition of poetry, and sober Sufism resulted in treatises on jurisprudence, moral development, and philosophy. But the two are not completely separable: sober Sufism is described as the state that immediately follows drunkenness.[7] Balance between the two is considered ideal.

It was drunken Sufism that generally became popular with the masses and is better known in the West. A second-year associate in my law firm catapulted ecstatically into my office one day to tell me she had found *It*! She had discovered Sufism and the Way! What she went on to describe was drunken Sufism.

It is not surprising that drunken Sufism, emphasizing lush poetry and imagery, love, and oneness with God to the point of ecstasy, should catch fire in the imagination, not only in the East but in the West. Thousands in India, Indonesia, and elsewhere converted to Islam because of Sufism.

Volumes of Sufi poetry are widely published, and many English translations are available (see the Suggested Reading List in the back). The best Sufi poetry:

> gives rise to a marvelous joy and intoxication in the listener and conveys the experience of God's presence in creation. . . . The poets address the highest concerns of the soul and employ the most delicious and enticing imagery.[8]

The poet and writer Muhyiddin Ibn al-Arabi wrote poems in Arabic that express this idea of God's presence and love but in ways that blur the distinction between divine and not divine, God and not God. In the following poem, he rebels against the exclusivity of religious belief, of who is right and who is wrong:

> My heart can take on any form:
> For gazelles a meadow,
> A cloister for monks,
> For the idols, sacred ground,

> Ka'ba for the circling pilgrim,
> The tables of the Torah,
> The scrolls of the Qur'an.
> I profess the religion of love.
> Wherever its caravan turns
> Along the way, that is the belief,
> The faith I keep.[9]

Intoxication permeates his poem, "The Hadith of Love" (*hadith* means "saying of the Prophet"), from which the following passage is taken:

> He whom you desire
> is between your ribs,
> turned side to side
> in the heat of your sigh.
>
> I told them tell him
> He is the one
> Who kindled the fire
> blazing in my heart.
>
> It is extinguished only
> in our coming together. If
> it burns out of control,
> who can be blamed for loving?[10]

I can only imagine how early Islamic scholars reading poems of erotically expressed religious devotion would have been suspicious of Sufism! But in the twelfth century, a brilliant intellectual, lawyer, philosopher, and theologian named al-Ghazali legitimized Sufism and reconciled it solidly to the *Shari'a* and Islamic jurisprudence. Al-Ghazali also started one of the first Sufi Orders, which are sometimes called organizations or centers. Sufis today meet and conduct their devotional practices at such orders, which are led by a *shaykh*.

The Nation of Islam

Confusion abounds when it comes to the relationship between Muslims, "Black Muslims," the Nation of Islam, Islam, and Louis Farrakhan. The term "Nation of Islam" is confusing. I remember once asking my parents about the Nation of Islam and they told me simply, "Oh, that is something different." Only now, decades later, I realize that critical comments made to me in the 1970s about the Nation of Islam and Malcolm X were actually meant to criticize my religion. I never knew I was being criticized, because I never associated the Nation of Islam with my own beliefs! The reason is that the Nation is not a division of Islam.

The Nation of Islam began in the early 1900s as a separatist, nationalist movement for African Americans. It advocated beliefs, rituals, and practices that were unrecognizable as Islam and had almost nothing in common with it. However, these beliefs were inspired by Islam to some extent, as they were also inspired by Christianity and African-American pride.

The driving force behind the Nation of Islam stemmed from the despairing belief that African Americans, discriminated against and denied full participation in American society, would never gain equality or full citizenship benefits in the United States. African Americans needed to feel unity and pride in their race. The sole solution, it seemed to them, was to separate from white people, both physically and socially, by forming their own state.

I know what it is to be the object of hostility and prejudice, partly because I am Muslim and partly because I have brown skin, and I know that prejudice comes from the most primitive and contemptible part of human nature. Even knowing this firsthand, I can still only try to imagine the hopelessness that must have been daily routine for African Americans, despised in their own country, lacking full citizenship rights, and living in a country in which their own parents had been slaves. In which their great-great-great-grandparents, perhaps, had been *Muslim* slaves.

That is part of the reason for the confusing name "Nation of Islam." The organization itself had almost nothing in common with Islam. But centuries ago, up to 20 percent of the African men and women captured and brought to the American colonies as slaves were Muslim,[11] though they were nearly all forcibly converted to Christianity.[12]

Islam had spread to Africa in many ways—trade, conquest, and missionary activity—long before Columbus came to America or the pilgrims landed at Plymouth. Frederick Denny writes:

> Surviving accounts from the American South reveal that Muslim slaves, including some with Arabic literacy, struggled to sustain their religious beliefs and practices in a very adverse environment. We read of slaves who refused to eat pork or drink alcohol. In the twentieth century, African-Americans have steadily increased their sense of African cultural and spiritual traditions, including, for many, a desire to recover a lost Islamic heritage.[13]

I heard an African-American *imam* interviewed shortly after the September 11th attacks. The television interviewer asked the *imam* what he would say to the American who might be hostile to or frightened of the Muslim person living down the street. The *imam* pointed out that Muslims have been living in America since before it was a country, and nothing like the September 11th attacks had ever happened. We have been among you, living among you, in peace, for longer than you may think.

After emancipation from slavery, African Americans had a difficult time adjusting to and finding a place in white society; it was only natural that movements focusing on black identity should emerge. These arose to help black Americans deal with social and economic problems, prejudice, and their changing identity.[14]

Another reason for the connection between Islam and the Nation of Islam was that African Americans needed to find an identity separate from white identity. The Nation of Islam viewed Christianity as the white person's religion, with its Caucasian images of God and the angels. Therefore, the black person's religion necessarily became something else.

The Nation of Islam had its inceptions in 1913, when a man named Timothy Drew, born in North Carolina, changed his name to Noble Drew Ali and founded the Moorish Science Temple. His organization stressed racial pride for African Americans and viewed Christianity as a religion for whites and Islam as a religion for blacks.[15] Membership in the organization was restricted to non-Caucasians.

Religious rituals and philosophies were reminiscent in some ways of Sunni Islam but actually represented the Moorish Science Temple's own, original creation. Noble Drew Ali proclaimed himself to be a prophet of Allah, charged by the King of Morocco with the mission of bringing Islam to African Americans.[16] His philosophy was a mixture of the Qur'an, the Bible, and African nationalism.[17] His goal was to free his people from racial prejudice and discrimination.

In 1929, Noble Drew Ali died and two men stepped forward to fill the leadership breach. John Givens El and Master Fard Muhammad each claimed Noble Drew Ali had been reincarnated within him.[18] (Reincarnation, incidentally, is antithetical to Islamic beliefs.) The Moorish Americans separated into two groups, depending upon which man they believed. Those who believed John Givens El became the Moorish Americans of today.[19] Those who believed Master Fard Muhammad eventually became the Nation of Islam.[20]

The Nation of Islam accepted Master Fard Muhammad as a "black Christ figure to replace the old Christ," and he eventually took on the role of prophet.[21] Elijah Muhammad succeeded to this role of prophet in 1933. He believed that, because African Americans were denied the full privileges of American citizenship, they had no choice but to form a state separate from whites and, until that state was formed, work for racial equality.[22]

Elijah Muhammad taught his followers that Master Fard Muhammad had not been a mere prophet but God himself. He declared he himself was the messenger of Master Fard Muhammad (God).[23] In this most basic of beliefs, the Nation diverged from Islam, which requires belief in no god but God and Muhammad as His messenger.

One of Elijah Muhammad's many ministers was a man named Malcolm Little. He had grown up during the Depression, one of eight children, his childhood punctured repeatedly by a series of tragedies. When Malcolm was six years old, his father was murdered, and the Ku Klux Klan burned his family home to the ground.[24] His mother was institutionalized when Malcolm was still in elementary school, and his brothers and sisters were separated.

Brilliant and athletic, Malcolm Little did well in school and was president of his class, despite being the only black student. But he discovered crime in his teens, was arrested when he was twenty-one, and joined the Nation of Islam while serving a seven-year prison sentence.[25] Upon converting to the Nation of Islam, he changed his name to Malcolm X, the "X" representing his lost identity at the hands of white people. Freed from prison at the age of twenty-seven, he functioned as one of the Nation's ministers from 1954 to 1964, devoted to Elijah Muhammad and his teachings.

As a minister, Malcolm X resolved to improve himself and his African-American people. He read voraciously, studying the dictionary to improve his vocabulary. A gifted orator, he preached that Christianity was the white man's religion and that the white man was the devil.[26] He insisted that the Bible constituted "the greatest single ideological weapon for enslaving millions of non-white human beings."[27] He acquired a huge following bewitched by his message and the sheer mesmerizing impact of his personality. Malcolm X—handsome, charismatic, ex-convict, self-educated, hated, loved, and feared—became the spokesperson for the Nation of Islam.

But in 1964, he performed the *Hajj*, the pilgrimage to Mecca that is required of all Muslims. And there he was struck by visual evidence that the worldwide phenomenon of Islam does not tolerate racial divisions. As one member of the millions-strong, multi-racial community of Muslims performing the pilgrimage, Malcolm X shed the Nation of Islam's separatist, nationalist philosophy from his own.

In the words of his wife, Malcolm returned to America no longer a Black Muslim but, simply, a Muslim.[28] He dropped the "X" from his name because he had found his identity. He became El-Hajj Malik El-Shabazz.

Malcolm Shabazz defected from the Nation of Islam and began his own organization in an attempt to internationalize the plight of African Americans and Africans worldwide. What he would have accomplished will remain unknown. A year after his pilgrimage, three men shot him to death with eighteen bullets. He was forty years old.[29]

Those convicted for Malcolm Shabazz's assassination belonged to that faction of the Nation of Islam who had resented his defection and acceptance of Sunni Islam. Ironically, all three assassins later converted to Sunni Islam themselves.[30]

After Malcolm's death, his close friend, Warith Deen Mohammed, Elijah Muhammad's son, continued to preach along the lines of Sunni Islam. W.D. Mohammed clashed ideologically with his father, who excommunicated him several times but just before his own death endorsed his son's leadership of the Nation of Islam and his alignment of the Nation of Islam with mainstream Sunni Islam. W.D. Mohammed changed the name of his organization to the "World Community of al-Islam" and then again to "American Muslim Mission" in 1980. Since then, the organization has been one of Sunni Muslims.

For a time, it seemed the Nation of Islam had foundered after forty-five years of advocating African nationalist ideology. Many had hated and feared its racist, separatist message, but it had provided opportunities and cohesion for African Americans oppressed in their own country. Elijah Muhammad had established schools, job opportunities, small businesses, and social organizations for African Americans. His organization required specific rules of behavior designed to eliminate alcoholism and drug abuse. Not least, the Nation of Islam had fostered pride in African-American heritage and culture.[31]

It was inevitable that such a historical and passionate movement as the Nation of Islam would resist obliteration. In 1977, Louis Farrakhan pulled the Nation of Islam from its death throes and resurrected it. He did not accept Warith Deen Mohammed's dismantling of the original

Nation of Islam. He began his own organization, with his own followers. His offshoot organization is still called the Nation of Islam and continues the original African-nationalist, separatist beliefs and teachings of Elijah Muhammad.[32]

The Nation of Islam is much smaller than the American Muslim Mission, but the flamboyant, controversial personality of Louis Farrakhan magnetizes the media. Farrakhan's separatist, racist message is offensive, but his organization has done good things, too, particularly fighting crime and drugs in the inner cities and rehabilitating prisoners.[33]

Although the majority of the original Nation of Islam transformed completely by the 1980s and is now aligned with Sunni Islam, the details of its history continue to confuse people. Many Muslims I know do not even realize the transformation took place at all and still assume the people who used to be called "Black Muslims" differ from Sunni Muslims in their beliefs. And many non-Muslims are still misled by the name "Nation of Islam," believing Farrakhan's organization is a part of Islam, when in fact it never has been.

The Nation of Islam, both in its original form and under Louis Farrakhan, cannot be reconciled with Islamic strictures. Its pedagogy of Master Fard Muhammad as God, Elijah Muhammad as his prophet-messenger, reincarnation, white people as devils, racism, and separatism conflicts with Islam. The Nation of Islam has never been a division of Islam; rather, it began as and still is a nationalist movement for the uplifting of African Americans. Despite its name, much of its philosophy derives from a reinterpretation of the Bible.

Of the nearly seven million Muslims in the United States today—black and white and all shades in between—the vast majority are part of the *umma,* the worldwide, color-blind, nationality-blind Islamic community. Islam encompasses all races; in fact, Muslims believe Abraham's second marriage with Hagar, which produced Ismail, was a racially mixed marriage. Indeed, in his last address to his community, the Prophet proclaimed these words, reminiscent of Surah 49 of the Qur'an:

> All of you descend from Adam and Adam was made of earth. There is no superiority for an Arab over a non-Arab nor for a non-Arab over an Arab, neither for a white man over a black man nor a black man over a white man except the superiority gained through consciousness of God. Indeed the noblest among you is the one who is most deeply conscious of God.[34]

Wahhabism and the Taliban

When I began to write this book several years ago, it did not occur to me to include this section. The Wahhabis and the Taliban form so small a percentage of Islam—and one so ideologically remote from mainstream Islam—that I did not think of them as part of mainstream Islam at all. The Wahhabis reside almost entirely in Saudi Arabia, though their influence is spreading. The Taliban reside almost entirely in Afghanistan. But I have unavoidably realized, in recent years, that when many Americans envision Muslims, they picture the Saudis or the Taliban. I have been appalled to read articles and letters referring to Saudi Arabia as "Islam Central" or "the place where the purest form of Islam is practiced."

The Wahhabis advertise their form of Islam as the purest form, but the huge majority of Muslims consider the Wahhabis to be extremist fundamentalists and the Taliban to be *militant* extremist fundamentalists.

In 2002, I attended a lecture in which Michael Sells, now professor of religion at the University of Chicago, explained the fame of Wahhabism in the following manner: imagine the seventeenth-century witch-hunting world of Salem, Massachusetts. Now imagine that Salem suddenly discovered itself to be sitting on an oil field, swimming in riches. Imagine further that the community of Salem fortuitously happened to control the most sacred Christian holy sites in the world. Finally, imagine that Salem allied itself with the only superpower left on earth. It would be natural to conclude, in the face of all these factors, that the witch-hunting world of Salem, Massachusetts was representative of—perhaps even the purest form of—Christianity.[35]

All these factors would combine to give Salem a disproportionate and inaccurately large exposure to the rest of the world. We might conclude that witch hunts were the purest Christianity, as were burnings at the stake and tests of witchcraft by drowning. We might conclude that the witch hunters represented mainstream Christianity or, perhaps, the true message of Christianity.

Now substitute the Saudi Wahhabi offshoot of Islam for Salem in this example, and substitute Islam for Christianity. The result is an accurate description of the Saudi Wahhabis and why they erroneously seem to represent mainstream Islam.

Wahhabis are a miniscule part of Islam. They are anti-Sufi and anti-Shi'i. Wahhabism is not a new version of Islam—it has been around for several centuries—but it only became prevalent in the Arabian peninsula in the mid-eighteenth century, when the politically powerful al-Sa'ud family became Wahhabi. Thus was a culture born of a fusion between socially conservative Arabian culture and strict, conservative religion.

After Abd al-Aziz ibn Sa'ud formally proclaimed Saudi Arabia in 1932, Wahhabism became the state religion. Even then, it was only after the 1970s, when oil money began to flow into Saudi Arabia, that Wahhabism began to spread. Since Saudi Arabia has wealth, controls Mecca and the Ka'ba, and allies itself with the United States (or vice versa), Wahhabism seems the embodiment of Islam to many Americans.

Wahhabism has received disproportionate exposure not least because the Saudis use their money to infiltrate Muslim communities and promulgate their version of Islam as the true one. For example, Saudi money is being used to build mosques and Islamic centers in other parts of the world, which results in the spread of the Saudi version of Islam. In Indonesia, for example, mosques have traditionally been uniquely lovely structures representative of Southeast Asian culture. But the new mosques, built with foreign money, reject the local cultural architecture—as well as the local Islamic practices—in favor of the Saudi model.

The Taliban are radical, militant Wahhabis. In America, we commonly know the Taliban destroyed statues of Buddha and Buddhist artifacts. But the Taliban also destroyed *Islamic* artifacts. Ismaili, Shi'i, and Sufi artifacts were all destroyed. In fact, in the early part of the twentieth century, Wahhabis destroyed cemetery markers in Mecca and Medina. They nearly destroyed the tomb of the Prophet, as well.[36]

But Islam accommodates differences of Islamic vision! The several Islamic schools of law are all considered valid, and Islam rejects the "orthodox vs. non-orthodox" theory of religion. There is room for tolerance in Islam. Yet the Taliban, who think they are Muslim, destroyed Islamic artifacts and do not accept any form of Islam other than their own.

I realize I may sound contradictory. I condemn the Taliban for not tolerating other religions (and even variations on their own religion) as the Qur'an commands us to, but am I not simultaneously intolerant of the Taliban, implying they are not Muslim because of their vicious actions? Yes, I am. How can I tolerate so-called Muslims who ignore or even destroy what the Prophet was trying to achieve (a rise in women's status, for one thing), who themselves do not tolerate other Muslims, who desecrate what Muslims and non-Muslims hold sacred in violation of the Qur'an, who slaughter their opposition, and who destroy personal freedom? The Taliban's vision of Islam can only be tolerated, I feel, if that vision never injures others and is never imposed forcibly on anyone else.

The Saudis and the Taliban loom large in our perceptions of Islam because they have calculated it that way. Whereas the Saudis used their money, the Taliban and the attackers of the World Trade Center purposefully and deliberately used the media to build their image. For example, the Taliban *invited* Western media to Afghanistan to watch them shockingly destroy Buddhist artifacts. Similarly, the September 11th attacks (whoever engineered them) were coordinated so that all television cameras would be trained securely on the destruction of the first tower when the second plane crashed.

Thus, the Taliban and bin Laden both deliberately usurped the media and manipulated it to build themselves a specific media image. They represented this image as Muslim and representative of Muslims. We must recognize that we are all media victims of the Taliban and those like them. If we allow them to convince us they represent Islam and Muslims, if we allow them to stage a war between "Islam and the West," then we are playing into their hands.

The Wahhabis, the Taliban, and bin Laden are all connected in that they all come basically from the same mold—the conservative, ultra-extremist fundamentalist Wahhabi mold that is tightly interwoven with the conservative culture of the Arabian peninsula with pots of money and control over holy sites and exposure in the media. That brand of extremism gets a lot of press, but it is not what Islam is about; indeed, mainstream Islam rejects it. And it is a very small percentage of Islam, by no means representative of most Muslims, just as the witch hunters of Salem, Massachusetts, of the 1600s do not represent most Christians.

What saddens me is that the Saudis have been offering to build bright new mosques in Indonesia, Pakistan, and other places around the world, on condition that the mosque hire a Wahhabi *imam*. Thus, money controls everything, even religion.

6

Religious Hierarchy:
Who Makes the Rules in Islam?

The structure of Islam, or lack of it, confuses some of my friends. A devout Catholic from Mexico asked me distressedly, "But don't you have a church? Who makes all the rules? Someone must be in charge!" It was hard for her to comprehend a religion in which no central figure like the Pope made the rules. And, indeed, Islam *is* very different from Catholicism, at least as far as its structure is concerned.

Islam has no church and no priesthood. No saints, either, because we have no religious authority to sanctify individuals and authorize their canonization.★★ No popes, no ministers, no rabbis, no curates. No monks, no nuns. In short, no real structured clergy.

At least, we have no clergy in the sense that my friends usually ask about, which is, who marries people? Who gives the sermons? Who performs the funeral service?

Religious authority lies, more or less, with the religious scholars, who have always interpreted Islamic strictures. But there is no central authority, and scholars can (and often do) disagree on the religious guidelines. Although some attempts have been made to establish a top scholarly authority, such as al-Azhar University in Egypt, or the Shi'i designation of *Ayat Allah* (the Anglicized version is "Ayatollah"), no agreement has ever been reached. Not even all Iranians, much less all Shi'i Muslims, regarded Ayatollah Khomeini as their religious leader.

"But," protested my friend, "who marries people? Don't you need a priest for that?" Well, no. In Islam, marriage is a civil contract between two people, valid if signed willingly and witnessed. No religious authority need be present. Islam, Muslims have always been proud to say, is a direct individual link to God, unencumbered by religious hierarchy.

★★The Sufis do revere certain historical Islamic figures to the point that they have been called "saints," but these are not accepted as saints by most Muslims, and they are not saints in the Christian sense or any official sense.

"All right, then," said my friend with abused patience, "how do you all know what to *do*?"

As we discussed in chapter four, the rules in Islam come from the *Shari'a,* the guidelines of Islam. This includes the Qur'an, the *Sunnah,* and the guidelines developed by religious scholars interpreting the Qur'an and *Sunnah* over the centuries.

After September 11th, many people have asked me and my family why the Islamic "clergy" did not "stand up" and denounce terrorism and bin Laden. The answer is two-pronged. First, because Muslims do not have a central figure, such as the Pope, we have no one person who can climb onto a podium, purport to represent all of Islam, and inform the public about mainstream Islamic views. Second, despite the lack of an Islamic clergy, Osama bin Laden and terrorism were indeed denounced and condemned by individual authoritative religious voices, such as individual religious scholars, academics, and the *imam* at the respected al-Azhar mosque in Cairo. In fact, one Saudi religious scholar went so far as to issue a *fatwa* (defined later in this chapter) asserting Osama bin Laden could not call himself a Muslim.

Numerous Muslims, from American *imams* to Yasser Arafat, also denounced the September 11th attacks. Condemnations arrived from all over the Muslim world. The Lebanese guerilla group, Hizbullah, itself featured on the United States' list of terrorist organizations (although its members see themselves fighting military occupiers of a specific territory in southern Lebanon), issued this forceful statement regarding the September 11th attacks: "Although we are hostile to United States policy, we are horrified at these operations, which no religion in the world supports."[1]

In fact, immediately after September 11th, over two hundred Muslim individuals and organizations, representing nearly all of the *seven million* Muslims in America, issued statements categorically condemning the attacks as reprehensible and completely abhorrent to Islam.[2]

But these voices did not receive much media publicity. And because most people do not realize the religious scholars constitute the only religious authority there is in Islam, no one paid them or the others much attention when they did appear in the media to denounce bin Laden and the hijackers. They were waiting instead, perhaps, for an Islamic Pope. Even now, seven years later, I hear Americans asking why Muslims have not stood up and said anything. We have indeed reached out; but not everyone is listening.

It is nice for everyone to have a direct link to God, but the problem with having individual scholars and no central religious authority is that religion may easily become confused with family tradition or culture. American Muslims do not have many choices when it comes to mosques; I reside at a reasonable driving distance from only one and therefore cannot choose between mosques the way my Christian friends are usually able to choose between various churches. This means Muslims in the West do not necessarily have learned authorities around of whom to ask questions.

Shari'a is usually translated as "Islamic law," but as I mentioned in chapter four, this can be misleading, which I only realized recently. A friend asked me a question about the basis of Islamic law, and I told her it was like Judaic law: a body of man-made jurisprudence based on the religious texts. She replied, "Yes, but Jewish law isn't enforced—I mean no one tells me that I can't eat pork—except in Israel."

I was surprised, because it had not occurred to me that the term "Islamic law" implied a set of state laws; but given the state implementation of Islamic law in some countries within the last several decades, I understood her confusion. Historically, although religion and state were somewhat mixed throughout the Islamic empire, the religious scholars never governed the state, and religion largely stayed separate from the state. Even the so-called "Islamic states" in the world today do not all implement Islamic law in the same way. They all look completely different in structure (for instance, Saudi Arabia is a monarchy, Iran is a republic, and Pakistan has a military government).

Nobody enforces whether I eat pork or not, either. Although it is forbidden in Islam, ultimately it is my personal decision whether to comply or not. Islamic law (or *Shari'a*) actually just means religious guidelines developed by Islamic scholars, *not* by the state. If a country chooses to enforce religious law, as some countries do, that is a different issue. But Islam itself does not require that religion and the state be unified.

Do Imams Make the Rules?

The position of the (lower-case) *imam* is not really a formalized position and is used in both Sunni and Shi'i Islam. It is not necessarily even a clerical position. An *imam* may be a religious scholar, but alternatively may simply be someone who leads the prayer in a mosque and who has no religious training at all. So an *imam* could be almost anything: a simple prayer leader, someone who has some knowledge about Islam, someone who has spent a lifetime studying Islam, or (if capitalized) someone who was a divinely inspired successor to the Prophet.

When I was a child, the *imam* at our mosque (after the two-car garage, we increased enough in size to rent a community center complete with veritable parking lot) was an accountant with no formal religious training of any kind. He simply led the prayer, which means he stood at the head of the lines of people praying and recited parts of the prayer aloud. By the time I went to college, our mosque (now a former church) boasted an *imam* with, among other degrees, a PhD in comparative religion. We finally had someone to lead the prayers who could reliably answer questions, as well. However, because Islam allows for many variations on religious thought and accepts many views as possible manifestations of God's will, our *imam's* answers—though valid—might not have been the only valid ones.

The fact that *imam* can mean many things, from "divinely inspired successor to the Prophet" to "someone who does nothing but recite the prayer," can really be a problem. Often, those outside Islam automatically assume that *imam* is equivalent to priest or minister or some other religious authority and they ascribe to him religious knowledge he may not have. Likewise, *imams* and Islamic scholars are frequently assumed to be part of a hierarchy equivalent to the formal, religiously trained hierarchy in Christianity. But no such hierarchy exists in Islam, and so no part of it can really be equated with the structure of Christianity.

Muslims understand that any given *imam* may not necessarily know much about Islam. I know of one mosque in which most people consistently arrive after the *imam's* sermon but just in time for the formal prayer. Some of the mosques in the United States, where Muslims are scarce, engage *imams* who do not have sufficient religious or other education.

This kind of religious leadership is frustrating and problematic, especially if Muslims assume they are being given reliable information when they may not be. I do think the title of *imam* should be restricted to someone who has completed a certain amount of training. The American mosques that hire *imams* with formal, balanced training in religious studies or Islamic studies enjoy more popularity, conduct more interfaith events, and appeal more to American Muslims. Whichever the case, the opinions of an *imam* are not binding on any or all Muslims.

Can a woman be an *imam*? The debate around this issue reminds me of the debate about whether women can be priests. In Islam, the debate really contains two sub-issues: First, can a woman be a religious scholar and lead classes and the community of Muslims? And second, can a woman lead the group prayer?

The answer to the first question is yes. Islamic scholars have always agreed that women could train in religious studies, teach both women and men about Islam, and function as religious leaders of the community. The Prophet himself consulted with women in his community. A wonderful new program undertaken by the Moroccan government in 2007 trains women as religious scholars; called *mourchidat*, these women are qualified to instruct the Muslim community about the Islamic faith.

But the answer to the second question is more complicated. Most early Islamic jurists agreed a woman could lead a group prayer of other women. They did not agree on whether a woman could lead a group prayer that included men in the group.

In the seventh century, the Prophet did appoint at least one woman as *imam* of her household, which included men. For four hundred years after that, until around the year 1000 CE, two schools of Islamic law allowed a woman to lead a group prayer, even if the group included men.[3] In this case, the men stood to one side, for modesty's sake, so that they were not directly behind the woman *imam*.

Both of those schools of thought only survived for four hundred years after the Prophet; however, after that point the Islamic jurists (in the *fiqh* books of jurisprudence) generally agreed a woman could not lead men in prayer.[4] The main issue seems to be modesty: that a woman should be kneeling, rising, and bending over (with her hands on her knees) in front of men was and still is deemed inappropriate by some jurists, who believe no distracting thoughts of the opposite sex should interfere with prayer. The Moroccan *mourchidat* may not lead prayers.

Though many current Islamic scholars throughout the Middle East view a woman *imam* as disallowed, more than one Muslim scholar has argued that women may indeed lead mixed-gender prayers. At least one Muslim scholar has said that if the woman is the most learned in the group she can lead men in prayer if they stand to one side,[5] and another has argued that the Islamic sources support the view that women may lead a mixed-gender prayer.[6] Egypt's Grand Mufti, Shaykh Ali Guma, declared that "woman-led prayer of mixed-gender congregations is permissible, so long as the congregation agrees to it."[7] Some early Muslim scholars like Tabari and ibn Arabi (highly respected luminaries in Islam) had permitted woman-led prayer, as well.[8]

Amina Wadud, a woman and professor of Islamic studies, led mixed-gender group prayers in New York City in 2005. In her group prayers, men and women did not pray in separate groups but stood in a mixed group. Some men stood shoulder to shoulder with their wives.

As a Muslim, I am entitled to listen to the various opinions of the Islamic authorities, pray for guidance, and choose the view my conscience tells me is right. My view—which is one of the several valid Islamic viewpoints on this issue—is that we should follow the Prophet's example, as well as the view of early and modern jurists, to allow learned women (*or learned men*) to lead the prayer. I do not think we should consider men to be so weak that they could not concentrate on God with a woman leading the prayer. (We're all supposed to be looking at the floor in front of our feet when we pray, anyway!) I would love to be able to pray together with my husband and children, all standing together, rather than in separate rooms or even separate groups. When I first read of Professor Wadud's mixed prayer I felt a rush of sympathy and hope.

Western media portrays Islam as monolithic and intolerant, and all debates within it as "fierce." But throughout the centuries Islamic scholars have had a rich tradition of scholarly discussion and debate with words, not weapons. I am proud to see this aspect of my tradition in the flourishing debate surrounding the qualifications for an *imam*.

How the Rules Are Made

When I was growing up, I learned my religion from my parents. They always gave me reasons for the Islamic rules I was supposed to follow, they never tried to ostracize me from non-Muslim society, and they helped me try to function normally within it. They taught me how to pray, how to fast, and what to believe. How conservative or devout I and my friends were, growing up, depended entirely upon our parents and the few other parents who volunteered to teach Sunday school at the mosque (luckily, the community center we rented had several rooms by then). The *imams* were mostly there only to lead the prayers. So I grew up with no Muslim "clergy" at all, no one who made rules.

In college, some of my acquaintances assumed I could not date because my parents prohibited it and that I naturally harbored all manner of latent anger against them. Looking back, it seems to me that these acquaintances must have thought me the most vapid sort of mindless sheep (or perhaps just an oppressed Muslim woman). The reason I never fumed at my parents, on this issue, at least, was that I never held them responsible for my religious rules. I could not date, I knew the reasons I could not date, and I dealt with it, despite the many adults (from my hairdresser to my teachers to my co-workers) who told me dating was modern or good for me or educational. As far as I was concerned, no one but God was telling me not to date. Since the reasons made sense to me and it was God, after all, I followed them.

But if my parents did not make the rules and I grew up with no clergy who made the rules, either, what exactly is a *fatwa*? Because of Khomeini and bin Laden, the word, "*fatwa*," has obtained a place in Western vocabulary, where it is now used in all sorts of etymologically irresponsible ways. For example, I have heard news agencies defining it as a "divinely inspired order."

A *fatwa* is neither divine nor an order. It is not a law. A *fatwa* is the legal opinion of a recognized Islamic religious scholar (or, as developed in later years, of an institution such as a religious school) on a point of religious law that results from applying legal reasoning to a particular issue. The *fatwa* is an individual opinion and nobody need agree with or follow it. It is not binding or enforceable. I could climb up onto a box in Times Square or Hyde Park and issue as many *fatwas* or, for that matter, medical opinions on the causes of Alzheimer's disease as I wished. That would not mean I was qualified to do either or that anyone should follow my opinions.

Osama bin Laden, for example, can issue *fatwas* until he is blue in the face, but that does not mean anyone should follow them or even that he is qualified to make them in the first place. Khomeini was qualified to issue *fatwas*, but no one was obligated to follow them. Sunni Muslims did not follow Khomeini. Not even all Shi'i Muslims did and not even all Iranians.

One news service I came across asserted that Islam was "different" and therefore violent. After all, the writer continued, exhibiting a mind-boggling ignorance of history and comparative religion, it was impossible to imagine the Pope declaring war on an entire nation the way bin Laden had issued a "*fatwa*" against the United States. Actually, that is exactly what the Pope did in 1095, and what subsequent popes continued to try to do. But even disregarding that, the equating of Osama bin Laden and the Pope is just so much rubbish. Osama bin Laden has *no* religious authority. A more accurate equation would be Osama bin Laden to Timothy McVeigh, who bombed the Oklahoma Federal Building pursuant to the dictates of his Christian fundamentalist beliefs.

Moreover, a *fatwa* or other law in Islam does not result from religious scholars throwing out unjustified opinions. The religious guidelines are accepted as true rules when jurists (*muftis*) exercise independent reasoning (*ijtihad*) to interpret the Qur'an and *Sunnah*. They use established methods of analysis and legal justification (*not* their own sole opinions) to individually come up with a legal opinion, a *fatwa*. The *fatwa* is debated and discussed by other jurists; some might accept it, some might not. If all or part of the *fatwa* is accepted by a consensus, then it might become a part of the religious rules. But even then, dissenters' opinions are valued and recorded.

For example, some Islamic jurists believed that abortion was completely forbidden under Islamic law. Some jurists asserted it was always allowed. Some thought it should be allowed until the "soul entered the body." And some thought abortion was allowable within forty days of conception. (Remember, this was a long time ago, from the seventh to the twelfth centuries, so jurists did not have the medical knowledge we have now.) Who was right about God's intention? No one can know. So we, as Muslims, have a duty to examine the different valid viewpoints and then choose the answer that our conscience tells us is the correct one—because we as individuals will have to answer to God.

In the early days of Islam, when scholars were studying the Qur'an and *Sunnah*, scholarship became, over time, grouped into schools of thought, like schools of philosophy. By using the legal process, scholars adhering to one particular school produced an interpretive body of literature based on the Qur'an and *Sunnah* and containing the guidelines of Islam. The rules of Islam are in this interpretive literature, if anywhere.

The major schools of thought in Sunni Islam are the Hanafi, Hanbali, Maliki, and Shafi'i schools. The major Shi'i school is the Jafari school. All recognize the others as equally valid and possible manifestations of God's will.

Therefore, the practice of Islam can be personalized and varied because there is no central authority who makes the rules and because the differing rules of the various schools are all acceptable as valid. Osama bin Laden's "*fatwa*" against the United States amounted to, simply, an unrecognized individual standing up, espousing his unproved and unjustified opinions (on televised video, unfortunately), and attempting to fire up popular opinion against the United States. Bin Laden is not a recognized scholar or even a Muslim, according to one Saudi *fatwa*.[9] And yet I hear him referred to as a "prophet" or "pope" of Islam.

After Muhammad, certain positions of religious authority were developed over the centuries, but these were administrative. Scholars were appointed to give reasoned answers to questions about Islam, for instance. Judges called *qadis* were appointed to administer property, preside over divorces, rule on the validity of a contract, and so on.

Though many of the rules of Islam were set down during the first centuries after Muhammad, the rules can change, as when scholars reinterpret the texts and when an individual *fatwa* is accepted by the consensus of Muslim religious scholars. So the notion that Islam is backward or—more kindly—*traditional*, is not a true one. The *Shari'a* is flexible. But the perception persists, and the reason has to do with the exercise of *ijtihad*, or independent reasoning.

Ijtihad is a pointed illustration of the cultural and linguistic problems that exist in the perception of Islam. After the twelfth century, the books of jurisprudence assumed a formal structure that made Islamic law look as though it were unchanging. The Islamic jurists deliberately cultivated this illusion in order to stress the connection between the juristic literature and revelation (the Qur'an and the *Sunnah*).[10] In other words, the jurists conveyed the message, "We haven't changed anything—this is really Islam as it was originally revealed; don't worry." But in reality, they continued to develop the law.

What, then, has *ijtihad* to do with the cultural and linguistic gap? Western scholars did not recognize the illusion of immutability for what it was (an illusion) and assumed Islamic law had not changed in 800 years. The phrase, "the closing of the door of *ijtihad* [i.e., independent reasoning]" became increasingly popular in Western scholarship on Islam. What is meant by this phrase is that independent reasoning was stopped in the twelfth century.

This whole idea is demeaning to Muslims, but it is reinforced by academics, not to mention instant experts and some Muslims themselves. Accusing an entire culture of having stopped all independent reasoning 800 years ago is like saying no original thoughts occurred in that culture for 800 years. It sounds absurd. (It *is* absurd.) It leads to adjectives such as "backward," "declining," "stultifying," and "decaying." Norman Calder writes that "the pernicious results of these comments [regarding the end of independent reasoning] have haunted academic descriptions of Islamic law ever since" and that the mistake is being addressed in more recent studies.[11]

What I find interesting is that this particular phrase, "the closing of the door of *ijtihad*" is hardly mentioned in the early twentieth century.

But by the *late* twentieth century, it is widely prevalent to the point of being assumed and unquestioned truth. It was a catchy slogan that became increasingly reiterated.

Despite the *ijtihad* issue and the differing opinions regarding changes in Islamic law, many countries in the Muslim world have tried to implement reforms without straying from the original message of the Qur'an. At times, this is the result of a reinterpretation (called neo-*ijtihad*) of the Qur'anic verses. For example, Tunisia has prohibited polygamy outright by reinterpreting the Qur'anic verses. At other times, reforms result from re-examination of medieval Islamic scholarship. Certainly, Muslim intellectuals around the world are developing ways to implement reform within an Islamic context. And they are developing a variety of methodologies. There is much cultural and intellectual discussion and debate within Islam, despite the negative, homogeneous impression Western media gives us.

So if *imams* are religious scholars in mosques and the rules are made by religious scholars, where do Ayatollahs fit in?

Do Ayatollahs Make the Rules?

Even today, many Americans inescapably envision Ayatollah Khomeini when Islamic authority figures come to mind. For the first time in history, a Muslim religious authority forced himself into the American collective consciousness, and American perception of Islam was changed forever. Khomeini appeared nightly on television during the Iranian hostage crisis of 1979, personifying an alien culture most Americans had never thought about. We never learned much about him, except that he was enraged. And that he represented Islam.

The title of "Ayatollah" was traditionally granted to Shi'i Iranian religious scholars of particular achievement and distinction. Most Iranians are Shi'i Muslims, although the Kurds, who are Sunni, form a significant minority. As I mentioned at the beginning of this chapter, the term "Ayatollah" is a slightly Anglicized form of *Ayat Allah*, which means "sign of Allah." That is all. Ayat Allah does not mean "prophet" or "divinely selected *Imam*" or "saint." It does not mean "someone who kills Westerners so he can go to heaven."

In the last century, the title of Ayatollah was awarded increasingly frequently to Iranian Shi'i religious scholars and thus became less prestigious. Ayatollah Khomeini was referred to sometimes as *Imam* Khomeini, but the designation "*Imam*" just referred to his scholarly status. It did not mean he was the kind of divinely inspired *Imam* whom the majority Twelver Shi'a believe succeeded the Prophet. Only twelve in number, those capitalized *Imams* are no longer in the world, so when you hear the word "*imam*," it almost never refers to the divinely inspired *Imams*.

"Ayatollah" is a Shi'i designation, not a Sunni one. Ayatollahs have completed a required amount of rigorous religious training and are given the title by their Shi'i peers. Ayatollahs do not speak for all Muslims or even all Shi'i Muslims. Their opinions are not binding. But they are learned.

Leafing through a *Bon Appetit* magazine one day, I read, in the letter from the editor of all places, the following sentence:

> This was shortly after Louis XIV (who had about as much use for religious toleration as the average ayatollah) revoked the Edict of Nantes, essentially telling citizens who did not agree with his views that they could either leave the country (at their own expense) or be burned at the stake (government subsidy).[12]

This did make me smile. But would it have been acceptable for the editor to write that Louis XIV had about as much religious tolerance as your average minister? Or rabbi, or priest? I cannot imagine it would have been acceptable, nor should it have been.

Yet, in this one phrase, the editor produced a negative generalization about an entire segment of people—ayatollahs—about which he was almost certainly fundamentally ignorant. And whether Khomeini was intolerant is irrelevant; if Louis XIV's intolerant behavior is not generalized to be representative of the average Catholic then Khomeini's behavior should not have been generalized to be representative of all Muslim religious scholars who have reached the level of ayatollah. What is, after all, an "average ayatollah"?

The average ayatollah is the average religious Shi'i scholar who has achieved a particular level of religious education. Although Khomeini implemented a brutal regime, modern non-Muslim leaders have, too.★★ And although Khomeini became brutal, many ayatollahs strongly disagreed with his views.

But why do we care? Khomeini is dead, right?

Khomeini is worth explaining because he personified a turning point in history, and his influence reaches into the present day. Most importantly, for the first time in fourteen centuries of Islamic jurisprudence, a new

---

★★For example, Slobodan Milosevic and Ariel Sharon have both had actions brought against them for crimes against humanity and Robert Mugabe is letting his people in Zimbabwe starve.

Shi'i theory of governmental rule *by the religious scholars* was developed and implemented. Secondly, many Americans were barely aware of Islam (or even "Mohammedanism") before it exploded into the American consciousness in the form of the Iranian revolution in 1979. And suddenly, I was aware that the American attitude toward Muslims changed from one of vaguely benevolent ignorance to hostile ignorance. I could hardly fail to notice when people leaned from windows of passing cars to shout "Dirty Iranians!" at my Indian parents.

Six clerical designations range below "Ayatollah," the lowest being that of "student."[13] In terms of religious hierarchy, it may be tempting to equate or analogize those designations with, for example, hierarchy in Catholicism. But the analogy would be incorrect. As I discussed earlier, there never has been a "church" in Islam. In Islamic territory, the government wielded political power and the scholars determined what was "Islamic" and what was not. The scholars and the government stayed separate, though each often criticized the other. (This is why Andy Rooney's remark that Islamic religion and state must be the same is just so much nonsense.)

Inevitable differences existed between the government's implementation of Islamic law and the scholars' interpretation of it. And sometimes they did get somewhat mixed. But the religious scholars in Islam primarily remained only the religious scholars and historically did not accede to political power.

Khomeini decided to change that. He was a scholar to whom the designation "Ayatollah" had already been granted. While in France, exiled from Iran, he began to develop a *new* theory, that of a government run by jurists (*wilayat al-faqih*) and answerable to the Iranian religious scholars. His writings justified the clergy's right to rule and "worked at a new Islamic concept which was to change quietistic Shi'ism into an aggressive political theology."[14]

The Iranian revolution of 1979 was not an "Islamic" revolution. A diverse array of political and religious groups in Iran had banded together to overthrow the corrupt and brutal Shah, who had alienated just about every Iranian citizen at every socioeconomic level. After the Shah fled, huge differences in ideology remained as to what the nature of the new government would be. Groups ranging from secular activists to Islamic activists to Marxists to liberal democrats had helped overthrow the Shah.[15] The million-dollar question was, "Whose ideology would prevail in the new government?"

Khomeini and his supporters managed to fill the power void. They dominated the Iranian branches of government, and the 1979 constitution of Iran gave, for the first time, widespread political powers to the chief Islamic jurist. To Khomeini.

Khomeini developed a theory of Islamic law to justify a theocratic republic and to install himself as the one who makes the rules, but Khomeini's model of government is not traditional and is by no means unanimously accepted as the correct Islamic model. Certainly, Khomeini committed many acts that had nothing to do with Islam. In fact, many opposed his assumption of power, and many religious scholars revolted against the idea of appointing one religious scholar who governed the state and before whom all others, perforce, yielded.

Not only did Khomeini establish himself as religious leader, he used Islam to implement brutal practices in no way approved by religion. He secured his own power by removing dissenters from influential positions. He used Islam for his own ends, arresting, executing, and even "defrocking" to incapacitate those who opposed him.[16]

The defrocking is a perfect illustration of how Khomeini wielded tyrannical power in the name of Islam even when no religious justification for his actions existed in Islam. He disregarded the fact that the very concept of defrocking is totally irrelevant to and unknown in Islam, which lacks both a central authority to order it and any sort of mechanism to implement it. Many of those opposing Khomeini were the religious scholars, who were appalled at the bloodshed and violence the revolution had engendered.[17] Khomeini's solution? Defrock them, even though it makes no sense in Islam.

In America, Khomeini's crashing arrival into the 1970s media equated him with Islam and equated Islam with anti-American violence, a perception that still exists today. But Khomeini's vision of power and religious authority has never been universally accepted within Islam or even within Shi'ism. Again, not all Muslims, not all Shi'i Muslims, and not even all Iranian Muslims followed his dictates or agreed with his rhetoric.

No example of Khomeini's authority and its limitations could have been more sensational than the price he set on the head of Salman Rushdie.

Salman Rushdie

I once tuned in to a radio program that featured panelists discussing Islam. Someone telephoned the talk show host and said, "Yeah, but what about that guy who wrote a book and someone didn't like it and so they killed him?"

The caller was referring to Salman Rushdie, author of *The Satanic Verses*. Nearly two decades after the book's publication, he is very much alive and, as of 2007, Distinguished Writer in Residence at Emory University. But the caller's question encapsulated the sum total of what many people remember about *The Satanic Verses*. Indeed, many acquaintances have advised me to be careful about writing a book on Islam, because they have concluded, from the Rushdie affair, that Muslims do not believe in freedom of expression. Even if they do not recall particulars about the Rushdie case, they retain the impression that Islam is oppressive, repressive, and intolerant of free speech.

This issue was resurrected briefly in 2007, when the British government knighted Salman Rushdie for his contribution to English literature. This spurred a whole new spate of protests in Pakistan and Britain. Luckily, they were relatively short-lived.

Rushdie, an Indian-born British writer who had previously won the Booker Prize for his book *Midnight's Children*, was born Muslim but no longer belonged to the faith when he wrote *The Satanic Verses*. The title not only plays on the phrase "the Qur'anic verses," but refers to specific verses that legend says Satan himself inserted into the Qur'an, and which the Prophet Muhammad later removed. When the book was published, some countries banned it, some Muslims protested its publication, and, worst of all, Ayatollah Khomeini issued a *fatwa* that the author should be executed.

I believe censorship can almost never be defended. Freedom of expression and freedom of thought must not be suppressed. By extension, executing someone for their writings and their views is barbaric and should never be supported.

What could possibly have inspired such a violent reaction? To understand the Rushdie affair, we must understand, without justifying violence, why so many Muslims found the book so offensive. *The Satanic Verses* openly ridicules the Prophet and the Qur'an in a very obvious and precise manner and in a multitude of details. The book centers on two characters who, to put it simplistically, both reject parts of themselves in different ways and wrestle with the consequences. Both born Indian and Muslim, one character aggressively rejects his Muslim faith and the other aggressively rejects his Indian culture (and also, somewhat passively, his Muslim faith). He who aggressively rejects his religion is called Gabriel in the book.

Gabriel begins to dream a continual dream, ever playing inside his head, beginning where it last left off, like a video unfinished and unrewound. The dream eventually haunts him to his death. It is primarily, but not exclusively, in the dream sequences that Rushdie satirizes and ridicules Islam.

In the dream sequences, Rushdie manipulates religious stories from the Muslim tradition and turns them on their heads so that they stand for what is often totally abhorrent to Islam—unrestrained polytheism, extra-marital sex, prostitution, treachery, and corruptive additions to the Qur'anic verses by human hands. Rushdie does not bother with metaphorical disguises but is intentionally provocative and straightforward about his sarcasm. The book attacks Islam in a general way, but it also mounts an attack in myriad details, many of which someone unfamiliar with Muslim tradition would never catch. The result is that most of the insults to Islam are not only inevitably offensive to Muslims, they are *aimed* at Muslims.

The book refers to Muhammad as "Mahounde," which means "evil spirit" and which was a polemically derisive name that medieval Christians used for the Prophet. This name, Mahounde, carries a thousand years of venom within it. Rushdie also gives prostitutes the names of the Prophet Muhammad's wives.[18] He renames Mecca, the city toward which all Muslims pray, "Jahilia," which means "ignorance" and which refers to pre-Islamic Arabia. He portrays men circumambulating around a brothel the way Muslims circumambulate around the Ka'ba when they go to Saudi Arabia on pilgrimage.[19] Perhaps most inflammatory of all, given Islam's uncompromising monotheism, Rushdie portrays the Prophet Muhammad as accepting the existence of the pre-Islamic goddess Al-Lat in addition to Allah.[20]

Rushdie refers to or relates many stories from Islamic tradition but with so many distortions that the "followers of the faith of Submission," as Rushdie puts it, are portrayed as if they are the evil twins of the characters in Islamic tradition. They are personifications of all the worst aspects of humanity—lying, lascivious, perfidious, and venal. *The Satanic Verses* bitterly attacks the very essence of Islam in a manner that could not be more clear.

But attacking the very essence of Islam must be allowed.

As my usually gentle mother remarked disgustedly, "If you object to something someone has written, write something better to refute it."

Two images vividly remain in our collective memory when it comes to *The Satanic Verses*: Muslims protesting on the streets and Ayatollah

Khomeini's *fatwa* calling for the execution of the author. These two reactions turn on two different issues.

Muslims who protested against publication and for banning of the book did so for two reasons. First, the book simply offended Muslims and they wanted to ban it and boycott the publishers. Banning literature is not what freedom of expression is all about, but certainly in many other parts of the world (not just the Muslim parts), censorship on the basis of subject matter is not unknown. The Nobel Laureate Naghuib Mahfouz, while adamantly in favor of freedom of expression, also stressed that "different cultures have different attitudes towards freedom of speech. What might be endured in Western cultures might not be acceptable in Muslim countries."[21]

We cherish our right to free speech in the United States, but we must realize that it, too, has limitations; for instance, I may not yell "fire" in a crowded theatre, because public safety precludes my right to free speech. I may not shout "fighting words" at someone if they present an actual threat of immediate violence. Similarly, other cultures might view other factors as genuinely—not just expediently—outweighing the right to free speech. We may ourselves not agree with these other cultural factors as legitimate limitations on freedom of expression, but we can acknowledge that others might.

The second reason Muslims wanted to ban *The Satanic Verses* was to protest discriminatory laws in England. They argued that the book fell under the aegis of Britain's law against blasphemy, which applied only to Christianity and not to Islam or Judaism or any other religion. Under such laws, for example, a video was banned in the 1990s because it portrayed Saint Teresa sexually fantasizing about the crucified Jesus. Moreover, the British government did not allow Muslims to establish Muslim schools in the same way Christians and Jews were able to establish schools and even use public funds to maintain them.[22]

But even if banning a book may sometimes be understandable, Khomeini's *fatwa* sentencing Rushdie to a death sentence was absolutely not justifiable in any way. Khomeini was qualified to issue *fatwas* because his fellow jurists recognized him as so qualified. But as I noted earlier, that does not mean anyone—not even the Shi'a or Iranians—had to follow his edicts or that his edicts would become law or even were in compliance with Islamic law.

Most people did not, in fact, agree with Khomeini. The unadorned fact that Rushdie has survived for almost two decades without anyone murdering him, despite the 1.4 billion Muslims around the world, indicates that most Muslims did not consider themselves bound by Khomeini's opinions. There was even the added incentive of $2 million that the Iranian government offered as a reward for Rushdie's execution.

Many Muslim scholars in Western countries not only disagreed with Khomeini's *fatwa*, they vehemently condemned it, signing petitions to show their support of Rushdie.[23] These scholars included fifty Iranian intellectuals living outside Iran.[24] The scholars at al-Azhar University in Cairo, one of the oldest universities in the world and one of the great centers for Islamic studies, disagreed with the *fatwa* and said that at the very least Rushdie was entitled to a fair trial. A fair trial for *what?* you might ask. Writing a book, for Pete's sake?

Khomeini based his *fatwa* on the (disputed) medieval crime of apostasy, condemning Rushdie for renouncing Islam. The Qur'an itself minimizes apostasy, discourages it, does not really treat it as a crime, and does not specify a punishment for it. The Qur'an does *not* specify the death penalty. In fact, the Qur'an decrees that apostates must be encouraged and given the opportunity to turn back to Islam.

Yet, Muslim medieval jurists developed, as part of their Islamic juristic literature, a law of apostasy that did allow specific punishments and even death to the apostate, though in practice this was rare. Most modern Muslims view apostasy in its historical context and do not consider it applicable to the modern world. In fact, some scholars write that the crime of apostasy in Islamic law only came about because of a misreading of the early written discussions on the subject.[25]

Because of the potential for abuse, and because this law is inconsistent with the numerous verses on religious freedom in the Qur'an and *Sunnah*,[26] and because of modern notions of freedom of religion, this law, in the modern Muslim view, has absolutely no place in today's world.

Even if you consider Khomeini's *fatwa* against Rushdie from the point of view of the medieval Islamic jurists who developed the law of apostasy, Khomeini's *fatwa* was *still* totally wrong for three reasons, set out as the following by one Muslim scholar, Abdullahi an-Naim:

1) Khomeini had no jurisdiction outside of his state and no authority to punish a citizen of a non-Islamic state;

2) Even if you ignore the first requirement above and assume Khomeini had jurisdiction over Rushdie (and thus over all the Muslims in the world, which is ridiculous), the *Shari'a* requires that the person

be charged with the offense and allowed to defend himself before he is convicted and punished; and

3) At any time, "repentance and recantation of heretic views is always a complete defense against a charge of apostasy."[27]

Just to show how Khomeini did not adhere to the dictates of even medieval Islamic law, he responded to Rushdie's apology for causing anguish or affront by saying that the apology was not accepted and that even if Rushdie repented and recanted his insults, he should still be killed.[28]

Most Muslim governments did not support Khomeini's *fatwa*. The foreign ministers of forty-six Muslim countries met at the Organization for the Islamic Conference and, though they approved of banning the book, they did not endorse the death decree.[29]

Khomeini's *fatwa* was revoked under Iran's President Khatami in the late 1990s.

The important thing to remember is that Khomeini did not represent all or even most Muslims. He committed unheard-of brutalities unprecedented in Islam and Islamic law. Most of what he did was *politically*, not religiously, motivated. This includes the *fatwa* on Rushdie, which was yet another method Khomeini used to deliberately destroy bridges with the West.

In the United States, the public was freshly aware of Islam and conceptualized it as consisting entirely of Khomeini and his militant propaganda. We were given *The Satanic Verses* and all the uproar surrounding it as another vivid "proof" of a religion most Americans had never thought about before 1979. It was another reason to hate Iran at the very least and Islam at the most.

I find that first impressions are sometimes the hardest to overcome.

Women in Islam: Marriage, Divorce, Polygamy, and that Veil Thing

"You don't think Islam is sexist?" a partner in my law firm asked me at a client dinner.

"No, I don't, not Islam itself," I answered. "For example, Islam—"

"Well, then, what do you think of the whole Anita Hill versus Clarence Thomas debate?" he interrupted. "Don't you think he should have been disqualified from the Supreme Court?"

"Yes, actually, I do," I said, irritatingly aware of his implication, which was that if I did not consider *Islam* sexist, then I probably thought *nothing* was sexist, including Clarence Thomas.

I opened my mouth to elaborate and make nonsense of the connection he was trying to make between sexism in Islam and sexism on Capitol Hill. But I lost my chance to explain away the incredulous expression on his face, because he swept around the table to take a survey of who sided with Anita Hill and who with Clarence Thomas.

Aysha, the Prophet Muhammad's favorite wife—yes, he did have a plurality of them, but that will be discussed later—would have been astounded to hear Western criticism of Islam as oppressive of women. After all, Aysha gathered and led a full-fledged army against Ali in a battle to determine who would succeed the Prophet. Perhaps she was ill-advised, but she was not oppressed. That was 656 CE.

Muhammad's other wives commonly accompanied him, two at a time, when he traveled, even to battles and campaigns. He was known to often discuss political and social issues with them, and they routinely offered him their advice. One of them, Umm Salama, defended the right of women to go to war. The Prophet's wives might have been surprised to hear that, despite their participation in politics and social life, many people in later centuries would denounce their religion as "oppressive."

A few years ago, I heard a woman call a radio talk show to express gratitude that she was not Muslim, since Muslim women were nothing but "breeders of children."

I attempted to call the radio show to explain that in Turkey, Pakistan, Bangladesh, and Indonesia, all Muslim countries, women have been elected heads of state as either prime ministers or presidents. I never penetrated the busy telephone lines, but I tried until the announcer moved on to a different subject, waiting with the receiver in hand so I could point out that even in the Islamic Republic of Iran—a country unflaggingly portrayed as misogynistic—women work as lawyers and judges and governors and elected representatives in Parliament. Muslim women, I wanted to tell that caller, are lawyers and judges in Tunisia, Sudan, and Iraq.

How would the caller have explained, I wonder, the fact that even according to very early Islamic legal procedure a woman could qualify to be a judge (a *qadi*), albeit with certain limitations?[1]

When many Americans think of Islam and women, they think of the Taliban and the Saudis. This is as erroneous as assuming David Koresh's cult was representative of Christianity. Chapter five discussed how Saudi Arabia and the Taliban have disproportionately huge exposure in the media. The reality of women's status in Islam is very different from the one we Americans routinely see. One American professor writes, regarding the status of women in Muslim countries,

> [I]t is quite ordinary to meet a woman medical doctor, engineer, lawyer, or university professor. In fact, women comprised a greater proportion of medical doctors and engineers in the Middle East than they did in the West until very recent times.[2]

If we peruse history, we find that Muslim women have been queens, heads of state, and rulers for centuries. Fatima Mernissi writes of the research process that led her to discover these "forgotten queens of Islam:"

> One by one they paraded through the silent rooms of the libraries in an interminable procession of intrigues and mysteries. Sometimes they appeared in twos or threes, passing the throne from mother to daughter in the faraway isles of Asiatic Islam…. Many themselves led battles, inflicted defeats, concluded armistices…. Each had her own way of treating the people, of rendering justice, and of administering taxes.[3]

Benazir Bhutto was not the first woman to rule an Islamic state.

Many people whose paths have crossed mine have assumed that, since

I am Muslim, my education and career must have been the result of my shattering the proverbial, oppressive iron shackles. In actuality, I and nearly all the Muslim girls with whom I grew up were nagged incessantly by our parents to do well in school and become doctors, primarily, but also academicians, lawyers, engineers, and other types of professionals. The pursuit of knowledge is the duty of every Muslim, male or female.

When the Prophet told Muslims to pursue knowledge even as far as China (i.e., the *moon*), he included women. In fact, I was always told that Muslim tradition considers knowledge for women to be especially important because traditionally they would be more likely to pass that knowledge along to their children.

Our parents' circle of friends always included many Muslim, Indian-Pakistani-American women doctors. These women had not become doctors only after immigrating to America. They had arrived as doctors.

When my parents first arrived in the United States from India, some of their American friends, even women, advised them never to trust a woman doctor. My Indian Muslim parents were surprised, because women doctors of any religion had been accepted in India for decades.

Although cultures change, Islam itself certainly puts no restrictions on learning, either for men or women. Carolyn Fluehr-Lobban, an American professor, spent many years in Muslim countries and writes,

> A number of women in Egypt, the Sudan, Tunisia, Iraq, Jordan, Syria and Lebanon have been appointed to important ministerial posts or have been elected to public office within their respective governments, while others have served as their nations' ambassadors abroad or at the United Nations.[4]

One scholar notes that although some Islamic countries have a long way to go with respect to women's rights—which I believe is a *cultural* issue, not a religious one—women are benefiting from the Islamic revival movement. Islam stresses the pursuit of knowledge and education. Therefore, part of the Islamic revival movement—sometimes misleadingly or even erroneously called "Islamic fundamentalism"—is stressing the (mostly religious) education of women to the highest attainable level.[5] And this is a new thing; traditionally, it was only men who attended such classes. In Iran for example, an Islamic theocratic republic, well over half of all university students are women, though women comprise less than half the school-age population, and the number is rising.[6]

It is a huge social shift since the 1979 Revolution: Iran's Islamic government has managed to convince even traditional rural families that it is safe to send their daughters away from home to study.[7]

However, thanks to media images of Saudi Arabia and Afghanistan, even well-meaning, well-informed people have surprising misconceptions of Islam and Muslim women, to wit: if Islam shapes your worldview and you are a devout Muslim woman, how can you possibly be liberated? Educated? You cannot be.

The female heads of state of modern Muslim countries testify to the falsity of this impression, as do the Muslim queens of history. But we in the West do not see the queens. We do not see the Muslim women doctors, lawyers, prime ministers, presidents, professors, and judges. We see the veil.

I have lost count of the times I have flipped to an unsought picture of a woman veiled in eerily billowing black from crown to fingertips to toes with only a strip of netting where the eyes should be, the caption reading, "Islam and Oppression" or "Islam and Women." In some variations, kohl-lined, dark-lashed eyes staring out at the camera replace the netting. The much-publicized flinging of acid into the faces of unveiled women is not Islam. It is the primitive cruelty of the Taliban.

With respect to the status of women in Islam, religion and culture have become hopelessly and frustratingly entangled, primarily in the perception of Islam by non-Muslims in the West, but also in the perception of Islam by Muslims. It is true that some Muslim women are oppressed, just as some women are oppressed in non-Muslim countries. Their cultures, Muslim or non-Muslim, oppress them; Islam does not, although it has been *used* to justify oppression of women. To a great degree, therefore, the issue of women in Islam turns on the extent to which their position, in any particular culture, accurately reflects the intention of Islam.

Again, I do not pretend there is any single, monolithic Islam, or that my interpretation of it is the only one. There are certainly some phrases in the Qur'an, as with most ancient texts, which—if taken ahistorically and literally—treat women differently from men. But I want this chapter to at least separate some of the bewildering threads so that the possible differences between religion and culture become clearer.

The first section of this chapter discusses how the Qur'an treats women. It has three sub-sections:

a) the historical context that must be kept in mind with respect to women's rights throughout the world;

b) how the Qur'anic text itself treats women; and

c) how scholars developed the law, based on the Qur'anic text, but unavoidably imposed their own seventh-century, androcentric worldview onto the text and mixed culture in with the religion early on. The result was that women were sometimes disallowed what the Qur'an itself allowed them.

The subsequent sections of this chapter cover the veil, marriage and polygyny, divorce, women's Islamic rights to inheritance, and three practices I think of as The Three Gorgons: clitoridectomy, honor killings, and infanticide.

Women in the Qur'an

Historical Context of Women's Rights

Muhammad preached the message of Islam in a tribal, patriarchal society that treated its women reprehensibly. Arabs, polytheists as well as Jews, in the Arabian peninsula exercised unlimited *polygyny*, the practice of a man taking several wives. A man could unilaterally divorce his wife. Moreover, he could proclaim she was "as the back of his mother," which denounced her and made marital relations impossible but also did not free her to marry anyone else.

The law did not provide for women to inherit anything. Prior to Islam, an Arabian woman could be forced to marry her dead husband's brother; she was, humiliatingly, part of his estate and the brother inherited her. Domestic violence was an assumed male prerogative, as it was throughout the rest of the world, since a wife was a man's property. Slavery was standard practice worldwide in the seventh century, in all types of communities. Burying alive female infants was a common pre-Islamic practice in Arabia.

Understanding the seventh-century world is important because some Qur'anic rules operated specifically within that historical context with the aim of immediately eliminating certain heinous practices, such as infanticide. Other Qur'anic rules restricted existing practices with the goal of gradually eradicating them altogether. Still other Qur'anic rules were meant to be general, universal guidelines and starting points for women's rights, with the ultimate goal of equality between the sexes. To understand the message of Islam in today's world, we must examine the goals of the message in the seventh century. It is also helpful to remember that women in the seventh century did not have many rights anywhere in the world.

Living in the twenty-first-century Western world, gifted with extensive women's rights, we forget too easily that women's rights everywhere are a relatively new thing. For example, before 1848, a husband in the United States assumed all rights to his wife's property, even her wages,[8] and received automatic custody of the children.[9] American universities were closed to women until the nineteenth century.[10] Not until 1920, upon the enactment of the Nineteenth Amendment, did every American woman receive the legal right to vote.

In the movement against women's suffrage in the United States, I found some parallels to Islamic cultures. For example, much of the opposition to the women's right to vote came from clergymen, who variously cited passages from the Old and New Testaments to support their claims and stated that to allow women to vote would be unbiblical and would violate Christian principles.[11] Similarly, in countries where Muslim women do not have the same rights as men, quotations from the Qur'an or *Sunnah* are frequently used to support their sexist views.

In pre-nineteenth-century England, too, a woman had no property upon marriage because her husband automatically received full ownership of it.[12] A wife's infidelity constituted grounds for divorce, but a husband's infidelity was acceptable, even expected. A wife had virtually no right to divorce, and even a man could obtain divorce only by an Act of Parliament.[13] A man had every right to beat his wife, as long as he did not endanger her life.[14]

Given that the status of women all over the world until the last few centuries has been inferior, Islamic reforms concerning women in the seventh century were significant. Because of the Qur'an, women suddenly had a right to inherit property—daughters, wives, sisters, and mothers became mandatory heirs. Women could not be forced into marriage. They kept their property upon marriage. Women were parties to the marriage contract and no longer objects of sale. Husbands did not own their wives as property. Women could testify in court. Their husbands were not allowed to abuse them because the Prophet said the worst of his followers were those who beat their wives. Women could divorce their husbands under certain conditions, too, and receive maintenance for themselves and any children. The divorced mother automatically received custody of her small children (boys under seven years of age, girls under nine years) upon divorce.

All over 1,300 years ago, all because of Islam.

But I think parts of the Muslim world have gone backward since then.

So, who cares what the historical context was if Muslim women are denied their rights today? If Islam so greatly raised the status of women fourteen centuries ago, when women's rights were inconceivable and implementation of them was an Herculean task, then the message of Islam itself must be feminist. And that is the message, that feminist message, which Muslims should apply—though they too often do not—in today's world.

The Qur'an's Treatment of Women

The Qur'an raised the status of women both generally and specifically. Qur'anic verses treat women and men in exactly the same manner when it comes to spirituality, their relationship with God, and their personal aspirations.[15] The following famous verse clearly and deliberately puts women on equal footing with men:

> For all men and women who have surrendered themselves unto God, and all believing men and believing women, and all truly devout men and truly devout women, and all men and women who are true to their word, and all men and women who are patient in adversity, and all men and women who humble themselves before God, and all men and women who give in charity, and all self-denying men and self-denying women, and all men and women who are mindful of their chastity, and all men and women who remember God unceasingly; for all of them has God readied forgiveness of sins and a mighty reward.[16]

Other verses, as well, affirmatively equalize men and women. One of my favorite stories and a clear example of the Qur'an's approving tone regarding female equality and empowerment is that of Bilqis, the Queen of Sheba.

According to the Qur'an, the Prophet-king Solomon (Suleiman, in Arabic) persuaded Bilqis of the existence of the One God. She discarded her previous religious practice of worshiping the sun and began instead to worship the One God. But here's the kicker: after converting to her new religion (which Muslims consider to be Islam), Bilqis continued to be the Queen of Sheba. Nobody told her to abdicate, give her property over to her husband, veil herself, and stay inside her house to become a subservient breeder of children.

In fact, the Qur'an refers to Bilqis as a female ruler and shows no astonishment at her elevated status.[17] The Qur'an takes for granted and approves of her political and religious power. Moreover, the Qur'an, a seventh-century text, sets forth her wisdom and power as something to be *celebrated*.[18]

The Qur'an treats Moses' mother in somewhat the same manner. God speaks directly to her, signifying that women as well as men can be the recipients of divine communication.[19] God tells her Moses' life is in danger and that she should send the baby away down the river in a basket. The Qur'anic verses about Moses' mother are not only commendatory of her sacrifice in giving up her child, they are filled with compassion and sympathy[20] when God assures her that her child will be returned to her.[21]

The Qur'an is always respectful of women, and these are just two examples that contradict any interpretation that implies the Qur'an approves of sexism. Other examples, such as those of the virgin Mary, also populate the Qur'an.

In fact, the very beginning of the entire Qur'anic story, which takes place in the Garden of Eden, treats women as the companions of men, no more to blame for evil than men. As we discussed in chapter two, Satan approaches both Adam and Eve in the Garden, and they both disobey God. In a deliberate rejection of the prevailing norms and traditional views,[22] the Qur'anic Eve is not the cause of the fall, and she is not an evil temptress.[23] In Islam, from the very beginning of time as humankind has known it, women have stood on equal footing with men.

The Qur'an recognizes differences between men and women, of course, and enjoins men to treat women well and provide for them; after all, in ancient patriarchal societies, if men did not provide for women, the women died. The Qur'an recognizes the economic and social status of men was superior in the seventh century to the status of women, but it does not treat men as the superior sex in terms of humanity or ability. In fact, the Qur'an makes a point of insisting that not only all men, but all *people* are equal:

> O people! We have created all of you out of male and female, and we have made you into different nations and tribes so you might come to know one another. Verily, the noblest of you in the sight of God is the one who is most deeply conscious of Him, not one belonging to this or that race or nation.[24]

This verse addresses everyone, telling us God has made us different so that we can know each other, with the differences, and without any inherent superiority.[25] It is not someone of a particular race or nation that is superior but whosoever is aware of God.

Like all ancient texts, the Qur'an does contain verses that may appear to be sexist if the historical and literary contexts of the verse are disregarded. In all such cases, though some Qur'anic verses may treat women as disadvantaged and in need of protection—which they were at that time—the Qur'an does not treat them as inferior beings and does not state that women will forever need such protection. Even the verses that seem sexist today improved the status of women then.

The Development of Islamic Law with Respect to Women

I am always surprised that acquaintances, familiar with my devotion to my religion and unswerving contempt for discrimination against women, could assume that Islam is sexist. Perhaps I am simply an aberration, they suppose. Theirs is not a new supposition, though. During the Romantic period of Europe (starting in the late 1700s), criticism of Islam unfairly extended to the issue of women's rights. Norman Daniel writes:

> The rights of women were . . . usually seen in terms of subjection, enslavement and concubinage. Yet before the passage of the Married Women's Property Act of the 1860s it was justly said that in England women had fewer rights than the Qur'an allowed them.[26]

If this is true, you may ask, then why do we continually hear about the overwhelming oppression of women in Islamic countries? The oppressed women we hear about are a small minority of Muslim women, but the media loves to film them. Another reason is that culture is often confused—by Muslims as well as others—with religion.

The oppressed Muslim women frequently displayed in the media live primarily in a few countries, such as Saudi Arabia and the Taliban's Afghanistan. Once, while watching a newscast, I noticed that several flashing images of enveloped, black-veiled women were actually of the same woman from different angles. Until I noticed this, I had the impression of numerous veiled women everywhere.

Put another way, Indonesia and India house by far the largest populations of Muslim women in the world—and their images are not the ones we see in the media as the "oppressed women of Islam."

Once in a great while I see media coverage of strong Muslim women like Palestinian Jumana Odeh, pediatrician, social activist, and outreach speaker, or the current Queen Rania of Jordan—smart, beautiful, and an advocate of human rights. Nevertheless, the media does not show them in the context of representing all Muslim women (as it shows the veiled ones) but in the context of their association with politics or royalty. That they are Muslim is only, to the media, incidental and not representative.

Often, the oppression of Muslim women is not a result of Islam but two kinds of cultural influence: first, the culture of the early Islamic scholars who developed Islamic law and resisted implementing the feminist reforms the Qur'an enjoined, and second, the local culture that became mixed into religion somewhere along the last 1,400 years.

The Qur'an or Male Interpretation of the Qur'an?

The development of Islamic law in the first few centuries was implemented by men who did not always approve of Qur'anic reform. Just as wealthy Meccans had been resistant to Muhammad's oversetting of their tribal system, the new Muslims, born of that same patriarchal system, sometimes resisted the changes Muhammad and the Qur'an mandated. Umar, the unswervingly loyal companion to the Prophet and later the second of the *Rashidun* caliphs, resented the Prophet's prohibiting men from beating their wives.

"What do you mean," he must have raged, "I can't treat my wife however I want? *Everyone* beats their wives! It's the custom!" Even those who unequivocally followed the Prophet did not always find themselves capable of change, even while he was alive. They would have had little reason to become more amenable to change after he died.

The scholars interpreting the Qur'an and *Sunnah* after the Prophet's death naturally imposed (consciously or subconsciously) their own perspectives and views on their interpretations of the law. Muslim scholar Amina Wadud writes that it was inevitable that men's experiences would have been included in Qur'anic interpretation and that women's experiences would have been either excluded completely or interpreted through the male perspective or the male vision of woman.[27] Given that books these days assert that men and women come from different planets, it seems to me that 1,300 years ago men and women must have seemed to come from different universes altogether!

It can only follow that Qur'anic interpretation from the male perspective would have been different from what the female interpretation of the Qur'an would have been. The established interpretations of the Qur'an were constructed by seventh-century men (nowhere profoundly renowned for zealous advocacy of women's rights) and without the participation of women. And this is a crucial issue, because:

> [Women's] voicelessness during critical periods of development in Qur'anic interpretations has not gone unnoticed, but it has been mistakenly equated with voicelessness in the [Qur'anic] text itself.[28]

In chapter four, we touched on how translations of the Qur'an into English vaporize the feminine voice in the Qur'an, which is signified by Arabic linguistic "sound figures" and a particular gender dynamic. When translated into English, the Qur'an seems to speak in a male narrative voice, which is inaccurate, because Islamic theology has always resisted categorizing God as male or female. The feminine presence, then, is much stronger in the Arabic original than in English translations.

Linguistic analysis is essential in determining the answers to questions that have vital importance for me: is my holy scripture addressed to me as a woman? And to what extent? Does God speak to *me*? Or only to men?

If I believed the Qur'an did not address women at all, I could not have remained committed to my faith, especially as I grew up with a dearth of Muslim peer support and much peer pressure to be like every other teenager around me. But the Qur'an does address women. The proof is in the text.

Nevertheless, when early male Islamic scholars set about interpreting the Qur'an and developing its bare-bones rules, they saw the Qur'anic verses through the lenses of their own experience. The feminine presence, new and alien to them, was sometimes—perhaps often—left out. An example of this androcentric interpretation of the Qur'an is evident in the inheritance verses.

The Sunni religious scholars could not bear to give up their male-dominated laws of inheritance that existed in pre-Islamic Arabia. It made absolute sense to them that men should get everything, and it made no sense to them that women should get anything. What had women to do with protecting the tribe, after all? But the Qur'an had commanded that women must inherit. What were they to do?

They grafted Qur'anic inheritance reforms (which were advantageous to women) onto the existing pre-Islamic law (which was disadvantageous to women) and used the pre-Islamic law as a default whenever the Qur'an was not absolutely specific. Sometimes they invented twisty, convoluted interpretations of inheritance verses with the sole purpose of clinging to their fondness for primogeniture (the practice of leaving the entire estate exclusively to the eldest son).

In contrast, Shi'i religious scholars threw out the old pre-Islamic system of inheritance and built a completely new one based on the Qur'anic verses. Unsurprisingly, the Shi'i law of inheritance is more beneficial to women and closer to the Qur'an than Sunni law. That, too, however, bears the interpretive stamp of seventh-century men. The Qur'an did not cover every contingency, and that is where they could not help but impose their patriarchal worldview.

The fact remains that the Qur'an never neglected to address women. The concern for women's rights is one of the Qur'an's primary themes. As Michael Sells points out, translations and interpretations of the Qur'an that favor the male voice falsely promote the image of a sexist religion.[29] The fortunate thing is that, despite all these convoluted interpretations and machinations, Qur'anic reforms *still* gave women more rights than they were given by anyone else for centuries.

The unfortunate, tragic, and frustrating thing is that some countries oppress women by using Islam as an excuse. That is culture, not religion, and largely the reason, I assume, that Islam is perceived as sexist. This perception is one of the hardest to overcome. When I told an acquaintance that Islam was not sexist, she asked sincerely, "Oh! Would you move to the Middle East then?"

Well, no, I cannot think so. (And I did find it troubling that she expected me to move to the Middle East just because I was Muslim.) But that is *not* because I think Islam is sexist. It is because the United States is my country. It is because many Muslim countries are still part of the developing world and I appreciate my American conveniences and my American civil liberties. Some countries do repress women in the name of Islam, and I unquestionably would balk at living in those. But this is because their *cultures* are sexist, not because Islam is sexist.

Religion, as my parents always maintained, should be private and personal. That is why I, as a devout Muslim, vehemently resent the small handful of "Islamic" governments who impose their own views onto their populations, whether or not their individual citizens believe in their particular interpretation of Islam. I particularly abhor those imposed views when they miss the point of the message of Islam in their relentless dedication to the letter of a law intended for the seventh century. In showing themselves to be devout, Muslims who think religious devotion means creating another seventh-century Arabia are doing an injustice to the original tolerance and eternal aspect of the Qur'an.

Religion vs. Culture

Culture became entangled with religion from the very beginning in the development of the law. The scholars resisted reforms, so many customs of pre-Islamic Arabia remained in place if they were not explicitly prohibited by Islam. They became part of the religious interpretive literature.

Moreover, non-Arabic cultures were sometimes inculcated into Islam as a result of Islamic expansion. When the Islamic empire appropriated Persian and Byzantine governmental institutions, Muslim rulers gradually appropriated their cultural practices, as well, even those directly contravening Qur'anic reforms, such as harems, concubinage, veiling, and seclusion for women.[30] In time, these practices, borrowed from other cultures, as well as from pre-Islamic culture, became associated with Islam.[31] Nowhere is this more evident than in matters of the veil.

That Veil Thing

I find it inconceivable that the Qur'an could have given women so many rights and assumed as a matter of course their positions of social and political power yet still required them to be veiled completely and ostracized from society, as they are in a few Muslim cultures. If the Prophet allowed his wives to accompany him to battle and argue politics with him and the rest of the Muslim *umma*, he could not possibly have favored totally segregating them from male society in today's world. If the Qur'an had meant to completely separate men and women, Qur'anic narrative would not have approved of the power and position of Bilqis, the Queen of Sheba.

Whether or not Islam requires the *hijab*, which is the word now commonly used to describe the head covering that hides the hair but leaves the face uncovered, is a debated question. The basis for it is cultural rather than religious, although two Qur'anic verses have been manipulated to support it. In most Muslim countries, whether to wear a hair covering, a more complete veil, or no hair covering at all is a personal choice.

Cultural or not, the veil in today's world is associated with Islam. In the West, it is usually unthinkingly equated with oppression. I heard a clear demonstration of this attitude once on a radio program.[32] An American schoolteacher displayed before her high school students a picture of a nun and asked them what they thought the nun represented. The students used adjectives such as, "pure," "faithful to God," "chaste," and "religious." The teacher then replaced the picture with that of a Middle-Eastern woman wearing a *hijab*.

Again, the teacher asked her students to describe what they thought the woman represented. They used adjectives such as "backward," "stupid," and "oppressed."[33] Why such a difference when the head covering was virtually the same? Why is a nun with covered hair considered modest when a Muslim woman with her hair covered is considered oppressed and stupid?

Furthermore, when discussions of "the veil" air in the media, they almost always refer to Muslim women and almost never include Jewish women who cover their hair, Rastafarian women who cover their hair, or nuns.

This, I think, is really the crux of the matter: the issue of head covering is not the same as the issue of oppression. If we do not consider nuns to be oppressed people on the basis of their dress, then it is unreasonable to condemn Muslim women on the sole basis of whether they choose to voluntarily cover their hair.

Muslim women all over the world wear a variety of veils or none at all. Nevertheless, the image overwhelmingly prevalent in the media is not the head scarf covering the hair but the billowing, voluminous garment that envelopes a woman's every millimeter of skin and sometimes even shrouds her eyes behind a strip of netting. This sort of covering is called a *chador* or *burqa*. In some parts of the Middle East, women wear an all-encompassing veil with a gold mask covering their faces. Sometimes they wear gloves, as well, so that none of their flesh shows.

Does Islam require women to wear veils? If so, what kind? The Islamic scholars interpreting the Qur'an all agreed that the chest and anything above the knees should be covered, for modesty's sake. But beyond that, there was no consensus. Nearly all scholars agree that veiling of the most complete nature, such as covering the face and hands, is not required by Islam. As for the head scarf, some Muslims believe it is required, but some do not. Historically speaking, it is clear that veiling was a pre-Islamic custom among many cultures; later, the veil came to be associated with Islam.

In pre-Islamic times, in many parts of the world and for various reasons, women wore head coverings. For hundreds of years, until at least the medieval era, Jewish and Christian women wore veils, too.[34] Sometimes the veil denoted inferiority; for example, according to canon law, a veil during the marriage ceremony ensured that a woman knew her lowly status and inferiority to her husband.[35] The Christian church "corporately at various times made canonical statements requiring women to be veiled" until the ninth century, but not so much after that, though women continued to wear veils.[36]

In some cultures, such as the ancient Persian empire, veils indicated high status, wealth, and gentle breeding. It was how women of status dressed, in many cultures, including European ones, and it differentiated them from prostitutes or poor women. Head coverings were a practical matter, as well; both men and women even now in the Middle East don head coverings to deflect the unsparing heat of the desert.

Given that religious scholars were products of their environment like the rest of us, the cultural norm of veiling influenced how the scholars interpreted two particular Qur'anic verses. These two verses are still used to justify veiling.

The first is the "modesty verse." What may come as a surprise is that the Qur'an commands modesty on the part of *both* men and women:

> Tell the believing men to lower their gaze and to be mindful of their chastity: this will be most conducive to their purity—and, verily, God is aware of all that they do. And tell the believing women to lower their gaze and be mindful of their chastity, and not to display their charms in public beyond what may decently be apparent thereof.[37]

This verse specifies that women should not display their charms beyond what is decent. The phrase "what may decently be apparent" is deliberately vague and open-ended and allows for changes in what constitutes decency in a given time and place.[38] Even the early Islamic scholars did not agree on the required level of coverage—all agreed the torso down to the knees should be covered; beyond that, they disagreed. Some people and cultures do interpret decency as requiring everything but the face and hands to be covered, but that is not required by the Qur'an itself.

Modesty and chastity outside marriage are an important part of Islam, not only in matters of dress. Men and women both, for example, should not display their wealth in an ostentatious and immodest manner, such as by wearing excessive jewelry, also subjectively defined. Many Muslim men of my personal acquaintance do not wear gold or jewels or silk.

My husband and I did not know whether he should wear a wedding ring when we got married. Do we follow the letter of tradition and not get a gold one? Or should we follow the spirit of tradition and conclude that wedding rings are not ostentatious displays of wealth? In the end, we did get him a wedding ring—a platinum one—which he rarely wears because he always misplaces it.

"Platinum?!" said a friend of mine. "Gold might be forbidden, so you get *platinum?*"

I squirmed. "Well, you see," I explained, "if we follow the letter of the law, we're okay because it's not gold, and if we follow the spirit of the law, we're okay because wedding rings are not ostentatious." I smiled.

She looked askance at me, but my decision made sense to *me*. I am endeavoring here to ensure a pleasant eternity! I can only draw my lines where I feel personally comfortable.

Because of this requirement of modesty and chastity, some cultures disallow men and women from meeting unchaperoned. Chaperonage in Western cultures was common, too, until the last century. The purpose of chaperones is to discourage any extra-marital intimacy. Islam—like Catholicism—allows intimacy only between married people. I suspect that anyone raising an adolescent these days likely comprehends the advantages of chaperonage.

Some cultures extend the idea of chaperonage and segregate men and women completely, or keep women housebound and secluded. Again, this is *not* representative of the practice of the vast majority of Muslims. Rather, it is a cultural practice. Growing up in Southern California, I was not allowed the same degree of freedom as some of my non-Muslim friends (something for which I was actually grateful in later years), but I was never secluded or housebound or veiled. Neither was any Muslim woman I knew, either in California or abroad.

The modesty verse is the Qur'anic basis for dressing decently and without ostentation. But it does not say anything specific about women being veiled. The basis for the notion that the veil is a religious require-ment (and not a cultural one) is the continuation of the same verse:

> Hence, let them draw their head coverings [*khumur*] over their bosoms. And let them not display more of their charms to any but their husbands or their fathers or their husbands' fathers, or their sons, or their husbands' sons, or their brothers, or their brothers' sons, or their sisters' sons, ...[39]

This reference to *khumur* is what leads some Muslims to say that women must cover their hair. But what does the verse mean exactly? That is where scholars interpret the verse differently.

In pre-Islamic times, Arabian women wore a *khimar* (*khumur* is the plural form), an ornamental shawl or head covering.[40] The upper part of their tunics opened widely and showed their bare breasts.[41] This verse indicates that bosoms should be covered because they are not part of "what may decently be apparent."[42] Alternatively, I have seen this verse translated as simply urging women to draw their scarves more closely around them.

This verse does not necessarily mean that someone who is not wearing a head scarf must wear one.[43] Rather, it is simply an injunction to draw closer what women are wearing already, for the sake of modesty. In another time and place, perhaps the verse would have urged women to wear trousers if they were in the habit of wearing shorts. However, to conclude in that case that such an injunction meant that *only* trousers could be worn, to the exclusion of dresses, robes, and so on, would be missing the point of the verse.

The standards for modesty have changed in the interim fourteen centuries. It is debatable whether a veil is necessary to achieve the same purpose today—modesty and the protection of women—as it might have originally. The definition of modesty has always been subjective. In *The King and I*, the Rogers and Hammerstein musical, the English governess stares, shocked, at the immodest trousers of the wives of the King of Siam. The wives stare, shocked in their own turn, at the wanton expanse of neck, shoulders, and bosom that the English governess's dress reveals.

Even today, the definition of modesty depends on the country. Many women in Turkey cover their hair but wear skirts that show their ankles. Is hair more provocative or are ankles? In India, the bit of bare midriff revealed by a sari does not provoke as many shocked stares as a leg in a mini-skirt. Tight clothes can be immodest even if they cover the whole body. It all depends upon what people are used to seeing. That is why the Qur'anic verse is open-ended.

Another verse of the Qur'an has been used as a basis for veiling and secluding women, though it pertains specifically to the Prophet's wives:

> And [as for the Prophet's wives,] whenever you ask them for anything that you need, ask them from behind a screen: this will but deepen the purity of your hearts and theirs.[44]

This verse relates narrowly to the Prophet's wives, not to every woman, and stresses the Prophet's exalted and unique status in Islam. It also identifies the Prophet's wives as worthy of special respect and does not necessarily apply to all women and all men generally.

In this verse, it's the "screen" that conservative Muslims point to in justification of required veiling. The term *hijab* can be translated as "screen" or "veil" or "curtain" and can be interpreted metaphorically or literally.[45] Metaphorically, this verse is commanding exceptional reverence of the Prophet's wives and a certain respectful distance—a "screen" of respect, in other words. This is how many Muslims read it. If read literally, this verse enjoins separating the Prophet's wives from other people by physical screens or curtains. Whichever way this verse is read, its purpose was simply to protect and honor the Prophet's wives at a time of political tension and at a time when the pre-Islamic Arab society treated women badly. The purpose was never to subjugate them.

And finally, there's this verse:

> O Prophet! Tell thy wives and thy daughters, as well as all [other] believing women, that they should draw over themselves some of their outer garments [when in public]: this will be more conducive to their being recognized [as decent women] and not annoyed.[46]

The word "veil" or "*hijab*" isn't mentioned here. Rather in these verses, the words that are used are *jilbab* (cloak) and *khumur* (shawl). So the verses are not even referring to the same kind of clothing, much less a veil. Moreover, in the usage of the time, both *jilbab* and *khumur* meant clothing that covered the neck and bosom, but not the head, face, hands, or feet.[47]

Over time, these verses were read in light of the cultural norms of veiling. The result that some Muslims achieved, eventually, was the idea that Islam requires veiling or seclusion of all women from all men. This conclusion that Muslim women must be veiled was indeed a gradual progression that took centuries to coalesce.[48] One scholar notes that women prayed with their heads uncovered as late as the ninth century; moreover, women are supposed to make the pilgrimage to Mecca with their faces *uncovered*.[49] The point here is that veiling was not something even the Prophet forced on his wives; for the Saudi or Iranian government to do so is ludicrous. These verses constitute a very frail Islamic basis for requiring the veil or seclusion.

Because of this debatable interpretation, the majority of Muslim women do not, in fact, live veiled and secluded the way those in Western countries commonly perceive that they do. When I reiterate this point in conversations, I encounter profound skepticism, as though my lack of *hijab* and absence of downtrodden subjection is somehow pugnaciously adversative to Muslim womanhood.

For the sake of argument, suppose we accept that these verses command veiling and seclusion. Even then, the verses have one inescapable feature that is simple, crucial, and often ignored: the verses themselves are not sexist.

I mean that the verses pertain to both sexes. The modesty verse requires modesty for *both* men and women. The screen in the verse about the Prophet's wives comes down *between* both men and women. The cloaking of the Prophet's wives was to protect them from a society in which women were harassed. Nowhere does the verse say only women must stay home behind a screen while men should go freely wherever they please. The Queen of Sheba did not stay home behind a screen.

And though it is true that the verse enjoins women and not men to pull their garments closer about them, women in those days wore those particular garments, anyway. Men were already covered.

Therefore, the idea that it is the women who must be veiled and the women who must be modest while the men need not be is a cultural, androcentric idea that is not supported by the Qur'an. In fact, it smacks of that recurring cultural characterization of woman as an evil temptress driving men to sin, though the Qur'an specifically rejected that attitude in the context of Adam and Eve.

Recall that the Qur'anic verse mentioning the veil allows for an open-ended interpretation of modesty. What constitutes modesty today? A Muslim woman living in a Western country justified her decision *not* to wear a veil: "Where would you hide a grain of sand? In the desert! Where would you hide a tree? In a forest!" For this woman, modesty—the purpose of the veil—was achieved by blending in like camouflage, rather than by wearing the conspicuous head scarf.

Another acquaintance has recently stopped wearing a head scarf and says it's a relief not to be stared at so much.

I believe people should be allowed to wear what they want. Whether they are modest or not is a matter for their own conscience. And if it's a matter of protecting women from men's lasciviousness, then I agree with one female Muslim professor, who points out that now we have laws to protect against that.[50]

Aside from reasons of culture, modesty, and the two Qur'anic verses, the veil has survived in some cultures because of practicality. For example, a friend of mine who traveled in Yemen found that many Yemeni women wore their veils (which were the completely enveloping kind) more because of cultural custom than religious devotion. My friend added that it was only wise, anyway, to always wear something on your head when you live in the desert under a devastatingly hot sun.

Many women all over the world and from many avenues of life have begun to wear the *hijab*, even if they do not believe Islam requires one. Why would they choose to wear a head scarf? Is not the *hijab* a sign of oppression, subjection, and lowly status?

The purpose of the *hijab* was never a representation of inferiority and low status. This is proved by the millions of women who wear the *hijab* while pursuing their various occupations, from full-time mothers to academicians to politicians. The *hijab* has always represented modesty and religious devotion. Choosing to wear a *hijab* is not, in itself, oppressive or backward. In nearly all Muslim countries, the decision to wear or not wear the *hijab* is a personal choice.

Modesty is, of course, a primary reason women choose to wear some sort of *hijab*. But another reason, less known, compels some women to wear a head scarf: freedom.

Freedom from being ogled, freedom from harassment, freedom to be judged on their intelligence and personality rather than their looks. In Egypt, more women wear the *hijab* today than ever before, because more women are entering the work force—a sign of liberation—and are finding that they can more easily avoid sexual harassment and obtain intellectual respect if they wear a head scarf. When people see a scarf, they (to some extent) disregard appearance and focus on what lies underneath—intelligence, competence, and personality. The *hijab* sends the message, "Hands off. I'm not available, and stop treating me like a sex object."

The *hijab*, therefore, can be a way to become equal to men.

For women who choose to wear it, the *hijab* constitutes more than the freedom of not being accosted; it means not worrying about leading someone on or sending the wrong message. (It means not having to worry about bad hair days, either.) I know several American mothers, none of them Muslim, whose small daughters of preschool or kindergarten age wear shorts under their dresses. As one mother put it, "You want to make sure you're sending the right message."

A woman who dresses provocatively or revealingly stands a greater chance of receiving male attention (welcome or not) than one who does not. In a perfect society, women would not need to worry about sending those kinds of messages to avoid being harassed. But our world obviously is not perfect. My female friends in college (none of whom were Muslim) used to joke about how the intelligent, educated, probably even feminist young men who rarely deigned even to greet them would invariably sashay close for a lengthy conversation whenever any of them wore anything form-fitting or *décolleté* or otherwise brief.

Nuns who wear veils or head scarves send the message of purity and faith. The *hijab* sends the same message.

Moreover, the *hijab* sends the message that appearance and body image do not equal the sum total of our worth as human beings. In general, distancing ourselves from our debilitating fixation on body image would almost certainly be a good thing, in light of the shattering repercussions: nine million Americans suffer from eating disorders,[51] and eleven million Americans underwent cosmetic surgery in 2006.[52] I am by no means asserting that someone in a *burqa* could not suffer from an eating disorder. I am suggesting the possibility that, in a world in which pressure on females to achieve physical perfection invades even childhood, a veil can be freedom.

Pressure to look a certain way affects everyone, but it affects females disproportionately. Women are treated as sex objects much more than men; beer commercials come easily to mind as prime examples. Many Muslims resent Western societies denouncing the *hijab* as oppressive in unthinking blanket terms when, in their view, advertisers cannot seem to sell even a box of matches without posing a nearly unclothed woman somewhere in the advertisement.

I once heard a Jewish-American woman who had converted to Islam call a radio program and give her opinion that going shopping for a bikini was much more demeaning than wearing a *hijab*.[53] Another American woman, a former pastor's wife who converted to Islam, writes that her family thought she had succumbed to insanity and accused her of converting to a religion geared for men. She replied, "If it were geared for men, women would undress instead of covering up!"[54]

I am not taking sides here. I do not cover my hair and I challenge the notion that Islam requires it. Nonetheless, I want to clarify that, although Islam does not necessarily require a veil of any kind, the women who choose to wear one do so for a variety of reasons, none of which may be "oppression." It is having the choice that matters.

In Iran, for example, many women who wear head scarves (willingly or not) also have careers. Iranian women have been appointed to political positions, such as governor and vice-president.[55] Iranian women have also been participating in the reinterpretation and application of Islamic law to achieve legislative results beneficial to women. For example, upon divorce, a husband must "compensate his wife for the labor she has contributed to the management of his household." This has been the law in Iran since 1992 and has placed the power of the law behind the contention that Islam does not support the exploitation of women in any way, even for the sake of their husbands and children.[56]

It is possible for a woman to choose to cover her hair and not be oppressed. Oppression only arises when the matter of dress ceases to be a personal choice. The Taliban oppressed women because they forced them into total hiding, not only into their all-encompassing veils but into their homes and out of their jobs and schools. The Taliban oppressed women because they made them less than human. The Saudis oppress women by not granting them equal rights and by forcing them to dress in a way that should be a personal choice. All governments that require women to cover their heads are oppressing women by denying them their right to choose.

I must say that almost nothing, including choice in personal dress, is a completely unconditional freedom. For example, in the United States, we do not allow people to go about in public in the nude. We draw a line where we think indecent exposure begins and personal freedom ends.

We lack an absolute test to determine whether one country's line means oppression and another country's line does not. I do not wear a *hijab* myself. I endeavor to find the parameters of what my religion tells me. Where there is room for personal discretion, I draw my own lines of "modest" and "immodest" within those parameters. But I believe that to automatically stereotype something like the head scarf or even the *chador* as "oppressive," without ever delving into the specific circumstances, is an injustice.

Turkey, where 95 percent of the population is Muslim, has has long prohibited women from wearing the *hijab* in public institutions and has allowed security personnel to forcibly remove it from women's heads.[57] Muslim students in France, as well, have been prohibited from wearing the *hijab*, ostensibly on the grounds that all head scarves are "religious symbols;" yet, the *hijab* is simply a way of being modest. It does not represent Islam as a symbol. It is like choosing to wear long sleeves instead of short sleeves. Would the French law allow hats in the classroom if the hair were completely covered? A turban?

I hope we in the West are not so accustomed to perceiving the *hijab* as oppressive that the laws in Turkey and France prohibiting the *hijab* appear less oppressive than the Taliban's requiring it. The Turkish and French laws do not seem less oppressive to me. They restrict personal freedom.

Islam does not prohibit women from taking an active part in society, however they happen to be dressed, veil or no veil. Men and women are sometimes segregated in Muslim social functions because some Muslims consider segregation to be a part of modesty. The same justification is used to seclude women in some cultures. But, again, if we uphold the Prophet as the example to follow, we must remember he encouraged his wives and all women to be active participants in society. Segregation and seclusion are cultural developments, not religious ones.

The message and purpose of Islam gave women *more* freedom, *more* rights, and the goal of equality. Although some Muslim cultures may not reflect these goals, many Muslim women are standing up for their Islamic rights. The World Congress of Muslim Women, convened in early 2002, condemned practices that violate Islam, such as "domestic violence, female genital mutilation, and continued discrimination in work, pay, health, and education, regardless of race or religion."[58]

Understanding of Muslims cannot be achieved if we never penetrate the superficial presumption that the *hijab* equals oppression, no matter what the circumstances. For most women, the *hijab* is a personal choice, associated with modesty and religious devotion, and a separate issue from that of equal rights or career opportunities. When you see a woman in a *hijab*, do not assume she is downtrodden and subjugated, an uneducated breeder of children. She may be a mother, of course. She may also be a prime minister.

Marriage & Polygyny

While having lunch with three female law school classmates one day, a woman at the table suddenly told me she thought Muslims were disgusting because, she asserted, Muslim husbands took dowries from their wives and then killed them so they could marry again and obtain new dowries. Around this time, the media had been reporting on the tragic "kitchen fires" in India, in which wives had been killed so that husbands could remarry for another dowry.

I broke the sudden, awkward silence to tell her that, actually, in Muslim marriages no dowry at all is required for the bride. The dowry custom in India, I said, according to which the bride's parents give the groom money upon their marriage, is part of Hindu culture, not Muslim culture (though I am in no way implying that murder is acceptable in Hindu culture, either).

"Oh," she said huffily, and changed the subject.

The dowry was one of the first issues that Islam addressed in the seventh century. In pre-Islamic Arabia, a bridegroom paid a specified amount of money to the father of the bride. It was essentially a sale: the money (dowry) for the girl. But after Islamic reforms, the husband paid the dowry not to the father of the bride, but to the bride *herself*, so she would have resources in case of divorce or widowhood. By this simple innovation of paying the dowry to the bride herself, she became a contracting party to the marriage and not an object of sale.

Marriage in Islam is a civil contract between a man and a woman. If both parties consent before witnesses, then the marriage is valid. In Islam, marriage is not a religious sacrament, although the Qur'an disapproves of divorce and sets out procedures that must be taken before a divorce may be initiated. However, since marriage is a civil contract, it can be broken by the contracting parties under certain circumstances, especially if one or both do not uphold their duties under the contract. The Qur'an attaches no stigma to either the man *or* the woman in case of divorce: "And if the husband and wife do separate, God shall provide for each of them out of His abundance...."[59]

I am often asked who officiated at my wedding. An *imam*, I usually reply, but we discussed in chapter five how potentially confusing *that* word can be. Really, no one at all needed to officiate over our marriage under Islamic rules. To satisfy Islamic requirements for a marriage, we had only to freely sign a contract before witnesses. The rest of our wedding ceremony had to do with state requirements or simple celebration.

Both parties to the marriage contract can agree to certain stipulations. For example, a wife can insert a clause that requires the husband to consult her before taking another wife. Or, a condition may disallow the husband from taking another wife altogether. Custody and divorce issues can be included in the marriage contract. Essentially, it can embody any conditions and agreements that do not contravene the basic function of marriage. The Islamic marriage contract functions, actually, as a pre-nuptial agreement.

But why, those of us inured to monogamous marriages may ask, *why* must the woman insert a stipulation in the marriage contract to limit her husband's right to polygyny? Why is he allowed a right to polygyny (a man's right to take several wives) in the first place?

Part of the answer has to do with the culture of the seventh-century world. Polygyny was acceptable in certain societies. The Arabs and Jews of the Arabian peninsula practiced polygyny. The Old Testament assumes the legitimacy of polygyny.[60] By the time Islam came into being, though, the Christian view contrasted significantly by allowing monogamous marriages only, indissoluble except by death.[61]

Though a man in Arabia could marry an unrestricted number of women, women could marry only one man. The most common reason given for this discrimination was the importance of not casting doubt upon the paternity of children. But another part of the reason polygyny was lawful was that, in the tribal world of pre-Islamic Arabia, men were scarce. The acceptability of blood feuds and raiding resulted in untimely deaths, leaving women and orphans without provision. In those days, as for centuries to come, no (respectable) jobs existed for women. To take a wife was to provide for her.

The Qur'an restricted the allowed number of wives to four:

> And if you have reason to fear that you might not act equitably towards orphans, then marry women of your choice such as are lawful to you—even two or three or four; but if you have reason to fear that you might not be able to treat them with equal fairness, then only one ... to prevent you from deviating from the just course.[62]

Thus, a man may take up to four wives if he can treat them with equal fairness; if he cannot so treat them, then he is limited to one wife. This verse is primarily concerned with justice toward wives and orphans.

Some scholars interpret this verse to mean that polygyny applies *only* to orphans. This may sound bizarre, but it is clear from the Qur'an that mismanagement of the funds of orphans was a common problem. One way to solve this problem was for the guardian to marry the female orphans. The management of the funds by the husband was offset by the marital sharing of wealth.[63] We can thus conclude that this Qur'anic verse allows polygyny only when it comes to taking care of orphan wards.

Other scholars, however, interpret this verse as relating to all women, not just orphans. Correspondingly, some translations include the word "other," so that the verse reads, "marry from among other women of your choice," thus no longer limiting the verse to the orphaned women. Whichever way you read it, the above verse must be reconciled with this one:

> And it will not be within your power to treat your wives with equal fairness, however much you may desire it;[64]

The two verses taken together clearly indicate that polygyny is allowed but not approved. The first verse allows polygyny only if the husband treats his wives with equal fairness; the second verse says a man *cannot* treat his wives with equal fairness, even if he wishes to do so. Many Muslims read these two verses in conjunction to conclude that polygyny is impermissible.

This is what my Muslim friends and I were taught while growing up and learning our religious tenets: a man can have more than one wife if he can treat them equally, I remember my father saying, but since that is impossible, the Qur'an is actually obliquely limiting a man to *one* wife. We all regarded polygyny as a historical condition and no longer applied to the modern world.

Whichever the interpretation, it is clear that the Qur'an much prefers monogamy and allows polygyny reluctantly and fences restrictions around it. Polygyny could not be eradicated immediately, given the seventh-century social situation, but had to be restricted and disapproved so that it could eventually be eliminated.

As a practical matter, polygyny is only practiced by a very small percentage of Muslims, mostly in Saudi Arabia. It is not at all widespread. Once or twice during my childhood, I overheard my parents and their friends mention in hushed, scandalized, disapproving voices that someone they knew had a friend who knew someone else who had a relative in a distant country who had taken a second wife. Wide-eyed countenances and gasped exclamations invariably followed. That is the mainstream Muslim view of polygyny.

The Prophet himself was given a special dispensation for more than four wives, an exception to the general rule. But his was a special status bestowed upon him by the Qur'an and understood by his followers to be the mark of his prophethood. I am aware that this special dispensation may seem specious in the extreme. (Why does *he* get to have more wives?) It is not necessary to agree with the Muslim view to understand it. The reason for his marriages was not lasciviousness, which is the Western accusation usually leveled at him. It was political expediency.

For the twenty-five or so years that Muhammad was married to Khadija, while he was in the prime of life, he never took another wife, though it was the custom. After her death, he entered into most of his marriages to strengthen treaties and solidify relationships between tribes or political groups. Some of the Prophet's wives were also the widows of his companions who had fallen defending their new faith. After Khadija's death, Muhammad married nine women, eight of whom were widows or divorced and only one of whom was a virgin. The reason this is significant is that widows and divorcees were very often left with no means of support.

Widows remarried only with difficulty in those days, for various reasons. Men of many cultures throughout history have preferred marrying virgins to ensure the heirs are truly theirs. Widows were often older, sometimes past the age of childbearing, and considered second-hand goods. Divorcees, unsurprisingly, were in even greater straits. They confronted these same problems, but also had to contend with the denunciation of a second marriage. Christianity did not allow divorce and therefore considered a woman's second marriage to be invalid. She was considered to be her first husband's wife even after divorce and therefore adulterous.[65]

The marrying of widows and divorced women, as well as polygyny, contributed to the medieval Christian perception of Islam as licentious. This, in turn, gave rise to some of the medieval hostility toward Islam. The fact that a divorced Muslim woman could remarry was considered evidence of adultery and licentiousness. Muhammad's multiplicity of marriages, in addition to his marrying mostly widows and divorcees, was a double strike against him.

As for the Prophet's motivations, marriage for political reasons and the creation of political alliances has been common for centuries. Geoffrey Parrinder remarks impatiently that no man has been as maligned throughout history as Muhammad:

> This man was not married until he was twenty-five years of age, then he and his wife lived in happiness and fidelity for twenty-four years until her death when he was forty-nine. Only between the age of fifty and his death at sixty-two did Muhammad take other wives, only one of whom was a virgin, and most of them were taken for dynastic and political reasons. Certainly the Prophet's record was better than that head of the Church of England, Henry VIII.[66]

As for the one virgin Muhammad married, that was Aysha, who later led an army. Aysha was the daughter of Muhammad's best friend, Abu Bakr. She was contracted to the Prophet at a young age, given variously as somewhere between nine to twelve years. However, the marriage was a formality and unconsummated until she was past puberty. The sources variously cite her as somewhere between twelve and sixteen—and therefore, according to the standards of the time, an adult.

I mention this last point because Aysha's youth seems to have apparently appalled some non-Muslims, much to my surprise. So I thought

I would put things in perspective. It is unreasonable to be shocked at a seventh-century Arabian man's titular marriage to the young daughter of his best friend, consummated only after she was past puberty, when girls all over the world were also betrothed or married while very young and sometimes still in the cradle.[67]

In Europe, it was not uncommon for an adult man to be betrothed to a little girl.[68] As late as the eighteenth century, it was acceptable for children of thirteen or fourteen years to be married.[69] The Church, in fact, allowed child betrothals and child marriages in England well into the sixteenth century:[70]

> On another occasion, John Rigmarden, aged three, was carried in the arms of a clergyman who coaxed him to repeat the words of matrimony to a bride of five.[71]

People did not live so long in centuries past and in their twenties were already nearing middle age. Puberty meant adulthood.

In the United States of the mid-nineteenth century, the "age of consent," the age upon which a girl could legally give her consent to have sexual intercourse, was ten or twelve depending on the state; in Delaware, it was seven.[72]

In light of Western historical customs enduring into the eighteenth and nineteenth centuries, the Prophet Muhammad's seventh-century marriage to Aysha should raise only the most hypocritical of eyebrows.

Aysha, by the way, is portrayed in tradition as freckled, prone to jealousy, and vivacious. Jealousy seems unavoidable to me, in a polygynous marriage. However, one of my professors, herself a blonde Englishwoman, once said something about polygyny that made a deep impression on me.

She interrupted her own lecture to say, thoughtfully, that a woman was not necessarily better off divorced, deprived of her children, and left without a means of supporting herself than she was as a respected first wife among one or more other wives. Even 200 years ago in Western countries, women could not easily make their own living. In societies in which women can support themselves and need not automatically give up their children, this rationale for polygyny is irrelevant. But in seventh-century Arabia, and for centuries afterward, this rationale was indeed relevant.

As a Muslim, I accept that polygyny was a reality fourteen centuries ago and that Islam allowed restricted polygyny for certain social reasons. But, also as a Muslim, I think polygyny was disapproved of in the Qur'an and was meant to be gradually eliminated; I base this on the interpretations of other Muslim scholars, on the Qur'an's preference for monogamy, the Qur'anic emphasis on the impossibility of treating wives fairly, and the Qur'an's many verses equalizing men and women. Some Muslim countries have arrived at the same conclusion.

Tunisia has outlawed polygyny with a two-fold justification based on the Qur'an itself. First, since the Qur'an limits and disapproves of polygyny, we were meant to eventually eliminate it. Second, because equal treatment is a prerequisite for polygyny and because no one can possibly treat even two people, never mind four, in exactly the same way, polygyny is impossible. The verse on polygyny is actually the Qur'an's oblique manner of illustrating the impossibility of polygyny and the gradual eradication of it.

Turkey and the Ismaili Khojas of East Africa, as well as Tunisia, have both outlawed polygyny outright, although Turkey has done so on secular grounds rather than Qur'anic grounds.[73]

Reforms are taking place in other Muslim countries, as well, and although most countries have not yet outlawed polygyny as completely as Tunisia has, they have severely limited it. In many countries, including India, Iran, Iraq, Bangladesh, Algeria, Tunisia, Lebanon, Morocco, Jordan, and Kuwait, a woman may insert an enforceable clause in the marriage contract prohibiting the husband from taking another wife.[74] In Iran, if a husband does take another wife, he must show the court that the first wife gave consent to a second. In Malaysia, a husband must obtain consent from both his first wife and from the governmental religious authority before he can marry a second wife.

Even in countries prohibiting polygyny, a man who believes Islam grants him the right to more than one wife may illegally take a second wife if he believes no one will report him to the authorities. In many poor countries without decent social systems for people unable to support themselves, a wife might refrain from bringing an action against her husband because she depends upon him financially or does not wish to risk losing custody of her children as a result of divorce.

A woman of my parents' acquaintance in Pakistan, where polygyny is illegal without a prior court appearance and wife's consent, gave birth to four daughters, which so incensed her benighted husband that he acquired another wife and left his first wife alone to raise his children. She had no family to support her. She had no education, so even if she did find a job, which was unlikely, she had no one to take care of the four little girls. Daycare, even where it can be afforded, is not always available. She stayed married to her bigamous husband because she was financially supported and in no danger of losing her children.

The solution for this problem is not the continuation of polygyny, of course, but the bolstering of social systems and educating women about their rights under the law and under Islam. The Qur'an requires justice for women, and polygyny is no longer consistent—if it ever was—with this requirement. But a further difficulty is that sometimes the woman herself would prefer to be a first wife than to be a divorced one.

I recently heard a Saudi woman interviewed on public radio. She was a Fulbright scholar and had earned her PhD in sociology in the United States. The interviewer said to her, "You're educated, you have a doctorate, and yet—you're a second wife."

I found myself both agreeing and irritated with the interviewer. In this brief statement, the interviewer's assumption was clear: anyone with a doctorate must surely realize the interviewer's monogamous culture was the superior one, and a different value system was necessarily a backward one.

But the woman's response was enlightening to me. She said she was *proud* of being a second wife. When she and her husband met, in a workplace situation, he was already married. When they fell in love, he might have divorced his first wife, but he loved her, too, and loved his children by her. The first wife had no desire, either, to be divorced. So he married a second wife, who became part of their household.

Someone raised in the West may be understandably skeptical of this picture of marital harmony. In my view, the Saudi husband should simply have told his new *amour* that he was already married and suggest one of them switch jobs if such proximity was so fraught with unbearable sexual tension. But I have been raised in a monogamous culture and family, and my reasoning is a product of it. People raised in a culture that accepts polygyny as a way of life have a different set of values.

And, anyway, how often are people so noble? I know of a surprising number of people who have conducted extra-marital affairs or who have divorced their unsuspecting spouses to marry other people or who have been themselves the victims of philandering partners. Given that, is the Saudi woman's solution such a terrible one if all parties prefer it to any alternative?

Islam gave women many new rights of marriage, set forth monogamy as the ideal, equalized men and women before God, and urged equal rights for them. Not many ancient texts of any kind can boast such feminism. The Islamic message radically raised women's rights nearly 1,400 years ago, when it was so difficult to do. That same message translated to today's easier world can mean only equal rights for women, in the marriage sphere and elsewhere.

Divorce

Arabian women had no right of divorce before Islam. The husband could banish his wife—after all, he could have as many others as he wanted—and she would return to her own tribe. She would lose her children and receive no alimony. He could proclaim she was "as the back of his mother," which denounced her and made marital relations impossible but also did not free her to marry anyone else. The Qur'an imposed structure and limitation to all this unlicensed male freedom. But—once more—those early Islamic scholars chose to ignore or explain away some of it.

In terms of divorce, the Qur'an substantially and specifically increased women's rights, but cultural resistance subsequently restricted those rights. At least one verse of the Qur'an implies that women should have divorce rights equal to those of men,[75] but women were not given the unconditional right to unilateral divorce, which is what men had. Traditions of the Prophet seem to support equal divorce rights, too, although Islamic law did not interpret them this way.

For instance, I have heard since childhood the famous story of a young wife who came to the Prophet. She told him that although her husband's behavior was irreproachable, she disliked him excessively and wished to divorce him. The Prophet ordered her to return the dowry her husband had given her (a piece of land), and then allowed her a divorce.[76] To me and to some Muslims, this tradition teaches that the wife may unconditionally and unilaterally break the marriage contract for any reason, if she pays the penalty for doing so by offering to return the dowry, whether or not the husband accepts it.

The wife-initiated divorce (khul) transpired differently in Islamic law, however. The jurists decided that a wife could initiate the divorce and offer her dowry back, but they gave the husband the choice of either accepting it by accepting the dowry or preventing the divorce by simply refusing to accept the dowry.

Under Islamic law, husbands retained the unilateral right to divorce but had to follow a prescribed procedure. The wife kept her dowry if her husband divorced her, and she received automatic custody of small children.** She received the right to maintenance payments.

**She received custody of boys aged seven and under and girls aged nine and under.

As for the divorce procedure itself, the Qur'an required the husband to pronounce the *talaq*, "I divorce thee," three times at separate intervals, which forced him to rationally and coolly reflect upon whether he truly wanted to divorce his wife. After the third "I divorce thee," he was presumably certain of his decision, and husband and wife separated. The divorce was not final for three months, however, to determine whether she was pregnant. This may not seem like much, I realize, but the Qur'anic rules of marriage and divorce were addressing particular problems of the seventh century. One of these was the husband's right to divorce his wife instantaneously on a whim.

The Shi'a require a month to lapse between each of the three pronouncements before a divorce can be valid. But the Sunni scholars, resisting change, hit upon the happy notion of allowing the three "I divorce thee" pronouncements to be proclaimed all at once without a month or even a minute in between. Having completely undermined the purpose of the three-pronouncement rule, they incorporated their inspiration into the body of Islamic law. The operation of seventh-century prejudices and circumstances on interpretation of the Qur'an cannot be more obvious than in this example.

Pronouncement alone of the divorce words sufficed to divorce the married couple in early Islamic law, and *intention* to divorce was irrelevant. This fact resulted in amusing developments:

> In Turkey, for example, a convention developed during the rule of the sultans that allowed a wife to go before a *qadi* [judge] with two witnesses and claim that her husband had divorced her when he was drunk, a claim he would be unable to deny.[77]

The only problem arose if the husband actually followed Islamic strictures and abstained from intoxicants!

Under Islamic law, a wife could divorce her husband *without* his consent in three cases. First, she could insert a provision in her marriage contract stating that divorce (repudiation of the contract) would occur if a particular event transpired, such as if her husband married a second wife. Second, a woman could include a provision in her marriage contract in which her husband delegated to her the right to divorce him unilaterally. Giving a wife the unilateral right to divorce, even if she obtained it through the marriage contract, was revolutionary.

And third, a wife could divorce her husband without his consent by applying for a *judicial divorce*, whereupon she could take her petition for divorce to the court. The judge would pronounce the divorce on behalf of the husband, if the wife showed sufficient cause. The definition of "sufficient cause" depended upon which of the four main Sunni schools of legal thought the particular court followed. The most liberal view, that of the Maliki school, allowed a wife to divorce her husband for physical defects (such as failure to consummate), mental defects, failure to maintain, desertion, absence for more than one year for whatever reason, and ill-treatment. The Maliki view may seem somewhat restrictive by today's standards, but it constituted absolutely radical grounds for divorce when it came to thousand-year-old ancient doctrine.

Generally, therefore, although Islamic divorce laws improved the lot of women and although the Qur'an actually implied that women should have equal divorce rights, cultural resistance proved to be an obstacle.[78] This has been recognized by many Islamic countries, and many have consequently begun instituting reforms based on the Qur'an itself.

Of those countries adhering to Islamic law, Tunisia has instituted the most expansive reforms, including the Personal Status Code soon after it attained independence and became a republic. A divorce, according to this law, can be obtained only by judicial means. The husband and wife have identical rights of divorce, and the grounds for divorce are as wide as anywhere else in the world. They are based on the spirit of Islamic law and a reinterpretation of the religious texts.

A friend's Muslim aunt asked me whether she could divorce her husband under *Shari'a*. She knew she could divorce him under American law. I was chagrined to realize I had never before thought of this as a conflict. I always assumed I had the right to divorce for any reason. Brought up as I was to believe that Islam treats men and women equally, it never occurred to me that I should disregard California law to instead follow the minutiae of divorce law developed over a thousand years ago by Islamic male scholars.

This is a valid concern. Do we follow our ancient religious law or modern secular law (assuming there's a choice and that following ancient religious law would not result in anything illegal)? For me, this was an easy answer, but some issues are not so easy.

But must religions be incompatible with modern secular law? The religious law, the *Shari'a*, is flexible, as new laws are developed according to the religious sources. The religious message of the Qur'an and *Sunnah* can and should be reinterpreted separately from seventh-century prejudices, seventh-century limitations on worldview, and seventh-century social circumstances. Could a doctrine that provided such freedom for women in the seventh century really have meant to comparatively stifle their freedom in the twenty-first? I cannot believe it.

Inheritance

Anyone who has read Jane Austen's books knows that women in early nineteenth-century England could not inherit a single shilling if the estate were entailed to the nearest male heir, whatever their parents' wishes. The Bennet sisters in *Pride and Prejudice* were pressured not only by the awareness that their father's entire estate would pass to his insufferable distant cousin Mr. Collins (leaving the sisters nothing), but by the logical conclusion that one of them would need to marry the odious Mr. Collins to keep the estate within the immediate family. Luckily for them, fate intervened and they married (other) rich husbands.

Well, that was only 200 or so years ago, and in England, where tribal raiding and defense of the tribe—male obligations—were not essential to survival. To seventh-century Arab men, accustomed to viewing wealth as naturally flowing to the strongest male able to defend the tribe, the reforms were horrifying.

Suddenly, *even in the presence of a son*, the Qur'an decreed that a daughter must receive one-third of the estate. Not just a competence, which the Bennet sisters lacked, but one-third of *everything*. Imagine the difficulties of conducting any sort of decent tribal raiding with only two-thirds of the wealth you would have accrued.

Could a parent circumvent this law by leaving everything to a son and excluding the daughter in a will? No, because only one-third of an estate at maximum could be disposed of in a will, and a bequest could not be made to an heir already inheriting under Qur'anic rules.[79] The remaining two-thirds of an estate (after the one-third bequeathed by will) had to be disposed according to the provisions for intestate succession set forth in the Qur'an. Why? To ensure that women and near relatives would be provided for. In a tribal society, as well as Jane Austen's England, a first-born son would inherit everything because he had the most power to use it.

If the population of Regency England would have been shocked at such largesse regarding females, imagine how revolted those seventh-century male Arabs would have been! Before the Qur'an, women *could* conceivably own property—we know that Muhammad's first wife, Khadija, was a woman of property—but were not generally provided for under the laws of intestate succession. If the deceased did not make a will, only males inherited. (In fact, even male relatives did not inherit if their only claim was through a female relative.) This system, very much like the European system of primogeniture, retained the money where it would be most useful in the running of the tribe as an entirety.

The Qur'an introduced nine new mandatory heirs to the scheme of intestate succession: the wife, daughter, husband, father, mother, full sister, half-sister and half-brother on the mother's side, and half-sister on the father's side. Wife, daughter, mother, and sister—all immediate family of the deceased—had previously received nothing. Everyone except the father had been previously unprovided for, and even the father had inherited only under certain conditions. The portions of Qur'anic heirs were fixed and could not be wrested away.

A wife, or more accurately, a widow, enjoyed a vastly improved status. The Qur'an gave her one-eighth of the estate if other descendants were present and one-fourth of the estate if no other descendants were present. If this sounds paltry in modern-day terms, think of Mrs. Bennet in *Pride and Prejudice*, who stood to receive nothing when her husband died.

The Qur'an gave a daughter one-half of the estate if no son were present. Two or more daughters shared in two-thirds of the estate. If the heirs were a son and daughter, the son received two-thirds of the estate, the daughter one-third.

This means that Elizabeth Bennet and her sisters would have been entitled to receive two-thirds of their father's estate if they had lived in Islamic seventh-century Arabia instead of nineteenth-century England. Mr. Collins would have received at most one-third, possibly less if other relatives, like Mrs. Bennet, stood to share his part of the estate. As it was, the Bennet sisters got nothing.

The Qur'an covers only basic rules. Scholars confronted with new situations not mentioned in the Qur'an needed to search for solutions consistent with the Qur'anic verses. They developed the Islamic law of inheritance in terms of their own societal preferences for males.

"The Qur'an *couldn't* have meant for a woman to inherit all that!" one can almost hear them wailing. And they subsequently interpreted and developed the Islamic law of succession in accordance with this fervent belief.

When I began studying Islamic law, I came across an example of how an estate would be apportioned. This particular example shocked me, which is why I am including it in this chapter. We are taught, from childhood, various aspects of religion and values and religious law; but whatever wisdom we absorb depends upon our parents, our Sunday school teachers, and—rarely—religious scholars. The cloudy differences between religion, culture, and family tradition can be difficult to distinguish.

As I sat in a cold classroom in London, improbably riveted on the subject of Islamic inheritance law, I realized the lines between religion and culture have always been tenuous, eroded still further by ignorance and the lack of a global worldview. The following example on the blackboard may not have disturbed most people, but it constituted an epiphany for me.

Consider the situation where a wife dies, leaving a husband, mother, and father alive. Under normal Qur'anic rules, the husband would receive one-half of the estate, the mother one-third, and the father the remaining one-sixth. But the Muslim jurists of the seventh century simply abominated the possibility of a mother receiving more than a father. So they changed the rules for this particular situation.

They applied a rule called "agnatization," which roughly means that if a male and female of the same blood tie and proximity to the deceased (such as brother and sister) inherit together, then the male takes twice the female's share.

"What really should happen when a mother, father, and husband inherit together," the early Islamic jurists must have said, "is that the father 'agnatizes' the mother and takes twice her share."

But the father and mother share no blood tie! The father should not have been able to agnatize the mother!

"No matter," the jurists must have said, "the Qur'an cannot conceivably have intended for a mother to inherit more than a father, so we'll just use the agnatization rule anyway."

The result? The husband retains his one-half, but the father now receives one-third and the mother receives a humiliating one-sixth. The changed result was derived from an interpretation of the Qur'anic rules that directly reflected the seventh-century male outlook.

I remember myself leaning forward in that classroom, indignantly open-mouthed, pen stilled and notes forgotten. The realization that religion can be flexible, can be manipulated even by well-intentioned scholars doing their very best to adhere to the religious texts, and can be the result of cultural interpretation rather than the intention of God (which we can never be certain of, anyway), was *illuminating*.

I am reminded of my friend's question, asked in all sincerity: "Why do you live inside your religion? You have studied it, you are otherwise educated, and I think that the more one studies a religion, the more difficult it is to believe in it."

Since that day in class, I have not thought of my religion in quite the same manner. As one of my professors offhandedly, but most profoundly, said in a lecture, Islam is more fluid than people think. That does not, for me, detract from its beauty; it enhances it.

And the inheritance verses are beautiful: they are clear, succinct instructions on how to improve the status of women. The Qur'anic message of these instructions is, I think: "In case you patriarchal seventh-century Arabs missed the point of the verses generally commanding equality for women, here are unequivocal, concrete examples of how to start. Get on it."

But the cultural resistance to change and the mindset of that century never disappeared from the development of Islamic law, especially with respect to women. Islamic inheritance law never lost the original Arabian philosophy of distributing wealth to male relatives who could support the tribe. Male agnatic relatives remained residual in many cases, inheriting the entire remainder of an estate after the Qur'anic heirs were given their share. This undermined the Qur'anic purpose of enabling the deceased's closer, rather than more distant, relatives to inherit, and some relatives like orphaned grandchildren and siblings still fell through the cracks.

This is important for two reasons. First, even in the present day, it is difficult to differentiate between the religion of Islam and the culture around it. Clearly, the cultural resistance to Islamic reforms and Qur'anic concerns for women's rights was there from the beginning of Islam and has persisted.

Second, I frequently encounter people, from scholars to "instant experts," who compare the ancient law of the Qur'an with modern American law and immediately condemn Islam as repressive and sexist. But Islam cannot be sexist when its religious text so long ago granted women so much more than they received under most other laws for a millennium—despite male interpretation of the texts.

Reforms

Some Muslim countries have begun implementing reforms in family law, recognizing that the Qur'an's message was feminist for its time and that classical Islamic law sometimes contravenes the Qur'anic purpose of providing for the immediate family. These reforms are designed to benefit members of the deceased's immediate family, rather than skipping over them to benefit an unknown or removed male relative.

Reforms in modern Islamic countries attempt to correct injustices such as these by keeping to the spirit of Qur'anic reform rather than to the letter of it.

We can (almost) encapsulate inheritance law in terms of the *Pride and Prejudice* example:

a)   Under pre-Islamic law, the pre-modern law of England, and other European countries using Roman law, Mr. Collins inherited everything because the estate was entailed upon the nearest male relative.

b)   Under Islamic law as it was developed by the scholars and which is in place today in the traditional Islamic books of jurisprudence, the estate would have been allocated this way: the four Bennet sisters would collectively receive two-thirds of the estate; Mrs. Bennet, their mother, would receive one-eighth; and Mr. Collins would receive the remaining five-twenty-fourths.

c)   Under many new reforms in Muslim countries, the Bennet sisters and their mother would receive everything, leaving nothing for Mr. Collins.

So what happens if I wish to leave half of my estate to my daughter and half to my son? The Qur'an says my son should get two-thirds and my daughter should get one-third. Do I choose my religious law? Or do I choose state law and allow myself to will each of my children half of what I own?

This is part of that soul-risking balancing act. For me, the solution to this particular issue is clear: I would leave half to each of my two children because I love them equally. I think the Qur'an would support my decision because my daughter has just as much of a chance to succeed these days as my son does, Qur'anic reforms emphasized the importance of the immediate family, and the Qur'an treats women equally in its general injunctions. True, I would be in noncompliance with classical Islamic law. But that is a matter between God and me.

A Note on Slavery and Concubinage

Slavery

I have frequently come across the accusation that Islam condones slavery. I think the primary reason for this perception is unfamiliarity with the historical context and with the fact that slavery in Islam is a completely different institution from the slavery depicted in Alex Haley's *Roots*.

Until the nineteenth century, much of humankind endured some sort of "unfree" status—slavery, serfdom, or peonage.[80] Prisoners of war were often taken as slaves throughout the world. Slavery was so entrenched in the seventh century worldwide that the Qur'an, using its modus operandi of gradual elimination of undesirable practices, accepts slavery as the status quo, as does the Bible.[81]

Two or three times since the September 11th attacks, I have found myself unwillingly reading incidental and unrestrained diatribes vilifying the Qur'an for accepting slavery and Muslims for having practiced it in Africa and the Middle East. A review I read of a particular translation of the Qur'an compared the Qur'an very unfavorably to the Bible and condemned Qur'anic rules for the "care and feeding of slaves" as disgusting. None of these writers mentioned (perhaps they did not know) that both the Old and New Testaments of the Bible urge slaves to be obedient to their masters.[82]

The Qur'an accepts slavery but discourages it, constrains it with rules and conditions, and urges slave owners to free their slaves. The Qur'an does not specifically forbid slavery, though Muhammad himself set the example of setting slaves free.

Slavery is indefensible. But it was the status quo until only a few centuries ago, and the Bible and Qur'an were both received in worlds that took it for granted. In being repulsed by the practice of slavery, as we should be, we might forget to put the Qur'anic treatment or the Biblical treatment of slavery in its historical context.

Slavery as a label covered a wide variety of historical institutions. Peter Kolchin writes:

> In many pre-modern societies there were high-status slaves who exercised considerable authority; such elite slaves ranged from stewards who managed vast agricultural estates in China and early-modern Russia to high government officials in Rome and the Ottoman Empire. Throughout much of Asia, Africa, and Latin America, slaves served in the armed forces, at times—especially in the Islamic world—achieving high rank and wielding considerable power.[83]

Slaves in the Muslim world were not separated from their masters on the basis of skin color, as they were in the United States. As we discussed earlier, the very first *muezzin* of Islam was a freed Ethiopian slave named Bilal.

Under classical Islamic law, slaves could only be taken if they were captives in battle. Because of numerous other rules controlling treatment of slaves, Joseph Schacht comments that the Islamic law of slavery belongs more to the law of family than to the law of property.[84]

For instance, the Qur'an commands Muslims to allow slaves to purchase their freedom by allowing them to pay an agreed sum in installments.[85] How could they pay? Were they not slaves? Yes, but the Qur'an also provides that they be paid not only a portion of the wealth the slave owner has but also a portion of the wealth the state treasury has; this portion should be set aside for the emancipation and economic independence of slaves.[86]

In fact, under Islamic law, a slave can legally claim maintenance from his or her master.[87] In other words, the Qur'an requires slaves to be *paid*. Furthermore, under Islamic law, a slave has a legal capacity to sue his or her master.[88]

In the Ottoman Empire, slaves could apply for freedom and, even while slaves, attain the rank of vizier or senior pasha.[89] India and Egypt were both ruled for centuries by a series of sultans who were manumitted slaves.[90]

The Qur'an allowed sexual relations with slave women only in the context of marriage.[91] Forcing slaves into prostitution or concubinage is specifically forbidden in the Qur'an,[92] and the Qur'an enjoins Muslims to free and marry their slaves if, in effect, they cannot control their libidinous impulses (but see the section on concubinage, below). This Qur'anic injunction directly contravened the custom of the seventh century, which allowed for the sexual abuse of slave women. Under Islamic law, slave women could not be raped or forced into concubinage.

In classical Islamic law, minor slaves could not be separated from their parents or near relatives. Moreover, children born of a slave and a free person were free themselves. This is very significant: American slave masters were not required to maintain or recognize any of their children born of slave women, and separation from at least one parent was imposed on almost half of all slave children in the United States.[93]

Again, although slavery in any form is reprehensible, it is important to recognize that the Qur'an—and to some extent Islamic jurisprudence as developed by the Islamic scholars—attempted to mitigate the injurious effects of slavery with the ultimate goal of eliminating it. As with any huge lifestyle change, Qur'anic commands regarding slavery were strenuously resisted by the Prophet's Arab contemporaries. Sometimes, when possible, the early Muslims interpreted the Qur'an to mean "recommendation" instead of "requirement." In contrast, Muhammad himself freed slaves, married two of them, adopted them, gave them his own family, and helped them become leaders of his community. Fatima Mernissi comments dryly:

> As in the case of women, so in the case of slaves Islam interfered in the private life of individuals and overturned ancient customs. Freeing slaves was one thing, but treating them as equals was quite another.[94]

"Slavery" may refer to extremely divergent institutions, none of them defensible but varying in scope. The ghastly slavery conditions depicted in Alex Haley's *Roots* (Kunta Kinte, by the way, was Muslim[95]) do not correspond to either the more humane conditions of slavery in the Qur'an or to the actual practice of slavery in the Islamic world.

I do not strive to whitewash slavery in Islam, but to explain its parameters. Certainly in today's world, slavery should be prohibited not only by governments, but by religions. All Muslim countries have prohibited slavery. But given that the Qur'an *meant* for slavery to be abolished, the law of slavery as delineated in the Islamic books of jurisprudence should also be voided, as some Muslim scholars advocate. In the case of slavery, as in the case of polygyny, 1,300 years is plenty of time to prohibit a practice the Qur'an moved to eliminate.

Concubinage

Now wait, you might be thinking. If the Qur'an sanctions sexual relations with slaves only within the context of marriage, then what about the Ottomans? Did not Western Orientalists report in mesmerized detail on decadent Ottoman harems filled with concubines? Did not Suleiman the Magnificent fall in love with a concubine named Roxelana (as she's known in the West), marry her, and allow her to wield considerable power as the sultana?

Concubinage was one of those cultural practices that men had difficulty giving up. Islamic law absorbed the unsavory practice of concubinage from cultural sources like the Byzantine and Persian governmental institutions, and it became associated with Islam.[96] Early Islamic scholars did develop rules for concubinage in their books of jurisprudence. (Anything, including cultural practices, can be justified if you try hard enough.) But the Qur'an does not allow concubinage.[97]

The Qur'an allows sexual relations only within marriage.[98] Besides, it makes little sense that a religion so clearly abhorring of extra-marital sex would then sanction sex with as many unmarried concubines as a man could afford. Perhaps that is why concubinage was historically rare throughout the Muslim world (and shocking to most Muslims). The stereotype of the harem remains because of the Ottoman sultans, who wielded awesome world power and thus became the most fascinatingly well-known of Muslims in the fifteenth-century world. Besides, not everything the Ottomans did was Islamic. Akbar Ahmed comments upon the Turkish harem:

> The harem is extravagance, vulgarity, luxury—it is Orientalism, the stuff of European fantasy; it is not Islam. So much wealth, so much suffering, so much injustice are far from the idea of marriage and married life in Islam. The verses from the Qur'an that are so prominent on the walls do not condone the spirit of the place.[99]

I asked a friend, an Islamic scholar and Muslim herself, about concubinage, because a discussion of the subject is actually rather difficult to find (a good indication of how unimportant it is in Islam). Did she know, I asked her, of any thorough discussions on concubinage? I got this email reply: "Oh, *concubinage*! No, nobody talks about *that*! It's obsolete, and I don't know anything about it. It's just one of those things those *men*, those medieval *men* couldn't do without and so they had to go putting it into their books." I could hear her dismissively huffing with umbrage through the ether.

Having said that, concubines under (man-made) medieval Islamic law did have certain rights. It is like slavery—a bad thing, concubinage, and a product of its time. But if it must be there in the man-made books of Islamic jurisprudence, let me at least strive to paint an accurate picture of what it entailed.

Under classical Islamic law, a child of a concubine and her "master" was by law born free and was considered by law to be the father's legitimate child.[100] The child's mother became free, by law, upon the death of her owner; she could not be sold, and his descendants did not "inherit" her.[101] In addition, concubines, like other male and female slaves in Islam, were allowed to marry not only slaves, but free men and women. Their children would be free. And it is true that sometimes citizens in the Ottoman Empire desired for their daughters to enter the sultan's harem, hoping they got the chance at world power that Roxelana did. At the very least, they would be rich.

Bestowing such rights does not justify slavery or concubinage, by any means. But the situation in Ottoman Turkey did differ considerably from the African slaves in America, where they had no hope of freedom and where the law did not recognize slave marriages, slave families, or children born of white masters and black female slaves. In contrast, slaves and concubines in the Islamic world had a much better chance of obtaining freedom, autonomy, marriage, families, and even, as in the case of Roxelana Sultana, royalty status.

Concubinage was rare historically and is no longer practiced. But it is clear from the Qur'an—despite the way those early male Islamic scholars and rulers justified their desires in the guise of Islamic law—that it was never meant to be practiced in the first place.

Clitoridectomy, Infanticide, and Honor Killings

A friend of mine in London said she had read an article in the August 1993 issue of *Vanity Fair* magazine and wanted to ask me how accurate it was. The article purported to report on Islamic fundamentalism and misleadingly included a discussion of clitoridectomy, which is the removal of a woman's clitoris. Clitoridectomy is also called female circumcision or female genital mutilation, depending somewhat on the extent of the surgery. The *Vanity Fair* article implied very strongly that clitoridectomy was an Islamic practice.

Clitoridectomy is a loathsome procedure unequivocally antithetical to the principles of Islam, which views sex within wedlock as a normal, healthy practice. Clitoridectomy is prevalent primarily in some parts of Africa, where it is a cultural practice a thousand years older than Islam. In Egypt, for example, it is practiced as much by Christians as by Muslims.[102] In fact, in July of 2007, Egyptian Islamic clerics issued a decree announcing clitoridectomy as totally banned by Islam. The government announced plans to institute a total ban on the practice, which had been mostly outlawed in 1997.

But the popular media in the West still often portrays this practice as Islamic. The same *Vanity Fair* article also strongly implied that infanticide and honor killings were Islamic.

But infanticide is *prohibited*, in no uncertain terms, numerous times in the Qur'an. Not only did Islam generally prohibit infanticide, it forbade the pre-Islamic practice of killing female babies. Furthermore, Islam decreased the motivation for infanticide by granting females mandatory inheritance rights, thus ensuring that females would be more than simply financial burdens on the family.

The Qur'an describes the end of the world and the approach of the Day of Judgment and includes in this description these verses, which throb with total revulsion of infanticide:

> And when all human beings are coupled with their deeds
> And when the girl–child that was buried alive is made to ask for what crime, after all,
> she had been slain . . .
> On that Day every human being will come to know
> what he has prepared for himself.[103]

Several other verses of the Qur'an also damn those who would kill their female infants instead of celebrating their good tidings at receiving a newborn.[104]

I read a customer review of a translation of the Qur'an on Amazon.com recently. Instead of approving of the Qur'an's prohibition of female infanticide, the reviewer espoused shock that the Arabs "had to be told not to murder their female babies." The reviewer was right to be disgusted at the practice of infanticide, but she did not seem to realize that female infanticide *still* occurs in cultures of various geography and religions, such as China and India. The seventh-century Arabs were not alone in valuing girls less than boys.

"Honor killings" refers to the execution of a woman by her family when her honor has been violated—in other words, if she has relinquished her virginity outside of marriage. Honor killings are not Islamic and occur in non-Muslim cultures, as well. Islam does not require, sanction, or encourage honor killings. Islamic law does *not* punish by death an unmarried woman who has lost her virginity outside of marriage, and it requires a trial before a conviction of adultery. Islam prohibits execution without a trial, which is murder. And, in allegations of extra-marital sex, Islam requires *four* reliable eyewitnesses to the actual, physical act of intercourse itself before anyone, man or woman, can be convicted of adultery.

Four eyewitnesses to the sexual act? Under Islamic law, the witnesses must have seen actual penetration. Try presenting any prosecutor with that kind of burden of proof! Without a trial and those four witnesses, not to mention other mitigating conditions, honor killings are murder under Islamic law. (Extra-marital sex as a crime is discussed in greater detail in chapter ten.)

Female genital mutilation, infanticide, and honor killings may be practiced by some Muslims in the world, just as they are practiced by some non-Muslims. This does not make these practices Islamic or sanctioned by Islam. They are not. These are intolerable cultural practices that people of all religions are struggling to eradicate from society.

Addressing Some Commonly Leveled Accusations

One Woman + One Woman = One Man?

I came across a statement in a work of historical fiction set in early nineteenth-century England (before English reforms on women's rights). It asserted as fact that women in the Arab world were worth only half of men. Incidental to the plot, this statement appeared in the narrative, an assertion not of some racist nineteenth-century protagonist to further the plot, but of the author herself. I knew exactly the origins of this statement. Those wanting to prove that Islam is sexist routinely fling about, like indiscriminate weapons, two Qur'anic verses with which to make their accusations.

A daughter inherits only half of what a son does, they say. And a woman's testimony is equal to only half a man's. So a woman is worth only half a man in Islam.

I hope the section on inheritance makes clear why the first accusation is unjust. A daughter's mandatory portion under Islamic law, even if half her brother's, was much more than she had received previously and more than women in other cultures received for a long time.

The second accusation above refers to a Qur'anic verse that allows women to testify in court. This verse says that if two male witnesses cannot be found, two women and a man may be substituted instead, so that if one woman errs or forgets, the other can remind her.[105] Before this verse of the Qur'an was revealed, Arabian women could not testify in court at all. Allowing a male witness to be replaced by two females was progressive.

In some parts of Europe, especially influenced by Roman law, legal status depended upon gender; women could not appear in court at all until at least the eighteenth century, even if they themselves were the petitioners to the court.[106] They had to appoint a man to speak for them.[107] So this was a common limitation on women and must be kept in mind when reading an ancient text.

In addition, the Qur'anic verse must be read in light of certain facts:

    a)   This two-women-for-one-man formula was meant to apply *only* to certain types of financial contracts—this is the Qur'anic context—which fell outside the typical female sphere at that time;[108] this formula is not the general rule for witnesses in non-financial cases.

b)   Although the Qur'an requires two women, only one is to be a witness; the other is simply there to provide support. Therefore, it really is only one female testimony that replaces the one male testimony.[109]

But why does the woman need support and not the man? Why might she forget when the man would not? It is clear from the Qur'an that women were commonly taken advantage of or subjected to intimidation and coercion at the time. They had very little political power. The purpose of including the second woman was to provide safety in numbers.

Women today are not secluded or powerless, and they can be as conversant in financial matters as men. Therefore, the modern view is that the custom of needing a second woman to "help" the witness is obsolete, because that precaution was aimed at correcting certain inequities in seventh-century Arabia.[110] These days, a woman's testimony has the same validity as a man's.[111]

In all cases, it is possible to quote verses removed from their appropriate context and insist that the literal reading is the correct one; certainly, traditionists or conservatives might espouse this view and insist that women should never be conversant in financial contracts. The same can be done with any text. To ignore the textual context, the intertextuality of the Qur'an, and its historical context is ignoring the Qur'an's own history[112] and cannot, in the modern view, give an accurate reading.

For the novelist in my example to accuse Arabs as treating their women as only half of men illustrates a lack of knowledge about the treatment of women in Islam as well as elsewhere in the world. It shows utter willingness to stereotype and vilify Islam on the basis of rumor. It also demonstrates an ignorance of her heroine's own history and legal rights.

Have You Stopped Beating Your Wife Yet?

Another common accusation relates to a Qur'anic verse that gave men more rights than women, but more than women previously had. Specifically, the Qur'an allows a husband to strike (or slap) lightly his wife as a third resort in curbing her illicit behavior.[113] This may sound appalling to us, but it was—again—a severe restriction on the unlimited wife abuse prevalent in Muhammad's time and for centuries afterward in all cultures.

Having said that, I wish this verse were not part of the Qur'an. Am I blaspheming to say so? I do not intend to blaspheme. A part of me can understand why it is there, but another part wishes away the need to explain why the Qur'an contains apparent permission for a husband to strike his wife lightly.

Although, as a friend noted, sometimes studying a religion makes it harder to adhere to it, I find that sometimes studying it makes it easier. This verse, read without explanation, is upsetting to me. But studying the linguistics, the context, and the relevant scholarly writings made this verse easier for me to accept both as a provision intended for its specific historical time and place and as a provision that no longer applies today.

I found that a husband can slap his wife only in the case of *nushuz*. Unfortunately, the meaning of *nushuz* is disputed. (It figures.) It is significant to me that early Islamic (male) jurists translated *nushuz* differently in the case of a wife than in the case of a husband. Perhaps they were protecting themselves.

I say this because, in the case of a husband, *nushuz* means the commission of a "grave and known sin,"[114] that is, a clear and obvious sin. But in the case of a wife, *nushuz* is translated variously, depending upon the scholar, as "disobedience" (even though the Qur'an *never* orders a wife to obey her husband[115]), "dangerous rebelliousness," "marital discord," and "extreme sinfulness" like abusing the children or committing adultery.

The definition that makes most sense to me is the one that is the same for a husband as for a wife. After all, why should the same word be translated significantly differently for men and women if the context is the same? So *nushuz*, according to the view I agree with, means "a grave and known sin,"[116] whether it applies to a husband or to a wife.

Muhammad confirmed this definition of *nushuz* when he paraphrased the Qur'anic verse in one of his last speeches but substituted for *nushuz* the words "*fahisha mubina.*"[117] The Prophet said that a husband could only beat his wife as a last resort if his wife committed *fahisha mubina*, which is usually translated as a "grave and known (or clear) sexual sin."[118]

What we have so far is that this verse allows a man, in the case of a wife's grave and known sexual sin, to first verbally admonish her, then separate from her, then strike her lightly.

Why do I persist in saying "strike lightly" and not just "strike"? Because the grammatical form used in the Qur'anic verse means "strike lightly."[119] "Strike" would have necessitated another grammatical form.[120]

And actually, whether it even means "strike lightly" is questionable.

The word signifying the beating, *daraba*, can mean "to strike," but not necessarily in a way connected with force or violence: for example, *daraba* can also mean "to give as an example," or "to leave on a journey."[121] English has this variation, too: to "*strike* out on a journey" or "*hit* the road"!

I was surprised to read that one scholar translates *daraba* to mean "conjugal relations."[122] This is not so silly as it sounds! The relevant verse is translated thus: "As for women you feel are averse, talk to them suasively; then leave them alone in bed (without molesting them) and go to bed with them (when they are willing)."[123] I can readily believe there may be more possible, sometimes half-forgotten meanings to Qur'anic words than we might suppose.

Studying the linguistics is crucial in confirming that only striking lightly is allowed (if at all) and only in circumstances in which the wife is committing a grave and known, possibly sexual sin. But any slapping, even light, is an affront to personal dignity and a violation of respect. And besides, why does the husband get to decide when and if to punish? I found some answers to these questions in the historical context.

This Qur'anic verse severely restricted the standard, unlimited wife abuse that was prevalent in seventh-century Arabia. (Remember that European law until the nineteenth century allowed a man to beat his wife as much as he wanted as long as he did not endanger her life and even allowed the use of whips and clubs.)[124] This Qur'anic restriction was hotly contested by some of Muhammad's followers. Allowing a wife to be "slapped lightly" was a far cry from abusing her as property.

In addition, the "beating" verse is typical of the Qur'an's gradual progression toward change and of the way it often restricts undesirable practices with safeguards rather than forbidding them outright. Allowing seventh-century men to hit their wives lightly as a last resort in curbing egregious behavior does not mean the Qur'an intended for this practice to be allowed indefinitely. It was a disapproving message and a restriction.

One Muslim scholar writes:

> At a time when men did not need permission to abuse women, this Ayah simply could not have functioned as a license [to beat them]; in such a context, it could only have been a restriction ... And if the Qur'an meant to restrict abuse even during those most abusive of times, there is no reason to regard this Ayah as an authorization at a time when we claim to have become more, not less, civilized.[125]

As a Muslim, I must believe that God knows best. Perhaps an outright prohibition on the husband's power to discipline his wife would have been so shocking that no one would have followed it. I do not know. But I do know that, in addition to the grammatical meanings, the historical context, and the restriction of the beating to circumstances of grave and known sin, we have a multitude of historical records.

These records support the view that this verse applied only to the situation in seventh-century Arabia, and they inform us of Muhammad's particular abhorrence of any kind of violence toward women. For example, Muhammad prohibited the beating of women outright, saying "Do not beat God's handmaidens."[126] The Prophet told his followers that the worst of them were those who beat their wives.[127] His followers could not understand his attitude and viewed him as too soft-hearted, even weak, because he told men not to beat their wives.[128]

In addition, even the early jurists decided that the beating was symbolic and should be carried out only with a toothbrush or folded handkerchief.[129] In fact, UCLA law professor and Islamic scholar Khaled Abou El Fadl quotes a story about the genius Ibn Rushd (known in the West as "Averroes"), twelfth-century philosopher, theologian, Arabic grammarian, lawyer, physician, and astronomer:

> Ibn Rushd, the grandfather, was once asked whether a man who caught his wife performing lewd acts with a foreign man in bed could beat his wife and imprison her. Ibn Rushd responded that the husband may forgive his wife or divorce her, but anything beyond that would be a transgression.[130]

Ibn Rushd, by the way, wrote massive Arabic commentaries on *all* the translated works of Aristotle; he wrote extensively on Islamic law, medicine, and philosophy.[131] Given the prolific amount of brilliant writing he produced, I would say Ibn Rushd knew his Arabic and his Islamic theology more than passing well. If *he*, with his twelfth-century worldview, ruled that a husband could not beat his wife even if he found her in bed with a man who did not belong there, then I believe him! I am, indeed, grateful to be able to believe him.

Islam is old; the Qur'an is old. We forget history even fifty years old and we forget language three hundred years old. How then—if we are as conscientious as humanly possible—can we be sure of the meaning of every single word in the Qur'an? Given the Qur'an's equalizing message for women, given the historical context, given the grammar and the plethora of juristic writings and prophetic sayings condemning any kind of wife beating, given *all* that, I cannot believe the Qur'an meant to allow a man to strike his wife except as a limitation of the particular practices of the seventh century.

The books of jurisprudence are where the rules of Islam are. If even those medieval male Islamic scholars concluded that the Qur'anic verse allowing a beating meant a *symbolic* beating with a folded handkerchief, then I think I can claim to be in the mainstream.

Conclusion

Culture has become extremely mixed with religion when it comes to the issue of women. The images of veiled, secluded women come from only a few places in the world. Most of the Muslim women in the world are free to be active participants in society and to pursue whatever careers they wish. And that is what Islam and its Prophet encouraged us to be.

I agree with the Muslim scholars who insist that women in Muslim countries would get more rights if the populations of those countries were properly educated about Islam. Muslims sometimes assume that they are devoutly complying with Islamic law when, in actuality, it is cultural norms that bind them. For instance, I think many Muslim men worldwide would be utterly revolted if they knew that Islamic law actually decrees that domestic chores fall outside the scope of a wife's legal responsibility and allows for legal injunctions granting women domestic help at the expense of their husbands. Classical Islamic law allowed women to vote, too.

These are remarkable rights, especially for their time. Muslims miss the point of their own religious laws if they think being more Islamic means hiding their women in closets. And most Muslim countries do not in fact do so; we hear, disproportionately, of the ones that do. Sensationalistic reporting sells better and keeps a readily identifiable enemy before our eyes.

Even fourteen centuries ago, Islam radically uplifted women's status and gave them rights far ahead of their time. The Qur'an stresses equality continually: equality of men and women, equality of all races and tribes. In today's world, where equality is now considered a virtue and is more possible than ever, Islam's message of equality applies more than ever. Muslim countries must reform family laws that do not give women equal rights. Given what we know about the Prophet Muhammad, I think he would have been at the forefront of the battle for equality.

Jihad and Fundamentalism: Not the Same

Long beards, turbans, white robes, drawn swords, and holy war. Osama bin Laden's so-called "*fatwa*" against the United States, illegitimate as it was, bolstered the stereotype that Islam is violent. Nearly insurmountable confusion surrounds jihad, a term that has been misused and overused with abandon. Alarmingly, many people I know do not even realize their impressions are confused.

Although ignorance regarding jihad is the first obstacle to understanding, extremist groups certainly exacerbate the confusion by justifying their terrorist acts as jihad. Al-Qaeda and other terrorist groups use religious symbolism to further their goals, though suicide bombings, attacks against civilians, and other atrocities have nothing to do with jihad. But these days, the word has become commonplace in the American public discourse.

Jihad is not something I ever grew up knowing anything about or studying formally or informally. I never heard the word at home or in school until I was in my teens. But since then, jihad, which is usually incorrectly translated as "holy war," has become much more central to how non-Muslims view Islam.

In the first section of this chapter, I endeavor to give an overview of the jihad doctrine. We first indulge in a few definitions and discuss the jihad doctrine in the Qur'an, in classical Islam, and as applied to the Arab conquests. We then discuss the modernist (that is, post-18th-century) doctrine of jihad and how it is perceived today.

The second section discusses "fundamentalism," amorphous as that term is. These are complicated topics necessarily discussed in brief; check the Suggested Reading List if you acquire an appetite for more.

Jihad

I want to put it right out on the table straightaway: under modern Islamic law, Muslims are allowed to use warfare only to defend themselves and to free themselves from tyranny. Period.

Definitions

Jihad is most popularly translated into English as "holy war." This simplifies and distorts the actual meaning of jihad, particularly since Islamic law does not actually include the notion of "holy war." One scholar states that in Islamic law, "War is never holy; it is either justified or not, and if it is justified, those killed in battle are called martyrs."[1] The Arabic word for fighting (as in a war) is actually *qital*, not *jihad*; the Arabic word for "war" is *harb*.[2] In contrast, the literal meaning of *jihad* is "effort" or "exertion."

Jihad literally means "to strive" or "to struggle." In its most common and comprehensive context, it means to "strive toward a praiseworthy aim."[3] The most important jihad is the struggle to purify oneself of wickedness. The struggle need not arise exclusively in a religious context, and it is frequently used in a generic, non-religious sense.[4] For example, the leader of one African country declared a jihad against economic hardship in his country. A recent graduate of Harvard described his struggle to achieve his education as a jihad.

When it is used in a religious context, jihad may mean "to struggle for the right to worship God" or "to struggle in the way of God." It can mean "self-exertion," or exerting oneself to become a better person. This may also include exertion in warfare, but its meaning is far more comprehensive than that.

Verbal persuasion can constitute jihad. For example, the Qur'an commands the Muslims to use the Qur'an itself as verbal persuasion, or jihad, against the unbelievers:

Hence, do not defer to the likes and dislikes of those who deny the truth,
But strive hard against them, by means of this divine writ,
with utmost striving.[5]

The words "strive hard" represent the word "jihad" in translation. God in this particular verse is commanding Muslims to strive hard to convince unbelievers by using the Qur'an itself ("this divine writ") as a means for debate and persuasion. Used in this manner, "jihad" has nothing to do with fighting or warfare.

The following passage illustrates the place of jihad in the Qur'an:

> Those who believe, and who have forsaken the domain of evil
> and have striven hard in God's cause
> with their possessions and their lives
> have the highest rank in the sight of God;
> and it is they,
> they who shall triumph in the end![6]

According to this definition, jihad may require fighting, but not necessarily. It primarily involves faith and activity in the service of God.

Why fight at all, ever? Because sometimes fighting presents the only recourse in the face of oppression, injustice, or persecution. Fighting is sometimes the only solution to stop the cruelty of a Hitler or a Milosevic. The Qur'an states:

> How could you refuse to fight in the cause of God
> and of the utterly helpless men and women and children
> who are crying, "O our Sustainer!
> Lead us forth to freedom out of this land whose people are oppressors
> and raise for us, out of Thy grace, a protector
> and raise for us, out of Thy grace, one who will bring us succour!"[7]

A particularly famous quotation of the Prophet illuminates two ways in which jihad may be used. After returning from a devastating military battle in which the Muslims had sustained great loss of life, Muhammad remarked wearily that he and his followers had returned from the lesser jihad to the greater jihad. When asked by his astonished listeners to explain, the Prophet replied that by "lesser jihad" he meant physical fighting. By "greater jihad," he meant the ongoing, daily, personal struggle to improve the soul and purge it of wickedness.

The Prophet is also reported in the *hadith* to have said that "the best form of jihad is to speak the truth in the face of an oppressive ruler."[8] Jihad is the struggle against oppression. If the only way of struggling against oppression is taking arms to defend oneself or one's religion, then this warfare is allowed, though circumscribed by stringent rules. But it is only a small part of jihad, and certainly—as the lesser jihad—not the primary definition.

Islamic law identifies four kinds of jihad:

a) jihad by the heart, which is the greater jihad and means purging oneself of wickedness;

b) jihad by the tongue, which means using verbal persuasion to correct injustice;

c) jihad by the hands, which means undertaking good works to correct injustice; and

d) jihad by the sword, which means the use of force to correct an injustice.[9]

Jihad by nonviolent means was preferred, even in early Islam, and violent means were a last resort. The Prophet's example and the Qur'anic verses illustrate this. In the West, the Prophet and the Qur'an are so equated with warfare that I understand this may seem apologetic. But keep in mind that the West has always received information about Islam and the Prophet in an adversarial context. One rarely hears good things about one's adversary.

Only a small part of the jihad "struggle" is the struggle against an oppressor. Only a small part of *that* small part is the right to take arms against an oppressor. That is how minute a part of jihad the warfare element is.

When the word "jihad" is used today, what is often actually meant is "use of force," rather than jihad. "Jihad by the sword" is what we hear about in the Western media. Therefore, that is what I will discuss.

Before proceeding, I want to make a note of two factors that in particular confound understanding of jihad. First, if jihad means defensive warfare with strict limitations and rules of engagement, then how can suicide bombers who injure unarmed civilians be exercising jihad? And second, was Islam not "spread by the sword"?

The answer to the first question is that suicide bombers are terrorists who use religious texts to justify their actions, and they are *not* acting within the rules of warfare in Islam. They are a political phenomenon outside Islamic law. This is further discussed in the next section on militant fundamentalism, but keep in mind the following tenets of Islamic law that bear upon the actions of suicide bombers.

Suicide is *forbidden* in Islam. The use of force against noncombatants is also forbidden in Islam. Moreover, terrorism, defined as the secret and clandestine use of force against civilians, is forbidden. In fact, early Islamic jurists found terrorism repugnant and implemented harsh penalties for it. Therefore, terrorist actions and attacks on civilians are prohibited and are outside the bounds of Islamic law for many reasons. The September 11th attacks were completely prohibited actions according to Islamic law.

There will always be those who use religion to justify criminal actions. That does not mean the religious texts or religious laws permit those actions. One writer remarks that "the meaning of the text is often only as moral as its reader."[10]

The second stumbling block to understanding jihad was one I came across for the first time in high school. I first heard Islam mentioned as part of a classroom lecture while sitting in my high school American history class. I experienced a spontaneous fight-or-flight reaction during a slide show (impossible as it may seem to anyone who has slouched or slept through a high school slide show) because of what I suddenly heard my teacher confidently say.

"Oh, yes," he said smugly. "Islam is *supposed* to be spread by the sword. It says so in the Qur'an."

"Have you read the Qur'an?" my sixteen-year-old timid self asked him pointedly.

"No," he said, unabashed but surprised that I had a voice. "Have you?"

"Yes. And it isn't supposed to be spread by the sword." It was one of the most courageous things I had ever done, face flaming, and I was *sixteen*, when every mistake seems catastrophically world-shattering. "Besides," I added, "what good would a conversion at sword-point be anyway?"

He ignored me and continued his slide presentation, and I neglected to argue further because I had been taught to respect all my teachers no matter how ridiculous I thought their statements. I never heard the rest of the slide show. I trudged from the classroom that day and poured all my shaking indignation and sense of deep injustice onto the shoulder of my best friend, who hugged me briefly, patted my head, and changed the subject.

Reminiscing, I suspect my best friend had little idea how to respond to something that was totally alien to her. Even my closest friends knew next to nothing about my religious beliefs—only those things that affected them, such as whether I could go on excursions during Ramadan or to parties ever. Or, sometimes, whether they could take me to church with them and convert me. But I spoke of my religion only when someone asked me a question or when it was relevant to everyday life. Whatever the Qur'an said about spreading religion by force would have been irrelevant to our daily adolescent lives.

The slogan my high school history teacher taught his class, "Islam was spread by the sword," has survived in Western consciousness for centuries.

Catchy and convenient, this is a concept that has been very difficult to overturn, despite objective scholarly Western studies that disprove it and despite common sense, as well: the *imam* of a California mosque once exasperatedly demanded how exactly Islam was supposed to have been spread by the sword in Egypt when Egypt became Muslim only gradually over four hundred years.

Once Islam is believed to be a "religion of the sword," it is easy to assume every violent action undertaken by any Muslim in the world proves Islam is a violent religion. It is a self-fulfilling prophecy, and anyone who has read *Harry Potter* knows what those can be like.

Many of my acquaintances still believe that Islam is a religion of the sword. At our last party celebrating Eid ul-Fitr, my husband donned his formal Indian clothes (grudgingly, with much rolling of the eyes and only after I begged). One of our guests commented on how his ensemble appeared more Middle Eastern than Indian.

Before I could respond, he added, "I don't know why I'm surprised that the Arabs attacked India—after all, they attacked more countries than anyone else did." He laughed.

"Actually," I said, smiling politely, "it was the Mongols who came to rule India, not the Arabs."

This led my guest to ponder aloud instead how exactly the Arabs had gone about "attacking Indonesia to spread Islam" there. I sighed.

"Actually," I said gently, moving away, "that was trade, not conquest."

I left him discussing, among other things, how Islam was spread by the sword. At *my* party, celebrating Eid ul-Fitr! My guest seemed not to sense any irony or potential offense in that, because it is assumed and built into the cultural Western consciousness: Islam was spread by the sword—what is there to argue about?

Well, for one thing, this is what the Qur'an says about conversion at sword-point: "There shall be no compulsion in the matter of religion."[11]

Use of Force in the Qur'an

I feel obligated to explain how the Qur'an treats the use of force because many people seem to have been searching bookstore copies of the Qur'an for violent verses in it. The Qur'an, as discussed in chapter four, must be read in its historical context. The Qur'an itself refers to history, and therefore to read it ahistorically is to ignore its own history.

As I mentioned in chapter four, of the 6,236 or so total verses of the Qur'an, less than 1 percent have anything to do with fighting. The

Qur'anic verses that do address fighting arise in the context of ongoing warfare and persecution. But because of the ubiquitous media use of the word "jihad," along with disproportionate media coverage of militant organizations who employ the word themselves (such as "Islamic Jihad"), not to mention Osama bin Laden, who legitimizes his violence by characterizing it as jihad, it might be natural, though incorrect, to assume jihad means unregulated holy war.

In fact, after listening to various media and reading various book reviews and newspaper articles, we might reasonably conclude that any Muslim who feels upset about anything at all can declare a "jihad," sling a Kalashnikov rifle over his or her shoulder, and shoot civilians with it. In actuality, jihad means warfare only in a few specifically defined circumstances and, even when it does, employs very strict rules regarding how this warfare may be implemented. It is not the unregulated right to wage unregulated warfare.

The Qur'anic verse I often hear quoted is, "Slay the infidels wherever you find them." The Qur'an states some version of this three times. However, every single time, the immediately subsequent verse commands peace if the other side stops fighting: "But do not attack them if they do not attack you first."[12] "But if they desist, then all hostility shall cease."[13] And

> Thus, if they let you be,
> and do not make war on you,
> and offer you peace,
> God does not allow you to harm them.[14]

Each time any "slaying" verse occurs, it is bracketed by verses like the one above, which commands peace and cessation of hostilities if the other side stops fighting. What does this have to do with jihad? These verses indicate defensive warfare. Moreover, the "slaying verse" is applicable only in the context of ongoing hostilities or a battle that is already in progress.[15]

The Qur'anic fighting verses were revealed to the Prophet after he and his followers had fled from Mecca to Medina, where they suffered persecution, treachery, and political strife. At this time, they had left behind their tribal protection in Mecca; indeed, the Meccans had communicated their intent to pursue the Muslims even after the move to Medina. Therefore, the verses urging fighting were revealed in the context of political tension and ongoing battles with the Meccans. Their purpose was to allow the Muslims to defend themselves according to the standards of the time.

The purpose of these verses, contrary to media impressions, was not to command Muslims to unconditionally go find themselves some unbelievers and kill them if they did not immediately convert to Islam at sword-point. If it had been, the Qur'an would not contain its numerous exhortations for peace and Muhammad would have attacked the various non-Muslim peoples living around him and killed them for the sole reason that they were unbelievers. That is something he never did.

Even when jihad in its battle context is allowable in Islam, the implementation of jihad is circumscribed by stringent rules of engagement. For example, Islam prohibits harming noncombatants, including elderly people, women, children, and people who take refuge in convents.[16] Cheating or treachery in warfare is prohibited. Rape is prohibited.[17] Terrorizing is not allowed. Even property may not be arbitrarily destroyed; Muslims may not kill goats or cows except for food and may not cut down fruit trees.[18] The Qur'an requires that the spoils of war go to orphans, families of the deceased, and the needy.[19] And always, always, the Qur'an insists on peace whenever possible and disallows aggressive warfare: "Fight in God's cause against those who wage war against you, but do not commit aggression—for verily, God does not love aggressors."[20]

When the Qur'an is evaluated as a whole and in its historical context, it allows only defensive warfare. This, I think, is one of the most important points about warfare in the Qur'an: the only way to interpret the Qur'an as allowing aggressive warfare is if one reads in isolation and ahistorically only the verses allowing warfare and simultaneously ignores the verses limiting warfare to self-defense.

In fact, the Qur'an severely curbed and restricted the violent norms of a time and place in which war was the normal state. Raiding was an economic pastime, no central authority enforced any rules, and war was a legitimate method of conducting intertribal relations. The Qur'an—contrary to the norms of the day—decreed war to be allowable only in defense of people or religious freedom, rather than as an entire system of international law, which is how it was used not only in Arabia but much of the world.[21]

The early Muslim scholars could have interpreted the Qur'an to allow warfare strictly in self-defense, as the Qur'an lends itself naturally to this conclusion. Many scholars did exactly that. The Islamic jurist Shaybani considered as a given, as his predecessors did, that Muslims could not declare jihad on non-Muslims unless the non-Muslims had clearly shown themselves to be a "hostile threat;"[22] the simple fact of their being "unbelievers" did not justify holy war.[23] But other scholars—accustomed to warfare as a way of life—did not agree, and the jihad doctrine as it was developed by the early scholars became broader than a strictly defensive war.

The Classical Doctrine of Jihad

After the death of the Prophet, the new Muslims found themselves with a new religion to defend, persecution to resist, radical reforms to implement, and new laws to interpret and develop. Islam was revealed and interpreted in a tribal and violent society in which war was a commonplace fact of life and an acceptable method of conducting international relations.[24] (Arguably, it still is, all over the world.)

No one had any rights in seventh-century Arabia unless they were supported by force or the threat of force.[25] This was true even outside Arabia in the seventh-century world, in the Roman and Persian Empires.[26] In fact, unless some sort of truce were in place, a state of war was the default relationship between the Arab tribes.[27] (Interestingly, one of the few reasons important enough for the tribal Arabs to declare a truce was the annual poetry contest in Mecca![28])

Muhammad had conducted defensive warfare and had followed stringent rules of engagement. But his successors, the caliphs, did resort to armed struggle, sometimes in self-defense, but sometimes not. The caliphs found that, after Muhammad's death, the social reforms he had instituted were disintegrating; for example, some of the Bedouin tribes who had sworn allegiance to Muhammad refused to honor their treaties after he died. The breaking of a treaty in seventh-century Arabia, as well as in other parts of the world, was a cause for war. The Muslims, faced with the need to keep the new Muslim community together, assumed positions of authority.

Rather than read the Qur'anic verses as sanctioning defensive warfare only, the early Muslims chose to interpret the Qur'an and the *Sunnah* in a manner more consistent with their own societal norms. The early medieval Islamic scholars, products of this warlike society, interpreted the Qur'an and *Sunnah* in light of their specific circumstances; they knew they had to be able to use force to survive. Therefore, they gave themselves authority to implement Islamic reforms by establishing Islamic rule. In promulgating Islamic rule—not Islamic religion—the early Muslims moved away from the idea of jihad as purely defensive.

But how could they get around the Qur'anic verses commanding Muslims not to be the aggressors? In order to interpret the Qur'an so that it gave them the right to promulgate Islamic rule, the early scholars interpreted certain later Qur'anic verses containing commands to fight as having *abrogated*—that is, nullified, or replaced—earlier verses that allowed use of force only in defense. This convoluted reading resulted in one of the latest surahs, revealed in the context of ongoing warfare, abrogating well over one hundred Qur'anic verses urging peace. This was clearly related to the pre-Islamic Arabian idea of a default state of war.[29]

Abrogation makes little sense to me (but then I am not a seventh-century male religious scholar accustomed to tribal raiding). Not only does it mean that parts of the Qur'an are read out of context while other parts are ignored, but it implies that God, in all His infinite wisdom, changed His mind. Abrogation was used to allow seventh-century Arabs to reconcile their holy scripture to their comprehension of society.

An interesting thing about the abrogation theory is that, though it was developed by the early Islamic jurists and is still accepted by many (but not all) Islamic scholars today, every lay Muslim who has not studied Islam formally and to whom I have ever mentioned the theory of abrogation has been astonished to hear of it.

But I come from a time in which most job opportunities are not in tribal raiding. I come from a time and country in which laws are enforced. The jihad doctrine evolved the way it did as a practical matter, as one scholar writes, because if it had not, Islam would have disappeared:

> Given the historical context, . . . Islam would probably not have survived if the Muslims were denied the use of force in propagating the faith and maintaining the cohesion and stability of the community. It was impracticable to maintain a nonviolent society at a time when violent force *was* the law.[30]

Because war between tribes had been allowable in pre-Islamic Arabia, the early Muslims simply substituted the *umma* (Muslim community) for the tribe.[31] However, even according to the early Muslim scholars, promulgating the territory of Islam by war was always a last resort, to be used only after the attempt to persuade the powers in nonviolent ways to adopt Islamic reforms.

In summary, although a contextual reading of the Qur'an as a whole may be read to sanction war only in self-defense and although some early scholars also considered jihad to be defensive warfare only, the Qur'an and *Sunnah* were interpreted by the early Muslim jurists to allow the promulgation of Islamic rule as well as defensive warfare. In a way, it was a restriction on existing practices: "Islam outlawed all forms of war except the jihad, ..."[32] Certainly the early jihad doctrine was consistent with the customs of the time, both in Arabia and in the nearby Roman Byzantine Empire.

The Arab conquests, the bulk of which took place in the first century after Islam (from approximately the mid-seventh century to the mid-eighth century), were a result of this new doctrine. Here we come to the "Islam spread by the sword" issue. But remember, even the expansively interpreted jihad doctrine allowed the Muslims to spread Islamic *rule*, not religion.

Certain questions inevitably arise in the context of the Arab conquests: Did the conquests have much or anything to do with the spread of Islam as a religion? Or were the conquests primarily related to the spread of Islamic rule? Or were they simply the kinds of wars that have raged throughout human history, wars motivated by territorial, secular ideas of conquest?

The Arab Conquests

As we discussed earlier, Muhammad was succeeded by four elected caliphs: Abu Bakr, Umar, Uthman, and Ali. After Ali, the Umayyad dynasty ruled from 661 to 750, before it was toppled by the Abbasid dynasty, which ruled from 750 to 1258.

Islam had spread through the world long before the Abbasids came. By the end of Ali's reign in 661, just twenty-nine years after the death of the Prophet, Islamic rule had spread from the two towns of Medina and Mecca to half the then-known world. It encompassed the entire Arabian peninsula, the whole of the Persian-Sassanian Empire, and part of the Roman-Byzantine Empire.

By 750, just a century after the Prophet, the Islamic Empire stretched from Mecca as far west as Spain and as far east as India. It included North Africa and skimmed the borders of China. Within a hundred years, the Islamic Empire sat astride three continents, more vast than the Roman Empire had ever been.

To a Christian populace in Europe, the rapid growth of Islam must indeed have seemed terrifying. It was the enemy. It must have been logical to assume the religion was growing because the Arabs were attacking and forcing the populations to convert to Islam at sword-point. Yet, this is incorrect in many essentials.

The *political domain* of Islam spread by conquest, by treaty, and by political coups. The Arabs were fairly small in number. How did they conquer two great empires? First, the Eastern Roman (Byzantine) Empire and the Persian Empire had been fighting for a long time, and local populations were tired. So often they helped the Arabs. For instance, Arthur Goldschmidt writes that some Jewish and Christian communities actually aided the Arabs in their conquests:

> The disgruntled Syrian and Egyptian Christians viewed the Muslim Arabs as liberators from the Byzantine yoke and often welcomed them. The Copts, for example, turned Egypt over in 640 to Amr's Arab force, which, even with reinforcements, numbered fewer than 10,000. Likewise, the Jews, numerous in Palestine and Syria, chose Muslim indifference over Byzantine persecution.[33]

Sometimes the Arabs did attack. Sometimes they did not bother to attack but submitted a proposal for a contractual surrender, which was accepted.

But the *religion* of Islam, contrary to popular Western belief, was not spread by the sword, as shown by evidence indicating that the early Arabs were not interested in converting the local populations. Gerald Hawting, a specialist on early Islamic history (and one of my former professors), writes:

> [T]he Umayyads and the Arab tribesmen who first conquered the Middle East regarded their religion as largely exclusive of the conquered peoples. There was no sustained attempt to force or even persuade the conquered peoples to accept Islam, and it was assumed that they would remain in their own communities paying taxes to support the conquerors.[34]

Not only did the Arabs not force people to convert, evidence indicates that during the Umayyad period from 661 to 750, the government actually tried to prevent people from becoming Muslim because many of the caliphs and governors wanted to retain the idea that Islam was for Arabs as the chosen people. They enjoyed being part of an "elite."

This notion changed, nevertheless, as the conquerors and the conquered peoples began to intermarry and the cultures began to intermix. It was then that people began to convert to Islam, not only for religious reasons, but for cultural and financial reasons, as well:

> But by the end of the [Umayyad] period, in spite of the initial attempt by the Arabs to keep themselves apart religiously and socially from

their subjects, and in spite of the refusal by caliphs and governors to allow the non-Arabs to enjoy the advantages of acceptance of Islam, large numbers of the subject peoples had come to identify themselves as Muslims.[35]

After the Umayyad dynasty, but still only a few centuries after the advent of Islam, the idea of a democratic Islam for everyone took hold and people were no longer prevented from converting to Islam. Muslims would like to believe that people converted solely because they did indeed consider the new religion to be the truth and God's word. But clearly, other factors figured in the conversions, as well.

One factor was the non-Muslim poll tax, the *jizya*. Non-Muslims paid the *jizya* in return for retention of their religion and culture, exemption from military duty, and protection from the state against aggressors. If they converted to Islam, the tax was no longer applicable. Another factor was *Arabization* of the local populations. As the Arab culture became intermixed with the culture of the local population, conversions to Islam increased as a result of the new cultural identity and intermarriage. Intermarriage tends to be forgotten but cannot be underestimated.

My guest at our Eid party, while commenting on the Arabs and Mongols, did at one point nod knowingly and remark, "Well, yeah. They stayed for the women."

The behavior of the Arabs in not forcing people to convert to Islam is consistent with the classical definition of expansionist jihad. Its aim is to struggle against oppression, fight in self-defense, and spread the political domain of Islam. When the Arabs conquered territory and the local government became Islamic, significant groups of Jews, Christians (such as the Copts in Egypt), Zoroastrians, and others retained their religions.

After the expansion of the empire, Muslims realized the impracticability of continually promulgating the territory of Islam, and they moved away from the idea of jihad as a permanent duty to spread Islamic rule. They settled down to peacetime activities such as trade, management of their vast empire, and the pursuit of learning:

> Muslim publicists seem to have tacitly admitted that in principle the jihad as a permanent war had become obsolete....the jihad marked the change in the character of the nation from the warlike to the civilized stage.[36]

Some historians believe, for various reasons, that the Arab conquests from the very beginning had been secular wars:

[R]eligious interests appear to have entered but little into the consciousness of the protagonists of the Arab armies. This expansion of
the Arab race is more rightly envisaged as the migration of a vigorous
and energetic people driven by hunger and want... .[37]

In other words, religion was a unifying force, but not the reason for the
conquests.[38]

Still other historians assert that religion could not possibly have
factored into the Arab conquests because Islam did not develop formally
as a religion for at least a century after the conquests. (Some Muslims may
be offended by this concept, as we are often taught to believe that Islam
descended, fully fledged, from God, and that it was complete upon its
receipt by the time of the Prophet's death. But all religions develop, and
they cannot help but be influenced by cultural norms.) Certainly, Islamic
law continued to develop for centuries after the Prophet. Perhaps the
purpose was both territorial *and* unified by Islam. At the time, the entire
world was a mixture of religion and state, and it was no act of virtue in
those days to separate the two.

Moreover, religion has always justified territorial ambitions. Muslims
have waged war against other Muslim rulers in the past, which is not
allowable as a jihad. Muslims have conducted secular wars, too, which
Islam also prohibits.[39] And Muslims in the present day conduct terrorist
campaigns in clear violation of any definition of jihad.

The Modernist Jihad Doctrine

Classical jihad doctrine, then, allowed war to promulgate Islamic rule.
However, within a few centuries, the Muslims abandoned this idea as
impractical. By the Abbasid reign in the eighth century, the Muslims had
stopped waging war and had settled down to rule their empire.

In the eighteenth and nineteenth centuries, scholars began revisiting
the doctrine of jihad, primarily as a response to the European colonization
of most Muslim countries. The issue was whether the Islamic law of jihad
allowed war to be waged against colonizers. In Islamic law, jihad must be
declared by the state or by a divinely inspired *Imam*.[40] But what if foreign
colonizers controlled the state? Could they be ousted by a jihad waged
by the local population?

This question became crucial, for example, in the British-controlled
India of the nineteenth century. The British preferred to hire Hindus
rather than Muslims, considering the latter to be part of the former

ruling class and therefore potentially rebellious. In an endeavor to allay friction, provide job opportunities for Muslims, and abet cooperation between the British and the Muslims, Sayyid Ahmad Khan outlined a definition of jihad that he asserted was based on Muslim scholarship from all different centuries.

Ahmad Khan maintained that jihad constituted war in the defense of the faith of Islam, lawful only against unbelievers who were "positively obstructing" the practice of at least one of the five pillars of Islam.[41] Jihad, he said, may not be undertaken against Muslims, no matter how irreligious. It also may not be undertaken against unbelievers who are simply neglecting to implement the practice of Islam. There must be a "positive oppression" (that is, an *active* oppression) of a religious, not political, kind.[42]

Many of Sayyid Ahmad Khan's Muslim contemporaries concurred with this view. Since the British were not impeding the practice of Islam, they concluded, no obligation to overthrow them arose.[43] Muslims could, in good conscience, be loyal subjects of the British.

In the nineteenth-century Middle East, scholars like Muhammad Abduh and Muhammad Rashid Rida also confirmed the view that jihad was a defensive war only. They, however, allowed for jihad against coloniz-ers because colonization clearly constituted an attack on the territory of Islam, whether or not a "positive oppression" existed.[44]

The modernist theory of jihad, therefore, is typified by these scholars, who restrict jihad to a defensive war. This is the conception of jihad to which the vast majority of Muslims ascribe. Every religion has its extremists who use religion to suit their various purposes. But, long ago, Islam as a whole moved away from the idea of holy war and now defines modern jihad as defensive warfare only.

Jihad Today and Man-on-the-Street Interviews

James Turner Johnson writes that Christianity rejected holy war after the brutal Christian religious wars of the post-Reformation era (post-1650) and that Islam rejected it, too:

> The Western rejection of war for religion fits well into this legal framework [of the only justification for war between states being that of self-defense], but so, indeed, does the classical Islamic juristic model of jihad of the sword, for today, according to that model, only war in defense of Islam is allowed.[45]

"Defense" of Islam in the above quotation means defense against an immediate threat only, one against which a defensive war can be waged. Both Sunni and Shi'i views define self-defense in terms applicable only to an immediate threat and not a general or possible threat.[46] For example, the reconquest of Granada by the Arabs today would not constitute an act in defense of an immediate threat, since it has been 500 years since the Spaniards captured Granada from the Arabs.

Taken together, then, jihad in the context of warfare is considered by most Muslims to be an act of self-defense in response to an immediate threat. In my view, the Qur'anic verse that most applies to the attacks on September 11th is this one:

> If anyone slays a human being,...
> it shall be as though he had slain all mankind;
> whereas, if anyone saves a life,
> it shall be as though he had saved the lives of all mankind.[47]

Obviously, holy war cannot function in the same role in today's world as it did in a lawless society over a thousand years ago. In a world with weapons of mass destruction and international law, war is at best a vestigial system of exercising authority. The fighting that the Qur'an sanctioned for defense and to fight persecution was intended for an ancient, tribal society in which it was necessary for survival. It is too often forgotten that the jihad doctrine requires written, verbal, and persuasive non-violent struggle *first*. Remember the "jihad of the sword" is the very last option, after other forms of jihad have been exhausted.

Given the many reasons that jihad in the overwhelming majority view means a defensive war, it is unfortunate that the term "jihad" is used carelessly and ubiquitously, as if it meant random and unfocused violence against any non-Muslims in the name of Islam. On the PBS show *NOW with Bill Moyers*, one man stated in a "man-on-the-street interview," jabbing his finger emphatically all the while, "The Koran specifically targets Jews and Christians for hate crimes."[48]

This is not only untrue, it is ironic, since it was many *Muslims* in America who suffered from hate crimes after the September 11th attacks. In actuality, the Qur'an treats Jews and Christians especially well and specifies several times that heaven is open to them (and others) if they perform good deeds and believe in God.[49] The Qur'an enjoins Muslims to not dispute with Jews and Christians and to be courteous to them. The Qur'an allows Jews and Muslims to retain their own religion: "to

you, your religion, to me, mine!" And the Qur'an allows Muslim men
to marry Jews and Christians.

The one Qur'anic verse that frequently is snatched out of context reads:
"Do not take Jews and Christians for your allies."[50] This verse must be
read historically and in conjunction with all the other verses about Jews
and Christians. It was revealed in Medina, during the time when alliances
between the various Medinan (multireligious) groups were splintering.
So this verse, as a matter of safety, advises Muslims *at that time and in
that place* to refrain from politically allying themselves with anyone but
Muslims. The verse was providing the "necessary psychological support
for the survival and cohesion of a vulnerable community of Muslims in
a hostile and violent social and physical environment."[51]

It does not make any sense whatsoever to read it as applicable to all
times and places, because other verses of the Qur'an command Muslims
to honor Jews and Christians. It is not possible that the Qur'an, which
forbids Muslims from even insulting non-Muslims and allows Muslims to
marry Jews and Christians, should then urge Muslims to never be friends
or allies with them—or, as the finger-jabber stated, commit hate crimes
against them. The nonsensical conclusion then, would be: you cannot
insult them, you must be courteous to them, you can be assured they
will go to heaven, and you can marry them; but you can also commit
hate crimes against them. *Please.*

On the same television show, the interviewer asked several people in
the same style of interview if they would consider themselves Christians
first or Americans first. They all said, smilingly, that they were Christians
first and Americans second. The interviewer then asked these same people
how they would feel if they heard someone say he considered himself a
Muslim first and an American second.

In an honest manifestation of a clear double standard, many of the
responses immediately metamorphosed from smiling to hostile. Several
interviewees stated that a person who said he was Muslim first and
American second would make them "apprehensive" or "worried." The
full statement of the finger-jabber was, "The thing that would anger me
about that [for a Muslim to say he was Muslim first] is the Koran specifically targets Christians and Jews for hate crimes." Another interviewee
said his reaction would depend upon the Muslim person's definition of
jihad, of all things.

I cannot help but equate these responses with the attitude of Victorian
British Protestants, who assumed that Catholicism was synonymous

with treason and that British Catholics were necessarily more loyal to foreign Catholic monarchs, such as those of France or Italy, than to the English.[52]

Several interviewees, to their credit, did not exhibit hostility. One gave the admittedly double-edged statement that he would not "hold it against someone for saying that." The other said he would give the Muslim person a big hug and ask him about Islam. And one, bless her heart, declared, "It is the same choice that I have made and expressed. I would not be worried or concerned that they're a Muslim first and an American second."

It should be perfectly clear from the discussion on jihad above that the statement of the finger-jabber was foundationless. But, even the person who said his response would depend upon the particular Muslim's definition of jihad completely missed the point, which is twofold. First, the Islamic doctrine of jihad is just as irrelevant in assessing the individual Muslim as the Christian doctrine of holy war is in assessing the individual Christian. Second, if Islam has been used by some Muslims to commit violence, Christianity, Judaism, Buddhism, and Hinduism have all been used by some followers of those religions to commit violence, as well.

Consider one of those who said he was a Christian first and an American second. Our opinion of him as an individual would almost certainly *not* depend upon his interpretation of the Christian doctrine of holy war. I doubt anyone would feel "apprehensive" of this individual Christian just because certain Christians have characterized their wars as holy wars.

But perhaps, you might say, the difference is that the Christian doctrine of holy war is a dead letter, whereas jihad is not; just look at Osama bin Laden as proof. My response is that jihad is a defensive war, as we have discussed, and therefore offensive jihad *is* a dead letter, just as much as Christian holy war is. I have had acquaintances respond by saying, "Yes, but what about all the violence committed in the name of Islam? That proves jihad is not a dead letter."

Bin Laden's terrorist activities have nothing to do with jihad. He and other terrorist groups use jihad to justify their violent actions, which are expressly prohibited in Islam.

Violence in the name of Christianity or other religions has not disappeared any more than violence in the name of Islam has. It would be ridiculous to hate all Christians because the extremists who blow up abortion clinics and kill the doctors base their actions on Christianity. It would be incorrect to be fearful of all Christians because various Ku Klux Klans commit murder on the basis that "blacks and Jews symbolize the greatest threats to white Christian civilization."[53] If we do not consider that either the holy war doctrine in Christianity or violence executed in the name of Christianity matters in our assessment of the individual Christian, then the jihad doctrine or violence in the name of Islam should not matter in our assessment of the individual Muslim, either.

Well, all right, you might say, but those Christians who blow up abortion clinics are totally outside the mainstream, right? Of course. But so is bin Laden and his ilk. Islam is the second-largest religion in the world, encompassing over a fifth of the world's population. The bin Ladens of Islam are as miniscule a percentage and as outside the mainstream as the Timothy McVeighs of Christianity.

They are portrayed as representative of Islam by the media, but the media has an interest in covering only those extremists and keeping the "Islamic threat" before our eyes at all times. We must have a sensational enemy, because fear and horror sell really well. As historians Jonathan Bloom and Sheila Blair state:

> In the middle of Islam's second millennium, therefore, there are, as there have always been, many Islams. To stereotype such a multifaceted and vibrant tradition in a few careless images based on the extreme positions of a few is foolish indeed.[54]

In fact, one scholar points out that there is a lesson to be learned from examining Islamic history when it comes to incidents of extremism. These have occurred in Islamic history, as they have in most religions. But the "essential lesson taught by Islamic history is that extremist groups are ejected from the mainstream of Islam; they are marginalized, and eventually treated as heretical aberrations to the Islamic message."[55] Even the notorious Khawarij of the seventh century, as well as the later Assassins, eventually embraced moderation and settled down to mainstream religion.[56]

The problem today, according to Dr. Khaled Abou El Fadl, is that no central authority is left—in these post-Islamic-civilization times—to speak on religious matters. Traditionally, in Islamic civilization, the state and the religious institutions were separate, and the latter served as intermediary and advisor to both. But now religious authorities are weak, the state is strong, and the result is virtual anarchy on religious issues.

I was discussing this issue with my husband, who said, yes, let's disregard extremist terrorists like bin Laden, but what about *governmental* authorities that undertake violence on the basis of religion, such as the Taliban? My answer is that the Taliban were no less outside mainstream Islam than bin Laden is. No government recognized the Taliban by the time the United States began bombing Afghanistan in an effort to roust the al-Qaeda organization, and only three in the world had done so before that.

The Taliban were not the only modern government to use religion to undertake violence. Consider the Christian Serbs' ethnic cleansing and religious genocide in Bosnia. With the blessing and support of Christian Church leaders, Christian Serbs massacred village upon village of Bosnian Muslims, destroyed 1,400 mosques in the region, mutilated children and burned them alive,[57] raped women and children in organized "rape centers,"[58] and incarcerated civilians in "death camps" in which they were mutilated and killed.[59] The Serbs then turned to Kosovo to do the same thing to the Muslims there. William Dalrymple writes:

> The horrific massacre of 8,000 Muslims—some unarmed—at Srebrenica in 1995 never led to a stream of pieces about the violence and repressive tendencies of Christianity.[60]

That isn't all. Western governments have mostly turned blind eyes to the Russians' "cleansing" operations of the Muslims in Chechnya, which have been going on for years.[61] In 2002, in the Indian state of Gujarat, over 2,000 Indian Muslims were murdered, thousands more displaced, and hundreds of Muslim women gang-raped and mutilated in a religious ethnic cleansing in which the government was complicit; even afterward the Gujarati government was committing human rights abuses with respect to Muslim prisoners.[62] The conflict in Northern Ireland turned to a significant degree on the issue of Protestant and Catholic religions. Hitler quoted the Bible.

People of all religions commit crimes. People of all religions sometimes base their crimes on their faith. In the Qur'an and in Islamic law, jihad is defined, with strict rules, and cannot be interpreted as a sanction to commit crimes like the September 11th attacks or suicide bombing. Connecting jihad with deplorable crimes like September 11th makes no more sense than connecting the Christian doctrine of holy war with Timothy McVeigh's bombing of the Murrah Federal Building. No one in the media has seriously made the latter connection, despite the fact that McVeigh's bombing was inspired by the extremist Christian ideology of the Christian Identity movement in the United States, a fascist, anti-Semitic group that does include blowing up federal buildings and abortion clinics as part of maintaining a Christian identity.[63]

By the same token, no one should make the connection between jihad and criminal activities. They simply do not go together.

What further confuses people is that some groups like Hamas and Islamic Jihad themselves characterize their activities as jihad. These groups believe they are engaging in a defensive jihad and defending themselves against armed aggressors occupying their lands. They view themselves as defending their country.

Under Islamic law, however, even groups who have legitimate grievances may not use terrorism to achieve their ends.

Fundamentalism (Whatever that Means), Peaceful and Militant

The term, "fundamentalism," has achieved an indisputable place in the media spotlight in the last few decades. But its usage is so varied and vague that its meaning at any given time is very difficult to define. John Voll gives a concise definition of fundamentalism, stating that it "involves the effort to purify or reform the beliefs and practices of adherents in accord with the self-defined fundamentals of the faith."[64] Therefore, generally speaking, fundamentalists look to the original religious texts—the fundamentals of their religion—and redefine their religion.

Fundamentalism had its inception in the context of early twentieth-century Christian fundamentalist movements. In the context of Islam, "fundamentalist" is often used synonymously with "extremist" or "terrorist." The late Edward Said wrote that the word "fundamentalism" constantly looms over the words of journalists covering Islam and "has come to be associated almost automatically with Islam, although it has a flourishing, usually elided, relationship with Christianity, Judaism, and Hinduism."[65]

An important point to remember is this: in the late 1970s and early 1980s, fundamentalism worldwide across *all* religions rose markedly.

Sometimes, "Islamic fundamentalist" is carelessly used to simply identify an enemy. For example, after the first Gulf War, the United States began enforcing the United Nations resolution to force Saddam Hussein's forces to stay out of the no-fly zone. These enforcement measures were characterized as "fighting Islamic fundamentalism." But Saddam Hussein was not an Islamic fundamentalist by any stretch of anyone's imagination. Indeed, the purpose of this particular U.N. resolution was to protect the

Southern Iraqi Shi'i Muslims, who could more legitimately be characterized as fundamentalists than Saddam Hussein's army.

The term "fundamentalism" sometimes implies that all fundamentalist
movements are the same. In actuality, they differ with respect to ideology
and practice, though they all seem to want to "go back to the basics" in
some way. They each have their own interpretations of religious laws
and values. Some use violence, though the majority do not.

Some authors now acknowledge the imperfection of the term "fundamentalism" but use it anyway for lack of a better phrase. In terms of
Islam, "revival movements" and "religious activism" are sometimes more
accurate terms, not least because the word "fundamentalist" evokes all
kinds of pejorative connotations of violent, backward extremism. This
assumption is damaging to movements of legitimate Islamic revival that
have nothing to do with violence or oppression or extremism. The
extremist, violent terrorists acting in the name of religion are called
"fundamentalists," but that view—an aberrant minority opinion—in
itself contains many different variations and is the one that usually makes
it into the media.

The peaceful fundamentalists also have a variety of views. *One* of
these peaceful fundamentalist views is that every Muslim has a duty to
help achieve an Islamic state, though not by violent means. This view
entails peacefully overthrowing non-Islamic governments and Islamic
governments that do not conform to what the fundamentalists believe.
This overthrow can occur via the democratic voting process.

If installation of an Islamic government even via the democratic process
is frightening, keep in mind that many countries, including Israel, Poland,
and some Latin American countries[66] mix religion and state. And, anyway,
when countries like the former Soviet Union did *not* mix religion and
state, we characterized them as godless and portrayed ourselves as "one
nation under God." I am in favor of the separation of church and state,
and I deeply feel that a secular state is the only one that can work in
today's world. But I think we should shed our double standard when it
comes to Islamic states.

Some fundamentalist groups do resort to terrorism, but most operate
within the bounds of the law. The vast majority of Muslims, remember,
consider jihad to be defensive and do not strive to overthrow non-Muslim
governments or Muslim non-fundamentalist governments. Algeria is an
example in which the Islamic party tried to use the democratic process
and managed to win in the first free parliamentary elections in the Arab

world—only to have the whole election canceled and the winners imprisoned.

The Islamic Salvation Front had been providing social services and welfare services to Algerians, as well as a network of schools.[67] In 1990 and 1991, Algerians, deeply dissatisfied with their authoritarian government, voted for the Islamic Salvation Front in two democratic elections. The Islamic Salvation Front won in free elections and would have gained control of the parliament had the (non-religious) military not canceled the elections and imprisoned over 15,000 members of the winning party.[68] The government continued to close down Islamic Salvation Front institutions and seize their assets.[69] This military crackdown caused the Islamic Salvation Front to split into a moderate wing and a military wing. The military wing, called the Islamic Salvation Army, and the Algerian government both developed extremely violent militias, which engaged in a brutal civil war for a decade. Both the government militia and the Islamic Salvation Army committed horrible atrocities against Muslims and non-Muslims, civilians and combatants.[70] In the meantime, the Algerian government refused to engage in a peace process sponsored by the San Egidio Catholic community in Rome—though other parties, including the Islamic Salvation Front, were willing to do so.[71] In 2000, the Islamic Salvation Army finally disbanded.

It is a tragic story, and it is distressing that Western countries generally supported an authoritarian military government that squashed democracy and committed unrestrained violence and human rights abuses. The online CIA World Factbook[72] gives a version of the story but neglects to mention the second election, the government's cancellation of elections, its mass arrests, and its seizure of assets. Rather, it gives the impression that the entire decade-long civil war was essentially Islamic extremists attacking the government.

The Algerians tried to use the democratic process, though they failed.

Some fundamentalists are not peaceful and claim "jihad" in order to wage war or use violence against civilians. However, in doing so, they collide into several doctrinal problems with respect to Islamic law. These groups' practices contravene explicit rules of Islamic law, such as:

- ☀ Secret and clandestine use of force is prohibited;[73]

- ☀ Only combatants in war may be killed;

- ☀ Noncombatants such as women, children, the elderly, monks, rabbis, and civilians in general may never be killed;

- ☀ Suicide is prohibited;

- ☀ Jihad must be waged by the state or a leader of the worldwide Muslim *umma*, or community (no such leader exists today);

- ☀ Cheating and treachery in warfare is prohibited;

- ☀ Property may not be destroyed except under certain conditions in warfare; and

- ☀ Waging war against fellow Muslims is impermissible.

A glance at these rules should clarify how completely removed from Islamic law the actions of a suicide bomber are. Khaled Abou El Fadl refuses to associate jihad with suicide bombings, which he defines as:

> murdering people without differentiating between the aggressor (*muhârib*) and the non-aggressor (*'ghaira muharib*). *Fiqh* (Islamic jurisprudence) has prohibited this kind of random killing (*'qatlul ghîlah*). *Qatlul ghîlah* is a form of murder, where the object does not have any chance to defend himself or herself. . . . This is a violation of jihad, which is allowable only to free Muslims from tyranny or in defense from attacks. Suicide bombing is something not based on moral principles, but a form of murder that comes from revolutionary ideologies from the 1960s.[74]

It should be clear by now that bin Laden's actions contravene Islamic law. Given that killing civilians has always been outside the bounds of what is allowed under Islamic law, the September 11th attacks did not qualify as jihad under this or any definition of warfare under Islamic law, modern or medieval or anywhere in between.

Bin Laden justified killing civilians by characterizing the American people as combatants and as complicit in the wrongdoings of the American government, because the American people have not risen against their leaders and stopped their government's actions around the world. This view is spurious and universally rejected. It would obliterate the definition of "non-combatant," as any and all civilians could be deemed as being complicit in the wrongdoings of their leaders.

As I mentioned earlier, even groups like Hamas, Hizbullah, and Islamic Jihad—which are on the U.S.'s list of terrorist groups—condemned the

September 11ᵗʰ attacks and considered them to be terrorism, which is forbidden in Islam. In fact, although the classical Muslim scholars of the first centuries of Islam were surprisingly tolerant of political rebellion, they imposed the harshest penalties on terrorists.[75] In their definition of terrorism, the classical scholars included abduction, poisoning of water wells, rape, arson, attacks against travelers and wayfarers, and assaults under cover of night.[76]

How, then, do modern terrorists fit into the classical Islamic viewpoint? They actually do not. The ideology of most modern terrorist groups does not come from Islamic tradition but from post-colonialist national liberation ideologies of the nineteenth and twentieth centuries.[77] The terminology, ideologies, symbolism, and organizational structure "are exported from national liberation struggles against colonialism and did not emerge from the Islamic heritage."[78] Much of the Muslim world's political struggles, both violent and nonviolent, have been reactions to the colonization of their countries, the repression (in some cases) of Islam, and arbitrary borders imposed on them by Western powers after the first world war.

If terrorism violates all these rules of Islamic law, how do terrorist groups justify violence in the name of Islam? Anything can be justified on the basis of a single isolated line of text, whether it be from the Qur'an or any other type of document. (Lawyers are irritatingly wordy and specific—I can say this because I am one of them—because they are attempting to forestall misreading of the text. It's not always possible, though.) Justification does not mean it is a *legitimate* justification. Terrorism, the clandestine use of force against civilians and carried out by individuals or a state, has never been sanctioned in Islamic law.

I must point out, however, that terrorism is sometimes not easily defined. People who are oppressed, suffering, and desperate, and who have no government to help them free themselves, have more motivation to construe self-defense broadly, to find isolated verses in the Qur'an to support them, and to look to historical precedents to bolster their views. That does *not* mean their actions, like bombing civilian shopping districts, are justified under Islam.

Moreover, although people like Osama bin Laden use religious symbolism and terminology to legitimize their attacks, their purpose is not to wage war against all non-Muslims. I hear frequently the view that bin Laden fights the U.S. because we're a country of Jews and Christians.

This is incorrect. Bin Laden does not oppose the U.S. because it is a non-Muslim country (he does not balk at killing Muslims, either) but because he sees the U.S. as responsible for the turmoil in some of the Islamic world today. He began his career fighting *for* the U.S. in Afghanistan against the Soviets.

It is not only the terrorists who manipulate definitions. These days, the accusation of "terrorist" tends to be indiscriminately applied to whoever the enemy happens to be. The Islamic law definition of terrorism includes some very specific prohibitions, as enumerated above. Moreover, it is clear in Islam that "the injustice of others does not excuse one's own injustice." If someone, individual or state, uses terrorism against you, then you may *still* not use terrorism against them to retaliate.[79]

Islam is commonly portrayed to be encouraging of terrorism. Let me put a twist on this perspective. During the first Gulf War, the United States intentionally destroyed the Iraqi water supply and then denied the Iraqis the importation of materials needed to rebuild the supply and purify the water. Thousands of Iraqi civilians were subsequently deprived of clean water, and waterborne illnesses became epidemic.[80] According to the World Health Organization and UNICEF reports, over 1 million Iraqi people have died as a result of contaminated water, and over half have been children younger than five years old.[81]

According to Islamic law, poisoning the water supply is considered terrorism and killing civilians and children in warfare is strictly prohibited.

A Note on Religious Tolerance and Non-Muslim Rights

What I find most disturbing about extremist and fundamentalist movements of all creeds is their lack of tolerance for other religions and cultures. In particular, Muslims who are intolerant of other religions and cultures are violating the very principles of religious tolerance set out in the Qur'an.

The Qur'an prohibits discourtesy to Jews and Christians, forbids insulting those who worship an object other than God, and allows people to be ruled by their *own religious laws*, as in this verse:

> Say: O you who deny the truth!
> I do not worship that which you worship
> And neither do you worship that which I worship …
> Unto you, your religion, and unto me, my religion![82]

The Qur'an also states:

> There should be no compulsion in religion.
> Truth stands out clear from Error.[83]

And finally, the following verse of the Qur'an clearly enjoins respect of religious freedom:

> If it had been thy Lord's will,
> all who are on the earth would have believed, all of them.
> Wilt thou then compel mankind, against their will, to believe?[84]

In this last verse, the Qur'an says that if God had wanted to, He would have simply made everyone believers and been done with it. He left the choice of believing or not believing up to us, so how can we, as mere humans, presume to compel others? According to the Qur'an, to compel someone to become Muslim would be to disrespect God's plan. To practice freedom of religion is to respect God's plan. One historian writes:

> To my best knowledge, among all the other revealed texts, only the Qur'an stresses religious liberty so unambiguously. The reason is that faith, to be true and reliable, must be a voluntary act.[85]

How tragic it is, then, that some so-called "Islamist movements" diminish personal and religious liberty!

One of the very first things I remember about Sunday school at the mosque was my terrifying teacher pinning us with his stern stare and telling us that faith obtained by force was not true faith. For true faith, he said, there must be freedom. Otherwise, all that you get is a hypocrite.

Islamic history and theology support religious tolerance. Throughout history, Muslim states have been multireligious. William Dalrymple writes:

> As late as the 18th century, European visitors to the Moghul and Ottoman Empires were astounded by the degree of religious tolerance that they found there.... If that coexistence was not always harmonious, it was at least a kind of pluralist equilibrium which simply has no parallel in European history.[86]

Edward Said, who was a Palestinian-American professor at Columbia University and by birth and upbringing a Christian, once commented in a radio interview that "In general, Islam of all the monotheistic religions—well, there are only three—has been historically the most tolerant."[87]

Non-Muslims in the Islamic world historically had their own religious and cultural laws. Examples of this exist even from the time of Muhammad, who judged the non-Muslims in Medina by their own religious laws. Throughout the early Islamic Empire, part of the compensation for the *jizya* tax was the right to be judged by non-Muslim religious and cultural laws, to be protected from warfare by the state, and to be exempt from the *zakat* tax, which was levied only on Muslims.

The *jizya* tax, according to the modern view, is not an Islamic requirement for today's world, where no differences at all should be made on the basis of religion. The Qur'an allowed it as a solution to the particular historical circumstances; the Qur'an did not mandate it as a necessarily theological practice. This tax was a relic of the time and place, where it was standard custom in both the Arab and non-Arab world. (For example, in Victorian England, everyone who did not belong to the Church of England was required to pay a fee.[88]) The modern view eliminating the tax is based on the vision of religious freedom espoused in the Qur'an, the many verses on religious tolerance, and our changed world. In fact, the constitutions of many modern Islamic countries, such as Egypt, rightly declare that all citizens shall be treated equally, without respect to race, origin, religion, language, or creed.[89]

Precedent for religious tolerance exists from the very beginning of Islam. As we discussed earlier, when the Prophet Muhammad fled with his followers to Medina to become the leader of the community there, he entered into an agreement with the Medinans called the Constitution of Medina. Muslims consider this to be the first constitution announced by a state and ensuring freedom of conscience in human history.[90]

Four groups comprised the population of Medina in 622 CE. The original Medinan population consisted of Jews and Polytheistic Arabs. The non-Muslims followed their own religious laws, and all residents of Medina were free to practice their own religions. They all agreed to a *political* alliance, especially since the Meccans had made clear their continuing persecution of the Muslims. Eventually, this community in Medina did become internally stressed, but for political reasons, not because of rejection of a multi-religious community.

Historically and in practice, despite the inevitable discrimination that occurred between peoples, Muslims were tolerant of other religions and promoted multicultural, multi-religious societies. The historian Norman Daniel, in his study of the relationship of the West with Islam, writes, "In the long run only Islam effectively tolerated other religions within itself…"[91]

For example, when the second caliph of Islam, Umar, conquered Jerusalem in 638, the Muslims left Christians free to practice Christianity and visit the holy places.[92] The Jews, who had been banished from the city by the former Christian rulers, were invited back and allowed to worship as they wished.[93]

Is the Use of Force Unique to Islam?

I confess that I remember little of my eighth-grade social studies class. The only reason I remember the teacher at all is that one day he jolted his large frame to a halt mid-lecture, turned to me (sitting in the second row), and demanded before the entire class whether jihad did not mean that I as a Muslim (how did he know I was Muslim?) was supposed to go kill people who were not of my religion. This was a rather shocking question for anyone, but particularly for a thirteen-year-old whose fear of classroom debate was greater than her fear of death. Luckily for my fragile adolescent self-esteem, my teacher's challenge did not seem to rouse any of my eighth-grade classmates from their customary apathy.

He repeated the question, and I replied that Muslims were allowed to defend themselves if they were attacked. The teacher then smiled and pounced: "That's not the Christian point of view. Jesus didn't defend *him*self."

He neglected to mention the many holy wars and occurrences of forced conversion in Christian history. Neither holy war nor terrorism is new or unique to Islam.

The idea of a just war, of which holy war is a type, can be traced back to antiquity.[94] Aristotle considered some types of wars as just by nature.[95] The Romans had their own doctrine of just war and, in medieval Christendom, St. Augustine espoused a theory of just war that had been influenced by Cicero.[96] The early Muslims developed their ideas of just war along the lines of the Christian, Roman-Byzantine doctrine of just war.[97] St. Thomas Aquinas, who had read Islamic writings, came up with a doctrine of just war similar to the jihad doctrine, and he in turn influenced later writers, including Grotius, the "father of the modern law of nations," whose ideas were followed until the late eighteenth century.[98] A just war is not a new concept or one limited to a particular race or religion.

But this has been forgotten or perhaps never learned. I recently read on the internet a customer review of a well-regarded translation of the Qur'an. Anyone can leave a customer review. This particular customer did not review the translation but instead expressed his opinion that, "in contrast to the Bible, the Qur'an was a manual for murder and mayhem."

This particular review, like many others, left me feeling helplessly frustrated because clearly the customer not only misunderstood Islam, he probably had not read the Bible or Torah, either. Violent passages abound, after all, in the Old Testament. God Himself in the Old Testament commands extermination of entire populations:

> When the Lord your God brings you into the land which you are entering to take possession of it, and clears away many nations before you, . . . and when the Lord your God gives them over to you and you defeat them; then you must utterly destroy them; you shall make no covenant with them, and show no mercy to them.[99]

To fixate on these passages and ignore the many Biblical passages that urge peace and forgiveness would be an injustice to the peace and forgiveness ethic of Christianity. The same is true of the Qur'an.

Dishearteningly, my own friends have sometimes resisted my attempts to equate my religion to theirs. If I explain that the rules of war in Christianity were the same as in Islam, the reaction is "Oh, no. They're completely different." When I explain that the rules of martyrdom are essentially the same in Islam as in Christianity, the immediate reaction is "Oh, no. They're completely different." The reasons they offer me in the rush to repudiate commonality are, without exception, illustrative of severe misinformation relating to Islam.

It is this *distancing* that frightens me. You are not like us, I hear in their hasty reactions. You are different; you believe in an alien religion.

So the purpose of the comparison is not to point fingers but to bridge the distance. It is to clarify the inequity of the views that many people probably share with my former history teacher (that Islam was supposed to be spread by the sword) and my former social studies teacher (that Christianity is about love, but Islam is about violence). "Holy war," or war conducted in the name of religion, was acceptable in ancient times and has been exercised by all the major religions, whether offensively or defensively.

"Well," challenged a woman I know, "that just shows that religion is a bad thing, because people have always used it to fight each other."

Certainly I feel that those in power cannot be trusted with religion. But I doubt that in an absence of religion, we would cease fighting one another. In the former Soviet Union, Albania, and China, religion was prohibited, places of worship were destroyed, religion was suppressed, religious clerics were murdered, and Muslims (along with other religious groups) were persecuted in the cause of *anti-religion*.[100] One scholar observes that of all the people killed in the ten worst wars, massacres, and killings in the history of the world, only 2 percent were killed in religiously motivated conflicts, specifically in the Thirty Years War in Europe.[101]

Consider a *Star Trek* example. I remember an episode in which Captain Kirk (still my hero) encountered a race whose faces were half black and half white. This race fought bitterly with another race on the same planet whose faces were also half black and half white.

"Why," Captain Kirk asked a member of the first race, "do you hate each other so much?"

"Because of how he looks," spat out the alien. "Can't you see how repulsive he is?"

"He looks just like you," my hero said in bewilderment.

"*His* face is black on the *left* side," the alien said contemptuously. "Mine is black on the *right* side."

The violence of humankind needs little to provoke it. Religion is one of many excuses.

9

Theft and Adultery in Islam: Reflections on Disney's *Aladdin*

I lived in Los Angeles and walked to New Orleans every day one summer. I donned a blue floor-length dress, fastened to it the name badge sporting the small Minnie Mouse in the corner, and walked through the employee entrance to Disneyland and into New Orleans Square. I developed an appreciation for Disney's *Sleeping Beauty* during that time, so when *Aladdin* was released on video, my husband and I rented it one day.

We were shocked at what we saw. *Aladdin* enlightened me about the kinds of racial and religious biases to which America's two-year-olds and their families are routinely being subjected.

We watched the movie open with a song about Arabia, with lyrics like, "It's barbaric, but it's home." Never mind that cities in "Arabia" such as Baghdad were the literary and scholarly centers of the world while Europe was swamped in the Dark Ages. (The *Aladdin* story is set in the Middle Ages or thereabouts.) But *Aladdin* offended in many more ways than that.

The names of the villains were Arabic, like Jafar; the names of the good guys were Anglicized versions of Arabic, like Jasmine (from "Yasmeen"). In the movie, the good guys, such as Aladdin and Princess Jasmine, were given fair skin and American accents. The cartoonists gave the villains dark skin and "Middle Eastern" accents.

The genie, a positive character, of course, and portrayed by Robin Williams, was so far removed from an Arabian identity that he not only had an American accent, he *jived* with it. The irony here is that the very idea of a genie comes from the Arabic folklore of the *jinn*, which, as we saw in chapter two, comes from the Qur'an and pre-Islamic Arabia. If anyone should have been given an Arabian identity, it was the genie.

Small children watching *Aladdin* (and memorizing it) will receive several distinct messages: people with dark skin are villains, whereas people with light skin are good guys; people with Middle Eastern accents are villains, whereas people with American accents are heroes; Arabia, which is what we now call the Middle East, is barbaric; and people with Arabic names are bad guys, whereas people with Anglicized or American names are good guys.

Oh, and one more: people who mistakenly take apples from the marketplace will get their hands cut off right away.

That is what nearly happened to Princess Jasmine. She walked into the open-air market, did not realize she had to pay for the apples, and took one. A giant of a dark-skinned, accented man seized her wrist with one hand and brandished a huge scimitarian knife with the other and would have cut off the princess's hand right then and there (no trial, of course) if she had not been saved at the last minute.

Where did such an idea come from? *Aladdin* touches on one of the two most publicized crimes in Islam: theft and adultery. Even in junior high, some of my friends knew that in Muslim countries a thief would get his hand cut off and that an adulteress would be executed.

For the most part, Islamic law is very much like what we in the West think of as law. It prohibits us from stealing, killing, and cheating in contracts. It emphasizes fairness and kindness and justice. But the two areas where it seems very different is in the areas of finance and criminal law. I do not discuss finance in this book, but I thought it worth discussing the small part of Islamic criminal law relating to theft and adultery. These are the only two crimes I discuss in this chapter, because they are the two most sensational and subject to abuse.

Theft

It is true that amputation is the punishment for theft under classical Islamic law. Theft and adultery are both crimes that are mentioned in the Qur'an, so they fall in the category of *hudud* crimes; as such, they must always be defined as crimes.

However, although the Qur'an does specify the crime of theft, words surrounding the definition and punishment have been debated at various times. For example, with respect to cutting the hand of a thief, Ahmed Ali points out that the Arabic word "cut" can have many meanings, depending upon the nouns with which it is used, most relating to the idea of "stopping." For instance, you can "cut someone off" verbally (just as in English) or "cut them off the road."[1] Even in the Qur'an, it has more than one meaning.[2] In the Qur'anic verse dealing with theft, "cut" might mean "to stop their hands from stealing, using deterrent means."[3] This makes sense in light of the very next Qur'anic verse, with its assurances of forgiveness for those who repent and reform.[4] As Ahmed Ali points out, consistent with this reading is the fact that flogging was the penalty for theft in the early Islamic Empire.[5]

However, under classical Islamic law, the jurists did generally view amputation as the punishment for theft. But at the same time, they circumscribed the crime of theft with restrictions and conditions "that were practically impossible to fulfill before a limb could be amputated."[6] This was deliberate.

For example, based on a precedent set by the Caliph Umar in the mid-seventh century, some scholars determined that amputation only applied in a world where hunger and want no longer existed. Since no one has ever claimed that we live in a world without hunger or want (except perhaps Marie Antoinette in suggesting that everyone eat cake), the amputation punishment cannot apply.

In addition, the definition of what constitutes theft is construed narrowly. Only certain types of property qualify. Pickpocketing does not qualify, and taking something from its usual place of custody does not qualify. The stolen property cannot be that of a relative. The alleged thief cannot be part-owner of the allegedly stolen property.

Strict rules of evidence apply, as well. There "must be evidence that is *absolutely clear*"[7] of the theft. Mitigating circumstances—defenses to the crime—such as whether the thief took something by mistake (clearly the case for Princess Jasmine in *Aladdin*) can void punishment. And finally, if the thief repents, then he should be pardoned.[8] A confession of guilt can be withdrawn, in which case the punishment does not apply; and "it is even recommended that the *qadi* [judge] should suggest this possibility to the person who has confessed."[9]

The letter of the law of theft in Islam is much more complicated than Disney would have us believe. Where, in *Aladdin*, was the requisite trial? Where was the determination whether a mistake had been made (it had)? Or whether this theft qualified for amputation (it did not) or whether we lived in a world free of hunger or want (we do not) or whether the thief repented (of course she did)?

No director in his right mind would nullify the intended suspense and horror of the theft scene in *Aladdin* to discuss the rules of Islamic law and jurisprudence with the five-and-under movie viewer. But the impression left on the minds of those two-year-olds memorizing the songs from *Aladdin* must be one of lasting prejudice.

Islamic criminal law, including the punishment for theft, was meant to be a limitation on the violence of the time, just as the Old Testament's "an eye for an eye, tooth for a tooth" doctrine of Judaism was a limitation on the violence of that time. This punishment is no longer a limitation on violence, so its application can be interpreted as meant for its specific historical context. The overall message of Islam was to be *more* humane. In my view, Muslims who blindly follow only part of the letter of the law, without applying the conditions and policy restrictions that *also* apply, are not following Islam.

The "eye for an eye, tooth for a tooth" doctrine in the Qur'an is an affirmation of that in the Old Testament, in which it occurs three times.[10] This is how the Qur'an phrases it:

> In the Torah We decreed for them a life for a life, an eye for an eye, a nose for a nose, an ear for an ear, a tooth for a tooth, and a wound for a wound. But if a man charitably forbears from retaliation, his remission shall atone for him.[11]

Even as the Qur'an sanctions this doctrine, it reiterates that forgiveness and waiver of the punishment is always the better course. So although we have a right to let the punishment fit the crime, it is better to forgive.

Punishment in Islam (as in Judaism) must be examined in its proper historical context. For example, the "eye for an eye" punishment was also a limitation on existing tribal punitive practices in the Arabian peninsula.[12] Tribes tended to engage in blood feuds, where revenge was a necessary and acceptable part of punishment. Blood feuds sometimes continued for years, with each tribe exacting revenge for the last offense. Islam, just as Judaism before it, limited the punishment to a life for a life and not a hundred lives for a life.

In addition, some passages of the Qur'an can be interpreted to be homiletic in nature (explained in chapter four as overstatements intended to illustrate the seriousness of a crime but not necessarily meant to be taken literally). This hypothesis may be more easily understood if we illustrate it in the Biblical context. The Old Testament specifies the death penalty for stubborn and rebellious children:

> If a man has a stubborn and rebellious son, who will not obey the voice of his father or the voice of his mother, and, though they chastise him, will not give heed to them, . . . then all the men of the city shall stone him to death with stones; so you shall purge the evil from your midst.[13]

The modern view is that the penalties in this passage, and others like it, need not be implemented, because they serve to illustrate the moral severity of the crime and because they are homiletic, not because the penalty must be applied. This is also the modern view with respect to some passages of the Qur'an that specify punishments.

If the historical context of the Bible and the Qur'an doesn't seem relevant enough because it was too long ago, consider the Western world 200 years ago. Novels set in England were among my favorites when I was growing up, and I often came across the saying, "May as well be hanged for a sheep as a lamb." In England as late as the nineteenth century, some 200 crimes were punishable by death, including sheep (or lamb) stealing, minor theft (five shillings' worth), and stealing anything from someone's person, whatever the value.[14] Most of these laws were repealed by the nineteenth century.

Although Qur'anic verses cannot be repealed like English laws, the *Shari'a* is flexible—the Qur'an and *Sunnah* can be continually interpreted to apply to every society. One Muslim scholar refers to the *Shari'a* as a work in progress[15] because it contains within it the tools for new interpretation—for example, by independent reasoning (*ijtihad*). After all, if the Qur'an is forever it can apply to all different societies, but not necessarily in exactly the same way. That would be to restrict the Qur'an to its historical time and place. How could it be eternal if it applied only to one particular seventh-century society?

What I find profoundly tragic is how some Muslims blindly adhere to the idea of amputating for theft while completely ignoring the rest of the conditions that are meant to be applied before that punishment can be implemented. The reality is that the burden of proof in Islamic law is so stringent—more so even than is typical of American law—that the amputation punishment for theft (and generally other punishments under Islamic law) should almost never be applied. Nevertheless, although the Islamic punishment for theft is very restricted, we cannot trust human beings not to abuse it.

These Qur'anic punishments were originally limitations on violent, seventh-century society and aimed at that particular society. The original revolutionary message of Islam was to be *more* forgiving and *less* punitive. If we literally apply Qur'anic punishments to a society and get a result that is more punitive and more violent, that result is contrary to the goals of the Qur'an. I think amputation should never be applied as a punishment, and I believe there is more than one Islamic justification for this view.

Because many Muslims are beleaguered by lack of education (religious and otherwise) or the confusion of culture with religion, the kind of misplaced religiosity that requires ancient punishments to be applied goes over credibly. The groups who demand the implementation of Islamic law in a rush of religious fervor may not even realize how stringent the standard of proof is in Islamic law and how, in our imperfect world, humans cannot be trusted to abstain from abusing it in the name of religion.

Classical Islamic law is a policy-oriented system, not a rigid penal system.[16] Repentance is always a defense for theft and voids the punishment. The standard of proof is extremely high and can be applied only in a just society, where no need for theft exists. These are the earmarks of a criminal justice system whose goal is deterrence, not punishment.[17]

Given all this, *Aladdin* could not help but sadden me. I had to rent it again to confirm the information in this chapter, and I procrastinated for months, trying to overcome my revulsion. What grieved me most of all about *Aladdin* was the realization that small children would never even get a chance to be objective when it came to Islam, not when they were approvingly fed racism in their cartoons. They would grow up with the stereotypes, and yet another generation would harbor built-in misconceptions that voices like mine would not be enough to overcome.

Adultery

I once received an email message from Amnesty International, asking me to write on behalf of two women who were reportedly sentenced to be stoned to death for adultery in Iran. The message urged me to write a letter to authorities in Iran to prevent the stoning of these women. The form letter they wanted me to send urged the Iranian authorities to be merciful. Details of the charges and trials were unknown.

I sent the message and added my own entreaties.

I believe in the Qur'an and the *Sunnah*. But I know how incredibly difficult it is to prove the crime of adultery under Islamic law. And even if by some freak of cosmic convergence it *is* proved, numerous defenses, conditions, restrictions, and mitigating factors severely limit the application of its punishment. So almost certainly, whatever the circumstances, those two women did not need to be sentenced to death.

The Qur'an specifies the punishment for extra-marital sex as one hundred lashes, and it is the same for both men and women, married or unmarried.[18] Somehow, however, Islamic law came to regard death by stoning as the penalty for unlawful intercourse if perpetrated by married persons. Unmarried persons still received the punishment of one hundred lashes.

Nowhere in the Qur'an is death or death-by-stoning specified as the punishment for adultery. But death has been inflicted for adultery under the guise of Islam. Why? Stoning as a punishment for married persons who engage in adultery crept into Islamic law years after the Prophet's death. One reason for this may be that stoning is the punishment for adultery prescribed in the Torah, and the Qur'an has many elements in common with the Torah.

A second reason may be that the stoning punishment became connected with Islam through a *hadith*. This *hadith* relates that two Jews who had committed adultery were brought to the Prophet for punishment. This occurred in Medina, where he was the political leader of the community (though the religious leader of only the Muslims) and where, according to the Constitution of Medina, everyone was governed according to his or her religious laws. The Prophet asked the Medinan Jews what the penalty for adultery was according to their religious laws. When informed that the punishment was stoning, he ordered the stoning. This story may have been why the penalty was adopted—though *not* unanimously—in Islam.

Years after Muhammad's death, Islamic jurisprudence adopted the view that one hundred lashes were for unmarried persons engaging in sex and that stoning was for married persons who committed adultery.[19] This seems very strange to me; in a way, this is the abrogation doctrine, again, with the *Sunnah* abrogating a verse of the Qur'an. But the *Sunnah* should not be able to abrogate the Qur'an. As God's word, the Qur'an is the first and highest source of Islamic law. Yet, this distinction between married and unmarried persons who engage in illicit sexual relations remained on the books of Islamic jurisprudence, although it continued to be controversial.

Whatever the penalty for adultery or extra-marital intercourse, convicting someone of this crime requires overcoming nearly insurmountable obstacles. As mentioned in chapter seven, for a conviction of adultery—and this applies to men *and* women—the prosecution must produce four reliable eyewitnesses who have seen the act of sexual intercourse itself. *Four* eyewitnesses!

Not only must four eyewitnesses testify to seeing the act of sexual penetration with their own eyes, they must testify that it occurred in an unlawful context, that it was an "unlawful penetration." In addition, if the accused confesses, a confession of unlawful intercourse must be made on four separate occasions.[20]

It's a nearly impossible burden of proof to meet, I would say. *Purposefully* nearly impossible, because in Islamic criminal law, a policy-oriented system, the goal is deterrence, not punishment.

The Qur'an provides further deterrents to accusations of adultery: falsely accusing someone of illicit sexual relations is itself a serious crime. The Qur'an decrees eighty lashes as punishment for someone who accuses another of unchastity without bringing in the four witnesses. Also, the accuser's evidence may not be accepted in the future.[21]

The witnesses must satisfy certain character requirements, as well, to show their trustworthiness. If one of the four witnesses, for example, retracts his accusation, all four witnesses are liable for the penalty for false accusation for adultery.[22]

And that's not all. Even in the unlikely event that the above requirements are satisfied, the punishment may be mitigated according to individual circumstances.[23] For instance, age, repentance, duress, context, and capacity (mental or physical) may mitigate or abolish the punishment. Always, the Qur'an recommends forgiveness.

Although adultery, like theft, was considered a sin, the application of its punishment was deliberately restricted throughout the nearly fourteen centuries of Islamic history. The principle and punishment of adultery was "constantly restated (a sign of abhorrence), but the option of putting that penalty into effect was removed; the rules of evidence and procedure were carefully written so as to prevent the penalty from taking place."[24] Modern states that purport to be Islamic and that apply this penalty literally while ignoring all the deterrents and safeguards attached to it are not, in my opinion, following the totality of the *Shari'a*.

The punishment for adultery, like other Islamic punishments, can be applied only in an ideal Islamic society, according to some scholars.[25] If Islam governs all aspects of life, then to apply only one aspect of it, such as punishment, without also applying the safeguards, does not make theological or practical sense. One Muslim scholar writes:

> It is therefore nonsense to say that we must apply the Islamic penal system to present-day Muslim societies in their present circumstances. It is nonsense to amputate the thief's hand when he has no means of support but stealing. It is nonsense to punish in any way for *zina* [extra-marital sex] (let alone to stone to death) in a community where everything invites and encourages unlawful sexual relationships... .[26]

Most modern Muslims do regard Islamic criminal law as a system historically meant to discipline and contain behavior without the harshness
that had existed before it. Certainly, because of the numerous safeguards
and limitations on its application, a good argument can be made—on
theological grounds—that it need not be applied to today's world. The
combination of stringent proof required, mitigating factors, and limitations
on punishment clearly shows that a conviction for adultery can almost
never be attained. This is consistent with the original message of the
Qur'an, which limited violence and stressed forgiveness.

After all, the Qur'an says that he who repents and does not repeat his
sins should be pardoned.[27] Indeed, the Qur'an often reminds us that God
is merciful and that we should be merciful, too:

> But indeed, if any
> Show patience and forgive
> That would truly be
> An exercise of courageous will
> And resolution in the conduct
> Of affairs.[28]

Reverend Virginia Mackey writes that the theological substance of the
Qur'an blends the "Judaic Spirit of the Law with the Christian conception
of grace… ."[29] Forgiveness is a very large part of the Qur'anic message, but
too often it is not considered hand in hand with the penal sanctions.

Consider an example. The punishment in Islam for murder is death.
Nevertheless, the family of the victim may agree to take a monetary
compensation in lieu of exacting the punishment of execution of the
murderer. Or, the family of the victim may pardon the murderer altogether.
Forgiveness is encouraged. Even if the family chooses execution as the
punishment, execution represents the taking of a single life for a life and
not many lives for a life, not an everlasting blood feud.

I remember a *Star Trek* episode in which Captain Kirk came across
two men who were condemned to fight each other to the death for all
eternity, continually killing, continually revenged, continually resurrected
for the cycle to begin anew. It gave me nightmares. That is what the
Qur'an, like the Torah, sought to curb.

Modern Islamic Criminal Law

The application of classical Islamic criminal law had been significantly
reduced by the beginning of the twentieth century, due to an awareness

on the part of Muslims that *Shari'a* law, as it had been developed by the Muslim scholars, was inadequate for the modern world.[30] Most of the Muslim world adopted Western-type criminal codes, not to emulate the West, but as a result of a natural progression:

> It may even be suggested that Western influence was the consequence rather than the cause of the diminished role of Shari'a in the administration of criminal justice.[31]

Today, only a few Muslim countries, such as Yemen and Saudi Arabia, purport to apply classical Islamic law. The other countries with majority Muslim populations—whether "Islamic states" or not—apply penal codes consisting of an amalgam of Western and Western-inspired laws. In Iran, Islamic criminal law has been applied since 1982. Some countries, such as Libya, Pakistan, and Sudan have inserted "Islamic" provisions into their codes; they apply their secular codes if the stringent proofs required by Islamic law are not met.

In chapter six, I discussed how the death sentence *fatwa* against Salman Rushdie was morally and legally wrong, according to Islamic law. Aside from the specific reasons set out in that chapter, Islamic law contains general principles that also should have nullified Khomeini's *fatwa*.

For example, established general legal principles in Islamic criminal law are those of fairness, justice, non-retroactivity (that is, you cannot be guilty of a crime that was not illegal when you committed it), the presumption of innocence until guilt is proved, and due process (everyone gets a fair trial). Also, the Qur'an does not require Islamic law to be applied to non-Muslims. Moreover:

> Islam has also laid down the principle that no citizen can be imprisoned unless his guilt has been proved in an open court. To arrest a man only on the basis of suspicion and to throw him into a prison without proper court proceedings and without providing him a reasonable opportunity to produce his defense is not permissible in Islam.[32]

Nothing in modern international law or the law of human rights conflicts with the spirit of the *Shari'a*.[33] The *Shari'a* is flexible as to application. But tying religion to the state in the area of criminal law leaves too much room for abuse of individual rights and too much temptation to ignore the conditions and safeguards required by Islamic law. In some Islamic countries, for example, women have been thrown in jail *by state authorities* for no reason than that someone has accused them of adultery. And yet, this violates Islam.

Detention before trial is only allowed by Islamic law for a limited period and in specific, narrow circumstances to ensure no further harm can be committed in case the accused is guilty; this is not unlike the bail system in America. Furthermore, Islamic law requires that the state provide the following to the prisoner: food, clothing, medical care, visits from a spouse that allow exercise of conjugal privileges, and—very importantly—safety from violating the prisoner's rights such as "the integrity of his beliefs, mind, body and dignity."[34]

Besides, "imprisonment" in Islamic law means removing the right of the accused to move about freely, not throwing him in jail. Someone accused may be imprisoned in his house. Some jurists insist that if any kind of doubt exists as to liability (which it must, before a trial), the accused cannot be detained.[35]

In the area of international human rights, Islam guarantees:

* The right to freedom from arbitrary arrest, detention, torture, or physical annihilation;

* the right to be presumed innocent until guilt is proved by a fair and impartial tribunal;

* the right to a public trial;

* the right to not be compelled to testify against oneself;

* the right to present evidence and call witnesses in one's defense;

* the right to legal counsel of one's own choosing;

* the right to a decision on the merits based on the evidence; and

* the right of appeal.[36]

In addition, Islam allows for a wealth of policy considerations to be applied throughout the legal process. These include rehabilitation and resocialization of those convicted, repentance as a mitigating factor, and considerations of public interest.

But all these limitations and conditions, which combine to form a system not unlike ours in the United States, are sometimes disregarded by states politically inclined to prove their religious adherence. Muslims, as well as non-Muslims, are often familiar with only the sensational aspects of Islamic penal law. Even the most just law can only be just if implemented properly.

Conclusion

I hope by now it is clear why the theft scene in *Aladdin* was inaccurate and irresponsibly offensive. To portray an entire race and religion of people as barbaric and summarily brutal, to do it with such extreme inaccuracy, and to project this portrayal at small children is a disservice to anyone who wishes to promote dialogue between East and West, between Muslim and non-Muslim, and between people of different skin colors.

Islam and early Islamic jurists created a complex set of rules and laws to ensure fairness, increased rights for women, and limitations on existing tribal brutality. The Qur'an, as noted above, blended the spirit of Jewish law with the forgiveness ethic of Christianity and sought to deter and limit, not punish. Virginia Mackey notes that the Islamic rules that originally limited violence continued on through the centuries but the numerous restrictions, conditions, and exhortations to forgiveness contained in the Qur'an did not continue to be emphasized.[37] And that is the real crime, because the exhortations to forgiveness and forbearance are there, in the Qur'an and in the *Shari'a*.

An American Muslim
Reaction to September 11th

While I was writing this book, a friend told me she would like to see a section on my reaction to the September 11th attacks. It surprised me.

"What *about* September 11th?" I asked. "My reaction was just like everyone else's—horror and shock."

"I know that because I know your family," she said to me. "Most people don't know any Muslims and all they have is the media for their impressions."

My post-college life has been spent, among other things, listening to the media distort my religion and portray Muslims as extremists or terrorists or both. Battered with stereotypes, we Muslims confine our frustration, internalize our anger, and marshal our patience so we can present polite, understanding responses to the people who unhesitatingly malign our tradition. We even succeed, sometimes. But always, we wait for the next punch.

So when I heard on the radio one September morning that two jets had volitionally catapulted into the World Trade Center, my first reactions were, I assume, the same as everyone else's. I had trouble believing that the surreal images I later viewed on television were not simply special effects outtakes from some Arnold Schwarzenegger movie. When the reality began sinking in, I, like everyone else, worried about friends and acquaintances who might have been caught in the destruction.

But within a few hours, as I struggled along with other Americans to comprehend the tragedy, a litany began weaving through my brain, amidst the shock and disbelief and worry and increasing, sinking, dread: "Please, God, let it not have been Muslims who did this, please God . . ."

In addition to taking all those lives, the people responsible for that attack harmed Islam and Muslims more than the media had ever done.

And American Muslims were doubly harmed: like everyone else, we grieved for the victims, struggled with the images of their nightmare, and lost friends and relatives in the senseless destruction of the twin towers. But unlike everyone else, we braced ourselves for the backlash of hate mail and attacks on our persons and property, not from terrorists, but from our very own fellow citizens.

The Council on American-Islamic Relations received over 1,700 reports of hate crimes all over the country in the first six months. The South Asian Bar Association received call after call from ethnic Indians and Pakistanis and Sri Lankans reporting hate crimes and seeking assistance. An Afghani man who owns a pizza franchise near my house was beaten up by teenagers. Only a few miles away, an Indian man and his Australian roommate were attacked and stabbed by men shouting anti-Muslim accusations at them. My friend's half-Indian babysitter was refused service at businesses she had patronized all her life while growing up in a small Wyoming town. A Sikh gas station owner in Phoenix, Arizona, was shot dead. My mother's friend's niece received threatening telephone calls for days before someone set fire to her house. The FBI arrested two leaders of the Jewish Defense League in Southern California and charged them with planning to detonate explosives at various local mosques.[1]

My favorite Indian restaurant was torched one night at 2 a.m. Arson, the police said. No one made as wonderful a *saag aloo* as they did. The owners had recently changed its name from "Taj Mahal" to "Islamic Tandoori," so customers would know they served *halal* meat.

"Well," said a friend of mine, excusingly, "you never hear of other restaurants named 'Jewish Restaurant' or 'Christian Barbecue.'"

Since the prevalent tradition in this country is Christian, no one need advertise as a Christian restaurant. But I *have* seen plenty of "Jewish Delis" and "Kosher bakeries." Orowheat™ makes a "Jewish Rye" bread. And anyway, that's not the point. No one deserves to be the victim of violence for retaliation of a crime unrelated to them.

Two days after the September 11th attacks, a friend sent me an email to inform me that everyone in the country was going to display an American flag the next day.

"I particularly thought you should know," she wrote, "because if you don't display a flag, someone might think it's because you're Muslim that you're not doing it."

Oh, God. And where was I to find a flag when everyone in the country was out buying all the available flags in our vicinity in a frenzy of patriotism? My husband called every store within twenty-five miles of us. No, no more flags; sorry, we're all sold out.

If I had been a white non-Muslim, I would have given up. After all, I had done my best to obtain a flag by the next day and no one had any to sell. But, given that I am an Indian-American Muslim, I tucked my children into bed that night and then sat down on the floor to make one.

"Posterboard," I said to my husband on the telephone. "You know, the big white posterboard? Get that, will you? I think I have paint …"

I stayed awake until 2:30 in the morning painting red stripes onto white posterboard. I straightened, finally, not displeased with my efforts, rubbing my cramped neck, stretching my aching back, and trying to uncross my eyes. I smiled down at my flag with a sense of great accomplishment, as anyone would have done had they just finished painting a blue background painstakingly around the borders of fifty little white stars.

Fifty? I blinked my heavy eyes and counted again. And once more.

Thirty-five. I had painted only thirty-five stars on my American flag. I dropped onto the floor and wailed.

We put it in our big front window anyway, in the hope that no one would notice the fifteen missing stars. And when the army surplus store received a new shipment of flags a week later, my husband bought a ten-year supply. My three-year-old wanted every flag ornament and every flag sticker she saw. When I asked her why, she told me solemnly that people who did not display flags did not love America.

Neither, apparently, do people who are bilingual. That's the common perception, anyway. In the months following the September 11th attacks, I received glares and dirty looks when I spoke Urdu to my children in public.

I have no accent in either Urdu or English, having grown up speaking both. But being bilingual makes it much easier to learn other languages, and I have always wanted my children to have that advantage. I have wanted them to have that connection with their Indian-Pakistani culture, as well, and that extra appreciation for cultural differences of any kind.

But after a few days of my having to return the hostile stares of random strangers in grocery stores and medical offices, my husband sat me down and told me to stop. Stop speaking Urdu in public, he said. Don't risk your safety. Don't risk the children.

When the children asked me why we were switching to English in public, I disbelievingly heard these words issue from my mouth:

"Because some people think that if you speak a second language you're not American."

My mother was visiting us that week, and I was too afraid to let her drive home. I was afraid of her being stopped and killed on the highway because of her skin color and Indian accent. But I also worried about her being at her home alone, trustingly opening her door to strangers to let them use her telephone and borrow tools (something she tends to do).

"Well," said my father philosophically when he called, "it could be worse. If this were India, thousands of people would have been killed already in religious rioting."

Sitting at the kitchen table, my husband and mother and I tried to decide how to engineer her return home. My mother kept brushing away tears.

"When I lived in India," she said, "I used to tell myself that if anyone came to kill me, I would hide under the bed."

She was six years old at the time. Religious riots were a fact of life, especially near the capitol, where they lived.

"So many times," she continued, "I remember someone running to our door and shouting for us to lock all the doors and windows because a mob of rioters was coming."

How many times did my father, as a child, almost bicycle into a scene of violent rioting in India? Only by the grace of God, he has always said, is he still alive, because he has had too many close calls to count.

My parents had both lived through the Partition, the splitting of India into the two countries of India and Pakistan. My mother was three years old at the time. Her family did not leave India; her father refused to move, though friends and neighbors were packing up and fleeing. He was Indian, he said stubbornly. He had been born in the state in which he was now living, and India was his country.

"Is God not here in India?" he demanded. "Is God accessible only in a Muslim state of Pakistan? God can protect me just as well in India, if He wishes to protect me at all."

He died nine years later, having never left his country, when my mother was twelve and the oldest of six children.

My parents were afraid when they first came to America. But, in time, they relaxed and eventually forgot what it was like to live in continual fear. The racism they still encounter (like passing drivers shouting "Stupid foreigner!" at them) has been easier for them to cope with because it does not threaten their lives. I, raised in spoiled comfort to think of myself as a free American, have had much more trouble dismissing racism, even the non-violent kind.

But September 11th reopened that Pandora's box of anxieties that my parents had buried after their arrival in America. It were as if my mother had opened a familiar door to find—instead of the kitchen or closet—a constantly replaying, half-forgotten movie. She found herself trapped watching old images of violence, feeling the same persevering, unrelenting fear she had felt during the first part of her life in India. And we were reminded that non-violent racism is not so far removed from the violent kind; indeed, one is a precursor to the other.

When I voiced my concern about hate crimes, many of my acquaintances dismissed my concerns or were skeptical, as if I were whining for sympathy or fabricating. "Well," a friend of mine explained, "Americans are scared. And when we're scared we lash out."

I thought: am I not, then, American and scared? I am not going to be immune in a terrorist attack just because I am Muslim. Many Muslims died in the attacks. And I have the double duty of being wary of my fellow Americans.

Many Americans, including me, have only had a first taste of a constant threat since September 11th and it is terrifying enough. But my parents knew ongoing violence firsthand, in close proximity, filling their entire lives from infancy. The week of September 11th, my mother waited helplessly for the cycle of violence to begin all over again, in her new country.

Luckily, the violence was not too egregious, compared to India, anyway, though the Americans in this country who were injured or killed or ostracized as a result of hate crimes would disagree. Hate crimes tended to be underreported in the media, and I received most of my information from groups providing assistance to the victims. Whether there has been a backlash against Muslims depends on the definition of "backlash;" whereas it is true that physical violence has not been rampant, the verbal backlash comprising anti-Muslim feeling and anti-Islamic hatred has ballooned.

Even a year after the attacks, a Florida man was arrested in possession of explosives and detailed plans for blowing up nearly fifty Islamic centers and schools. As late as 2007, numerous mosques around the country reported incidents of vandalism or arson that were being investigated as hate crimes.

But it helped that some of those in the media were at first more responsible than they had been after the Oklahoma City bombing in

1995, at least before they were sure who committed the attack. It also helped that after a week or two, President Bush at least distinguished Islam and Muslims on one hand and terrorists on the other. That speech gave us hope; although, since then, the absence of similar reassurance has been deafening.

The attacks conveniently provided a blanket justification for anything negative anyone might possibly dream up to say against Muslims. Very few people realize what it is like to be the subject of daily socially acceptable lies, slander, defamation, and distortion. It is exhausting. I cannot dismiss the lurking fear that we have not progressed very far in fifty years, and the specter of internment camps broods sleeplessly in my mind.

Osama bin Laden and his ilk do not threaten only American non-Muslims. They also attack Muslims who do not conform to their vision of the world. They view American Muslims—and other Americans of all kinds—as complicit in the actions of the American government and therefore justifiable objects of their incorrect definition of "jihad." Bin Laden and his followers terrify Muslims living in Muslim countries, because most Muslims are not extremists or fundamentalists, and bin Laden's philosophies are anathema to them. And those Muslims are the ones in danger of their governments being subverted by extremists like him.

It is not a case of *us* and *them*. It is not a matter of Islam versus the West, because Islam is now a part of the West. It is not a matter of extremists against the U.S., because Muslims in Muslim countries stand in danger of the bin Ladens of the world, too. We American Muslims love our country and favor secularism and see that as reconcilable with Islam.

It is too easy to draw solid and grossly inaccurate lines. We all have a tendency to define ourselves in terms of goodness so that we can define other cultures or religions in terms of evil. The old villains of the early twentieth century always had heavy German accents. Later, it was the Japanese-Americans who were herded into internment camps. The Soviets (and Communists in general) replaced the Japanese and ushered in McCarthyism.

In the 1990s, I found myself reading a spate of 1970s spy novels, which featured Communist villains, always the one-dimensional, evil, inhuman variety. The Communists were indisputably our enemy, the Evil Empire. They were most emphatically not like us.

Anti-Islamic media rose in proportion to the decline of the Soviet Union. Once Putin was our friend, Saddam Hussein became our enemy. Never mind that Saddam Hussein was our friend when Iran was our enemy. Iran was our friend when the Vietnamese were our enemy. Bin Laden may be our enemy now, but he was our friend when he was fighting the Soviets in Afghanistan for us.

Unfortunately, bin Laden has been successful in spreading hatred and recruiting people to his cause. Much of the Islamic world today comprises developing countries and dictatorships.

> Internally, nearly all Muslim countries are governed by authoritarian regimes that stultify serious possibilities for free, vigorous discourse. Externally, Muslims are among the most powerless, dominated, and abused people in the world.[2]

In Pakistan, half the population is under the age of nineteen and most of them will grow up uneducated. The drug addiction rate there is higher than the literacy rate. So how can Muslims in countries like Pakistan even know what their religion says? How can they understand the world stage? People like bin Laden can recruit them easily by convincing them they're doing their religious duty.

It is up to us Muslims to educate ourselves about our religion so we can stem the divisiveness and prevent extremists from success. It is up to us Muslims to defend and explain our religion and reconcile it to the modern world. Most of us have indeed been trying. But we need media cooperation to give us a voice.

II

Why the Misconceptions Persist: Separating the Reality from the Murky Mythology

In the last several decades, Islam has become twisted in the public eye. The popular image of Islam as portrayed by the media becomes daily blacker, larger, more tortuously spiky and bent upon itself. And it is not simple ignorance that feeds the ever-growing image; it is a thousand years of myth-making. It is a yawning schism of linguistic and cultural differences. And, not least, it is the psychological need for an enemy.

Upon finding ourselves defined as the enemy or as followers of an evil religion, Muslims in America are only now beginning to object to the images. We, the millions of peaceful non-terrorist Muslims, were silent too long, and the stereotypes ran away with us. We did not realize in time that Khomeini, and twenty years later bin Laden, would force the issue.

My parents and those Muslim immigrants of their generation did not rank political visibility high on their to-do lists when they first came to America. Many came to study and were intent upon building their careers and families, struggling to assimilate to a new culture with a new language, and trying to understand the American system, so different from, say, the Indian one.

Many thought religion was a private matter, anyway. They had no wish to rock the boat. They were strangers in an incomprehensibly strange land, set apart already by their appearances and their accents. Those were reasons enough for prejudice.

My parents had trouble renting an apartment in Southern California. Landlords would glance at my mother's sari and turn them away. So my father's colleagues at the university where he was a professor found a house for them to rent. When they moved in, however, their neighbors left plastic bags of feces on their doorstep and threatened them with the police in case they ever "tried anything." My father was stopped many times by police officers when he bicycled to the nearest market in the evening to get last-minute groceries for his wife or medications for his small children. Why am I being searched, officer, he would ask. Oh, came the vague reply, we've had thefts around here.

Coping with American society was difficult enough without the added complication of religious differences. Explaining why we could not drink alcohol or eat pork was a cause of stress. Many of my parents' close friends were Jewish. I remember even at a young age feeling relief when we went to dinner at one of their houses, not just because they were nice people, but because I knew they would never serve pork.

Aside from all those disincentives to discuss Islam, many Muslims came from countries in which voicing religious or political views got people killed. Reticence was only prudent. So we never contested any stereotypes until it was too late.

But in the last ten years, American Muslims *have* been trying to find a voice in the media. We *have* been speaking up. The problem is that our voices get nosed out of the media by the many sensationalist voices of Islamophobes or the extremist voices of Muslims like bin Laden or Ahmadinejad, who are portrayed as representative of Islam.

But other reasons, too, contribute to the runaway images of Islam. In this chapter, I discuss four primary reasons for them: distortion of facts by the media, confusion regarding what is religious and what is cultural or political, the language barrier, and the centuries-old popular mythology that is so ingrained into the Western perception of Islam that any facts counter to it are not accepted as truth.

Media Distortion

Citizens of all countries are limited by their media and often conditioned by it. Particularly since the decline of the Cold War, the media has turned its dubious attention on Islam as the new enemy. Ludicrously unbalanced and fantastical characterizations of Islam in the media have been an increasingly insurmountable obstacle in any attempt to understand it. For the last decade, these impressions have been avalanching, so much so that I find *myself* being conditioned, though I should know better. How can someone unfamiliar with Islam overcome the media representation of it? The media essentially describes Islam in several predictable ways, and once we have some knowledge of Islam and the way it is discussed in the public discourse, we can be better critical thinkers.

Universalizing the Specific

The media constantly gives a disproportionate airing to the minuscule percentage of extremist Muslims so that we get the impression that all Muslims are just like them. After the September 11th attacks, 19 hijackers illogically became the symbol for the religion of some 1,400,000,000 people. When non-Muslims commit crimes, we do not assume all their co-religionists are criminals.

I had arranged to meet a friend for tea the morning after September 11th, and she told me she had already seen huge front-page newspaper pictures of Palestinians celebrating the destruction in New York. Predictably, one journalist wrote that "Muslims all over the world were celebrating the attacks." What no one bothered to mention was that these were just a few Palestinians. The town in which they lived was, at that time, under siege by the Israeli military, whom the Palestinians see brandishing American-made weapons.

And while these particular Palestinians were featured on the various front pages of American newspapers, very few news organizations covered the Palestinians who took part in candlelight vigils for the victims of the demolished World Trade Towers.

The coverage of a handful of Muslims celebrating—shown repeatedly in between coverage of mass destruction in New York—eclipsed the many expressions of condolence and the numerous condemnations of the attacks that came in from every Arab country and from Muslims all over the world, whatever their political relations with the United States. The September 11th attacks were condemned by so-called terrorist groups, Islamist groups (like Egypt's Muslim Brotherhood), heads of state, religious scholars (like the chief mufti in Saudi Arabia and others all over the Middle East), and groups like the League of Arab States and the Organization of the Islamic Conference; yet, these and other statements were rarely mentioned in the media. To this day, I have friends who suffer from the misapprehension that only those Muslims bravely struggling against the tide of mainstream Islamic opinion managed somehow (with great danger to themselves) to condemn the September 11th attacks. The opposite is true.

As I mentioned earlier, in addition to those condemnations, the spokesperson for Hizbullah, a guerilla group fighting the Israeli occupation of a strip of southern Lebanon, gave the following statement about the September 11th attacks: "Although we are hostile to United States policy, we are horrified at these operations, which no religion in the world supports."[1]

My parents and other Muslims I know were asked why members of the Muslim clergy did not denounce the terrorists. Several of my own friends asked me why Muslims did not make statements both informing the public about Islam and denouncing the terrorists. It is something I have heard for years: why do Muslims not condemn the bad things other Muslims do?

First of all, we do. Second, our condemnations can only be heard if the media publishes them. Third, why are Christians or Jews or Hindus or Buddhists all over the world not required to condemn all the crimes that their co-religionists commit (or else be thought somehow approving of such crimes)?

Muslims all over the world *did* denounce the terrorists and specifically condemn the September 11th attacks. Many offered explanations of Islam and how terrorism violated Islamic principles. Yet, even weeks after the attacks, hardly any news services mentioned these, even in passing. Very few news services bothered to relay the message that governments of Muslim countries and high-ranking Islamic scholars had almost unanimously condemned Osama bin Laden for his terrorist activities and rhetoric. I once heard a media spokesperson say on the radio that she received press releases from the Council on American-Islamic Relations every day, statements of condemnation or those explaining the Muslim position, but that they never made it to the airwaves.[2]

A leading Muslim scholar, Yusef al-Qaradawi, issued a *fatwa* immediately after the attacks, declaring that Osama bin Laden could not call himself a Muslim.[3] The conservative Saudi government also issued a *fatwa* rejecting suicide bombers and terrorism. Iran, which has had troubled relations with the United States since the 1970s, issued multiple statements of condolence. Iran's Supreme Leader, Khamenei, stated that "Islam condemns the massacre of defenseless people, whether Muslim or Christian or others, anywhere and by any means."[4]

Religious scholars within the United States also execrated the attacks. Muslim leaders in Southern California immediately denounced terrorism and explained that, in Islam, "To kill one person of whatever religion is to kill all humanity and to save one soul of whatever religion is to save all humanity."[5]

In fact, American Muslim individuals and organizations issued, either singly or as signatories, over *two hundred* separate formal statements condemning the September 11th attacks, together representing most of the *seven million* Muslims in America.[6] So there you are: the seven million Muslims in America condemned the September 11th attacks. They never made the headlines, though.

And I was still asked why Muslims did not condemn the attack. Why? Because the majority, mainstream Muslim voices are very rarely given a voice in the media, eschewed in favor of endless coverage of a few Palestinians celebrating someone else's suffering.

Characterization of Violence as Islamic in Nature

The media systematically attaches the prefix "Islamic" to any crime that has the vaguest connection with a Muslim or Islam. This has been going on for decades. Criminals exist in all religions, but they are not identified by their religions when they make the news.

After the September 11th attacks, it is easy to say with the perfection of hindsight: I told you so. We were right to suspect "Muslim terrorists." But al-Qaeda is only one organization, and terrorists of all kinds exist in the world.

For example, the armed wing of the Irish Republican Army attacked subway stations in London for years. The racist atrocities committed by some white supremacist groups, such as the Ku Klux Klan, are based on those groups' interpretations of the Bible. Jewish extremists have slaughtered worshipers in mosques. The people who blow up abortion clinics do so because of their religious beliefs. Buddhists used chemical weapons on a Japanese subway to kill and injure numerous passengers. David Koresh, who died with his Christian cult at Waco, was characterized as an extremist, not as a representative of Christianity. Over 900 followers of a Christian cult were massacred in Uganda in early 2000 by their cult leaders.[7]

But the media doesn't use the terms "Catholic terrorists" or "Protestant terrorists" or "Jewish terrorists" or "Buddhist terrorists" or "Hindu terrorists," and not because there have never been any. Violence is a characteristic of humankind. Yet Islam is continually used as an explanation for violence.

On April 19, 1995, Timothy McVeigh blew up the Arthur P. Murrah federal building in Oklahoma City. The media teemed with the opinions of those convinced that "Islamic terrorists" had done the deed. Composite profiles of the perpetrators portrayed them as dark-haired and dark-skinned, and witnesses described them as "Middle Eastern looking." They turned out to be light-skinned and light-haired and American.

But in the interim days, Muslim Americans all over the country were hurt and harassed. No one seemed to entertain the idea that the explosion could have been the work of a white, non-Muslim fundamentalist group or even a white, non-Muslim individual. Scholars who had written about Islam were contacted by journalists, as though anyone who knew anything about Islam was guiltily involved by association anytime a bomb exploded anywhere.

When it became known that Timothy McVeigh had been raised Catholic, no one killed Catholics in retaliation or fired bullets into churches. Very few people realized, then or now, because the media never featured it, that McVeigh blew up the building pursuant to the ideology of the Christian Identity movement, to which he belonged. Even if they had, I doubt anyone would have committed hate crimes against Christians. How ironic, then, that Muslim Americans were harassed for the actions of a Christian fundamentalist.

Even when Muslims are victims, they are not granted the same degree of media sympathy as non-Muslims are. Instead, surprisingly often when Muslims are victims, I hear the tired refrain of "Oh, they've been at each other's throats for centuries." That, of course, implies that the Muslim victims are incapable of rescue because they are genetically or historically fated to continue fighting for eternity, and it's best to just dismiss the whole thing.

This is evident when the fighting between Hindus and Muslims in India is characterized as "centuries-old hatred" even though widespread racial tensions only appeared in the nineteenth century. When the peace process is urged upon the parties in the Israeli-Palestinian conflict, a common but foundationless response is, "Why bother? Jews and Muslims have been at each other's throats for centuries." When thousands of Muslims in Bosnia suffered crimes against humanity at the hands of the Christian Serbs, Western pundits and politicians did nothing for years and dismissed the conflict as "ancient hatred," despite the evidence of five centuries of multireligious, multicultural existence in Bosnia.[8]

When the Serbs turned their attacks on Muslims in Kosovo, almost the first thing I heard in the news was, "this conflict goes back hundreds of years," again setting the stage for the lazy mentality of shrugging dismissal. The reality is that nationalist Serbs constructed the story of "ancient hatreds" in the nineteenth century.[9] They "projected [it] back to the battle of 1389, and then back even further, even to the creation of the universe."[10] The Western powers happily accepted it.

Occasionally, I do hear reasonable Muslim views on the news. But hundreds of repeated negative impressions of Islam add up to a wall of solid misperception that is very difficult to overcome.

Material Omissions

Omissions with respect to Islam appear in several different incarnations. Media pieces, even ostensibly objective ones, often omit an explanation of the *context*. An example is the frequent discussion of the fighting verses of the Qur'an, with all the conditions to fighting and the exhortations to peace conveniently omitted.

In addition, the media omits Muslim identities when the *victims* of violence are Muslim (though we have seen that Muslim criminals are routinely characterized as such). I once heard an entire piece on NPR, commemorating the tenth anniversary of the genocide in Kosovo. The journalist spoke at length of entire villages and families being destroyed, and the far-reaching effects thereof, but not once in the entire special, lengthy broadcast was it mentioned that the victims were Muslims.

If we only hear about Muslims as the perpetrators of violence and never as the victims of violence, then of course we will be conditioned to think Muslims are more violent than others.

Moreover, the media ignores the good things happening in the Islamic world and focuses on the reprehensible things. A recent example is the steady and peaceful progression toward democracy and women's rights in Kuwait, a Muslim country; this was largely ignored, despite that in June 2006, Kuwaiti women voted and could stand for election for the very first time.

Often, Muslims who make racist or reprehensible statements are given undue importance, and Muslims who make enlightened statements (from the Western point of view, of course), are dismissed. Columbia University senior research scholar Gary Sick, prominent Iran expert and National Security Advisor under Presidents Ford, Carter, and Reagan, comments:

> Ahmadinejad is the greatest gift that the Iranian hard-liners have ever given to the American hard-liners. The American hard-liners had a really difficult time when Khatami was president [1997–2005]. Same role, same office as Ahmadinejad, and when he was making friendly statements, many Americans dismissed it, saying "The presidency has no power, it has no real influence on anything, it doesn't get involved in the decision-making process, so ignore him." But when Ahmadinejad comes along and says all kinds of stupid things, the same people say, "He's the president of Iran, listen to what he's saying!"[11]

Similarly, when Professor Amina Wadud led mixed-gender prayers in New York City, the National Public Radio website described the reaction thus:

"In the days since, response from Islamic leaders at home and abroad has ranged from disapproval to outrage."[12] The report never mentioned those Islamic clerics who declared that mixed-gender prayers are permissible under Islamic law and even orthodox. How do these favorable views figure in the spectrum from "disapproval to outrage"?

The positive aspects relating to Islam, even critically important ones, like the reactions to the September 11th attacks, are usually ignored. Add to this phenomenon the fact that Arabs and Muslims have not had much of a voice in the media and the sum total is a picture completely lacking balance and accuracy. The following words of one American journalist can be applied accurately to Muslims, as well as Arabs:

> Palestinian Americans in particular, and Arabs in general, are the ghosts haunting U.S. newsrooms by their embarrassing absence. As journalists, we do not know them as a people, we have little connection with their slights and sorrows, and we can only, even with the best of intentions, experience their suffering as an abstraction. . . . Despite all the attention accorded affirmative action by news organizations on the grounds that diversity is necessary to better news reporting, the exclusion of Arabs has been ignored.[13]

Not all Arabs are Muslims, of course, and not all Muslims (or even most) are Arabs. But most Americans think of the Middle East when they think of Muslims.

Consider this question put to me, a new attorney, quaking but brave in her crisp wool suit, by a senior attorney who believed herself to be enlightened: "Why are Muslims more violent than other types of people?"

In the manner of a confession, she continued to tell me how attending Berkeley had "opened her eyes" but that now she was becoming increasingly prejudiced against all Muslims. I could not help but wonder what she had been like before she went to Berkeley.

The answer to her question, however inadequate, still is, "They are not." Muslims are not more violent than other types of people. But we have a media wall we find very difficult to surmount.

The Linguistics of Building an Image

As one scholar points out, so-called "experts" on Islam opine with inimical confidence about a religion that few of them seem to have ever encountered in person[14] or even in educational settings.

In order to understand how removed American media images of Islam are from most American Muslims, it is useful to understand the specific characteristics of the discourse. For example, linguistics professor Jeremy Henzell-Thomas lists entire paragraphs of stereotypes commonly applied to Islam, including fundamentalist, one-dimensional, incapable of integration or assimilation, backward, uncivilized, hostile, fanatical, terrorist, oppressive, negatively exotic, and "bent on imposing on the whole world a rigid theocratic system of government which would radically overturn every principle of freedom and liberal democracy cherished by the Western world." I cannot articulate how immeasurably grateful I felt when Dr. Henzell-Thomas recited in one sentence thirty-three examples of inane stereotypical adjectives purporting to describe Islam, and finished with the words:

> I have to say that I don't know a single Muslim who embodies even one of these characteristics, and I have Muslim friends and colleagues in all walks of life and from many cultures all over the globe.[15]

It is an indication of how accustomed I am to the besieging default hostility toward Islam that when someone makes a remark like this one, I disbelievingly blink and reread in astonished gratitude.

William Dalrymple does not exaggerate when he writes: "Anti-Muslim racism now seems in many ways to be replacing anti-Semitism as the principal Western expression of bigotry against the other."[16]

Words may never hurt me, on their own, but they may clear the way for sticks and stones to break my bones; this is what happened to the Jews in Nazi Germany and to the Muslims in Bosnia. The Christian Serbs used extensive media exposure to demonize Bosnian Muslims to make genocide possible. Anti-Semitism led to the definition of Jews as less than human in order to facilitate killing them without the hassles of conscience. Similarly, Serbian media and propaganda both internally and abroad dehumanized Bosnian Muslims to legitimize ethnic cleansing of them. Jeremy Henzell-Thomas writes that the Serbian media relayed messages that transitioned from a pseudo-scholarly analysis of a "straw-man" Muslim with no basis in reality to the advocacy of violence against that "straw-man" Muslim and then, ultimately, to genocide. From verbal stereotyping to the advocacy of violence to genocide:

> Such is the outcome of words used without truth or responsibility. To see so many stereotypes in the Western press so similar to those invented by the Serbs is quite chilling.[17]

It terrifies *me* when I listen to other scholars in addition to Dr. Henzell-Thomas draw parallels between anti-Islamic stereotyping, anti-Semitism, and Serbian anti-Muslim propaganda. I can only hope we have more people fighting against bigotry and racism in this country than the German Jews and the Bosnian Muslims had.

I recently heard a wonderful radio interview of Louise Arbour, who served as Chief Prosecutor of War Crimes for Rwanda and the former Yugoslavia from 1996 to 1999. In 2004, she was named the U.N. High Commissioner for Human Rights. Ms. Arbour identified three commonalities in the conditions that led to genocides: first, a campaign of hate propaganda, demonizing a set of people; second, fear-mongering, which convinces people that unless they commit genocide first, they themselves will be the victims of violence; and third, a culture of obedience which—under the pressure of the first two—eclipses individual moral judgment.[18] I must say, I feel profound relief that Americans are not a particularly culturally obedient people, because I certainly hear and see Ms. Arbour's first two points in abundance in my country.

Some of the ways in which language is used to enhance this sort of stereotyping are much more subtle than the outright lies. Many people who would realize that calling Muhammad a terrorist is defamatory may not realize that an objective-sounding report from a reputable news source could contain the same types of defamation portrayed in subtle ways.

Dr. Henzell-Thomas gives a few examples: the attack on the World Trade Center was characterized as an attack on the "civilized world, civilized people, and civilized countries."[19] That implies America is all those things but those outside America are not any of those things. That immediately leads to "us" and "them," with "us" being civilized and therefore superior. These labels are rarely even-handed: "Islamic mass murderers" was used instead of "terrorists," though "Christian mass murderers" was never used for the Bosnian Serbs.[20]

Hyperbole or gross exaggeration also contribute to such nonsensical notions as "Muslims are out to take over the world." Ridicule is yet another way to completely dismiss anything positive about Islam; one journalist laughed at the idea of a Muslim football team (how funny—did they wear turbans instead of helmets?). Condemnation can be imposed by association: if I say anything positive about Muslims and I myself am a Muslim, I cannot possibly have anything rational to say on the subject.[21] I have come across this one many times while writing this book. How can I be unbiased about Islam when I am Muslim? I am sure you see the logical conclusions looming: Americans cannot be impartial speaking of America, Christians are unqualified to speak about Christianity, and so on. It is absurd.

Pictures, too, are used to say a thousand *negative* words about Islam. It is not uncommon to see on a magazine cover or news piece the peaceful picture of a man or woman praying in a mosque, with an incongruous subtitle like, "Islamic Terrorism" or "Cradles of Fanaticism."[22] To pray, the picture obviously says, is to be a terrorist or a fanatic.

Dr. Henzell-Thomas lists an entire host of common euphemisms used when Muslims are portrayed in the media. The most common is "Islamic terrorist" instead of "terrorist." But also, an Iraqi civilian "killed in cross-fire" sounds much less violent than "shot by a soldier."[23] While people the media favors (non-Muslims) live in "neighborhoods" or "communities," people the media does not favor (Muslims) live in "areas," which sounds much less civilized. The "international community" usually just means "the West," but it gives the West more credibility to portray itself as the international community. We do not "attack" Muslims, we "respond" to them,[24] such as when we killed more Afghani civilians after September 11th than the total number of people who died in the WTC attacks.[25]

These are the more subtle points of discourse. The hostility of people like Jerry Falwell and Andy Rooney, discussed earlier in the book, is a much more obvious racism. The frightening thing about the more subversive prejudice is that it often *sounds* like it is respectable journalism. Imagine hundreds of such small points in every day's worth of newscasts about Islam, and that accumulates into a big picture that is hopelessly difficult to combat.

I can try to shout down the media, but that is hard to do. I have been writing "letters to the editor" for years and, whereas I have a high percentage rate of publication with respect to non-Muslim subjects, I have a zero-percentage rate with respect to letters explaining my Muslim position. How frustrating to then be asked why Muslims are not speaking up.

News can be very logical and dispassionate, yet still very misleading. For example, I heard a piece on public radio that discussed the religious schools at which the Taliban train. I heard these points:

a) The training at these schools is purely religious,

b) these are Islamic schools,

c) students are not encouraged to think independently,

d) the Taliban train here,

e)   the Taliban are bloodthirsty and out to kill Americans (established by a series of interviews within the broadcast), and

f)   these Islamic schools are proud of their Taliban alumni.

This, of course, implies: Islam as a religion maintains purely religious schools, which proudly teach the Taliban to be bloodthirsty. Ergo, Islam teaches people to be bloodthirsty.

Yet, Islam contains clear statements of tolerance of all religions and races, both in its theology and in its past historical record. William Dalrymple witnessed firsthand how Muslims and Christians worshipped together at the same pilgrimage site in Syria, as they had done for centuries, and writes:

> The Eastern Christians, the Jews, and the Muslims have lived side by side in the Levant for nearly one and a half millennia and have only been able to do so due to a degree of mutual tolerance and shared customs unimaginable in the solidly Christian West.[26]

Another problem with media coverage, in addition to bias in the language and the manipulated context, is that the voluminous coverage of Islam is presented in such a way that consumers believe they have understood it, never knowing that what they have "learned" is itself based on prejudiced material:

> In many instances [the term] "Islam" has licensed not only patent inaccuracy but also expressions of unrestrained ethnocentrism, cultural and even racial hatred, deep yet paradoxically free-floating hostility. All this has taken place as part of what is assumed to be fair, balanced, responsible coverage of Islam.[27]

For example, when Iraq invaded Iran in 1980 and the Iranians resisted, this resistance was characterized as "the Shi'a penchant for martyrdom."[28] This cliché, like others such as "the Islamic mentality," was used to describe something that everyone of every country should have been able to sympathize with—invasion of their country by foreign armies—and placed it instead into a completely alien context. If Americans resisted an invasion of the United States, they would be considered patriotic, not indulging of their "penchant for martyrdom."

Media portraits of the "Islamic world" are often drawn exclusively from Khomeini, bin Laden, isolated verses of the Qur'an taken out of context, and extremist militant groups like the Taliban. It would be equally delusive to assemble a portrait of the "West" or even of America exclusively from examples of the Ku Klux Klan, quotes from Pat Robertson, isolated verses of the Bible, and certain actions of the CIA.

I and my Muslim friends continually strive in a Sisyphean struggle to defend our religion. My former college roommate once reminded me that many Americans do not know any Muslims personally. All they have is the media. They do not have a Muslim friend whose behavior they can observe and of whom they feel comfortable asking questions. When we were undergraduates, she supported me through not dating, not drinking, not gambling, and not partying, though I was her first Muslim friend. And recently, twenty years after we doggedly attended the same Western Culture discussion section as freshmen, she told me something that I have held close to my heart ever since.

"I never told you this," she said, "but the reason that I became such a devout Christian was because of you. Because you inspired me with your behavior." I carry her words with me always and pull them out every so often so the light can illuminate their valuable fragility and so that I, in my turn, may be inspired. And be reminded to give thanks that not everyone believes the media.

Religion vs. Culture

Even when we do receive accurate facts, it is difficult for us here in the West—both Muslims and non-Muslims—to separate Islam the religion from the culture of the various countries in which it is prevalent. This is partly because the media routinely covers countries from Africa to Asia to Europe and portrays the dozens of societies, languages, ethnic groups, and cultures there as "Islam." We are fed specific images that are meant to be representative of all Islam. Veiled women are the obvious example, though as we've discussed, not all Muslim women veil themselves or are victims of oppression. The bearded, turbaned, white-robed, dark-skinned man carrying a Kalashnikov is the other example. The few hundred Sikhs in America subjected to hate crimes after September 11th are human testimony to the prejudice that a turban inspires.

One scholar points out that this sort of generalization is "of the most irresponsible sort and could never be used for any other religious, cultural, or demographic group on earth."[29] This is particularly the case with respect to women, as discussed in chapter seven, but politics and social problems in the Middle East and Africa are also incorrectly attributed to Islam rather than to social, cultural, political, and economic factors.

One of the interesting things about this vague language of generalities is that Islam is often characterized in opposition to the West, and not to Christianity. "Islam vs. the West" is a common phrase. This implies that the "West" has progressed beyond just Christianity and contains other elements besides religion, such as numerous societies and cultures and languages, whereas "Islam" is reducible to one (primitive) religion, never mind the myriad cultures, languages, races, and societies within it.[30] The imprecise and generalizing language exacerbates the difficulty of untangling the amalgam of religion and culture when it comes to Islam.

Contributing to the tangle is the fact that although many journalists report what they see, they do not always distinguish whether what they're seeing is cultural or religious. Further, most do not bother to unearth the reasons *behind* what they see. When we see the *hijab* and assume it means "oppression," we do not always look past the head scarf to see what kind of a woman is behind it and why exactly she wears it.

But it is not just Islamic culture and religion that gets confused. The other big myth in the making is the idea that Jews and Muslims have always been deep, perhaps even genetic, enemies. This is a projection of twentieth-century ideas relating to the Israel-Palestine conflict onto past centuries in perpetuity. And this conception festers on both sides, with each blaming the other: Muslims are growing up forgetting all the instances in which Muslims and Jews have not been enemies, and most Western people seem to have never known it at all.

It *is* a myth. Muslim Spain is just one example of how Jews and Muslims (and Christians, as well) lived in a multicultural, multireligious society for 800 years until the Spanish Inquisition, during which fifty thousand Spanish Jews and more Muslims fled to Istanbul and settled in the Ottoman Empire. During the Nazi occupation during the second World War, the citizens of Albania (a country of 70 percent Muslims) refused to give up any of their Jewish citizens to the Germans.[31] Because their Muslim and Christian neighbors sheltered them, all but five Albanian Jews survived the Nazi occupation of Albania.[32] Morocco still houses a Jewish community because the Moroccan king refused to hand the Jews over to the Nazis during the second World War. In 1992, Jews and Muslim Sarajevans together struggled to save the National Library from destruction by the Serbs because in it was housed "graphic and palpable evidence of 500 years of interreligious life in Bosnia."[33]

When Caliph Umar conquered Jerusalem in 638, the Muslims left Christians free to practice Christianity and visit the holy places.[34] The

Jews, who had been banished from the city by the former Christian rulers, were invited back and allowed to worship as they wished.[35] Jews lived with Muslims and Christians for over four centuries in Jerusalem, until the Crusades in 1099. Consider this letter, quoted by Sheila Blair and Jonathan Bloom, written by an elderly Jewish pilgrim to Jerusalem:

> Now all of us had anticipated that our sultan—may God bestow glory upon his victories—would set out against the Franks [the Crusaders] with his troops and chase them away. But time after time our hope failed. Yet to this very present moment we do hope that God will give the sultan's enemies into his hands.[36]

And though the Israel-Palestine conflict continues, many Jews and Palestinians are working toward peace.

So defy the myth-makers. Read a history book from the Suggested Reading List in the back and know that a "clash of civilizations" is not inevitable.

The Language Barrier

Language seems like such a paltry barrier in our slick new world of global communications. But it is a basic difficulty that can cause wars. We lack the universal translators, unfortunately, that the *Star Trek* crew had.

I remember the case of the Egyptian Air Flight 990 in October of 1999. The plane crashed on its way to Egypt, and all 200 passengers and crew were killed. This was tragic enough. But adding to the tragedy was the reaction of the media and some government officials who fastened onto a phrase the co-pilot uttered before the plane crashed, concluding that the crash was a result of a suicide. The equivalent of a suicide bombing, in other words. The phrase responsible for all the confusion was "*Tawakkalto ala Allah,*" which means, "I put myself in God's hands."

Now, this is a phrase I have heard all my life. My father says it when he has done all he can possibly do and it is time to leave the rest to God. He says it in varying situations, whether he is preparing a paper to present or planting a risky tree that may not survive in his garden. He says other Arabic (and English) phrases, as well, such as "God go with you" or "God bless you" or "God keep you well" or "Thank God." None of these indicate impending suicide. They mean, generally, "I trust in God." In God we trust.

Egyptians and Muslims in general found it frankly insulting that a phrase as common as "God bless you" generated disproportionate, headlong media speculation about a possible suicide crash and talk of a potential FBI investigation. Because of a commonplace utterance and despite ignorance of language and culture, the media and certain government officials energetically leapt to the conclusion that it was that mad Muslim "terrorist mentality" operating again.

I am continually reminded by even everyday circumstances to never underestimate the language barrier. In chapter four, I sketched some of the differences between Arabic and English. The flowery, metaphorical nature of Arabic is very different from the style of English. When someone brings you coffee, you must respond by saying, "May God bless your hands." An Arab will greet another by saying, "Peace be upon you." The response will be, "Upon *you* be peace." Throughout the Arab world, people of different religions say, "*Insha Allah*," or "God willing." Thus, during the first Gulf War, it was apparent to anyone fluent in English and Arabic that at least some of the frustration and misunderstandings between America and Middle Eastern countries came from the linguistic unfamiliarity on both sides. To take literally a sentence expanded with hyperbole is a dangerous enterprise.

The first days of the Iran hostage crisis constituted a prime example, too. Some 300 journalists rushed to Tehran, though none spoke Persian.[37] Not understanding the language, they did not receive or portray an accurate picture of what was happening, much less the reasons and motivations and historical conflicts behind it. As for the misperceptions the *Iranians* might have nursed about Americans, well, those cultural bridges are hard enough to navigate when both parties are speaking the same language.

Even now, many of the journalists who cover the Middle East do not speak any Middle Eastern language. A journalist covering France or Italy could hardly be well-regarded if she had no knowledge of French or Italian.

If we can never conceptualize Muslims in other countries as real people or hear their own stories in their own languages, we may never care about them. Until we become more familiar with the cultures and languages of the people we are purporting to describe, we are doomed to make avoidable mistakes.

The Historical Roots of Division

In addition to media distortion, cultural misunderstandings, and the language barrier, historical misconceptions still rooted in modern society are possibly the most powerful obstacle to American understanding of Islam. Virginia Mackey writes:

> [I]t is extremely difficult for many reasons for Western minds to understand Islamic tradition and culture. One of the major reasons is that historic rivalry between Christianity and Islam has prejudiced Western sources on religion and law. There are few of them and they frequently are contradictory. Hence this is an area in which there is a critical need for extensive interfaith dialog.[38]

Much of the bewilderment, confusion, hostility, and ignorance regarding Islam in the present has its roots in the centuries-old historical perception of Islam by the West, specifically Christian Europe. The Christian Europeans of the Middle Ages, not understanding the religion of Islam and astounded by its spread, invented a mass of material to vilify and flatten it.

The fearful Western notions of Islam that pervaded scholarship, as well as popular perception in medieval Europe (via both the propaganda leading up to the Crusades and popular tales and songs[39]), are understandable and even deserving of some sympathy. Both Christianity and Islam claimed to be the sole *correct* message of God, and one could not believe the other in every detail without committing apostasy.

The Christian West had a great deal of incentive to invent an entire mythology about Islam, more incentive than the Muslims had to invent misconceptions about Christianity, for several reasons. First, medieval Christians had more to lose by accepting the legitimacy of Islam—namely, an entire worldview, as well as Christian rule. Islam is the only world religion that has ever "threatened the political and religious ascendancy of Christianity."[40] In contrast, the Muslims were newcomers on the scene and did not have as much to lose in being on friendly terms with Christianity. In fact, Muhammad was related by marriage to Christians and had been counting on Christian support.

Second, it was not easy for Muslims to revile Christianity. Although the Christians vilified Muhammad because he was a threat to their religion, Muslims could not reply in kind, because they respected Jesus as one of their own prophets. While Christians considered Islam a false religion, Muslims considered Christianity to be part of their *own* religion, and they believed in most of it. This second reason, incidentally, figured in the 2006 protests against the Danish publisher of cartoons reviling the Prophet Muhammad. Muslims could not retaliate with, for example, vicious cartoons about Jesus, because Jesus is one of Islam's own prophets. This does not justify violence, of course.

Third, information about Christianity had been around for 600 years already. The Muslims knew what it was. The Qur'an told them to respect it and to respect Christians as "People of the Book" or "Followers of an Earlier Revelation." But to the Christian Europeans, Islam was a strange new movement.

The geographical and language barriers were not easily overcome in the tenth century. They still loom over us today. Christian Europeans had little idea of what Muhammad actually preached; the popular and scholarly tall tales surrounding Muhammad and Islam in the West grew to ludicrous proportions. Because of this initial hostility, Christian Western perception of Islam was never clear.

A friend with whom I discussed the subject of this chapter challenged me: "Yes, but what kind of sources are you using to get this information? *Eastern* sources, right?"

Assuming that I interpret "Eastern" correctly, let me say that I have used nearly all "non-Eastern," non-Muslim scholarly sources in this chapter, as in much of the book. I feel forced to make this point because implicit in my friend's question were several presumptions:

- Eastern sources are biased toward Islam, whereas Western sources are impartial (and not biased against Islam);

- Eastern sources are not legitimate, whereas Western sources are;

- Muslims are never qualified to speak impartially about their own religion; and

- Therefore, I am wrong when I assert that misconceptions and mythology are ingrained into Western perceptions and literature regarding Islam.

Whether in journalism or casual conversations, this "condemnation by association" attitude occurs frequently when it comes to Islam. Books are dismissed as biased toward Islam if they are written by Muslims or even non-Muslims who are viewed as not critical enough of Islam. This may not seem too ridiculous until we reach the logical conclusion that therefore no one should be allowed to write about their own religion.

V.S. Naipaul is "Eastern" and characterizes Fazlur Rahman, a brilliant, moderate Muslim scholar and lately a professor at the University of Chicago, as a rabid fundamentalist who came to the United States for missionary work and who asserted that the position of women should be the same as it was in the Prophet's time.[41] I was shocked at this characterization. Anyone at all familiar with Rahman's work could not possibly believe that Naipaul referred to the same man.

Fazlur Rahman, a respected academician and professor, advocated *modernization* of Islam. He launched an intellectual assault on conservatives and fundamentalists in Pakistan. He advocated modernization of the Islamic education system. He approached the study of Islam academically and without blind assumption of the veracity of tradition. In fact, he was expelled from Pakistan because he denounced the fundamentalists' conservative views on women and their blindly following the classical Islamic jurists.

Yet, each time a Muslim is branded, however defamatorily, as rabid and radical and fundamentalist because of the sole fact that he or she is Muslim, we take one more step in widening that divide between East and West, between Islam and non-Islam. A new obstacle is forged, a new brick is laid. We are building new walls between "Islam" and "the West."

Objective study of Islam in this country, and even in Europe, did not really exist until the twentieth century, when scholars began examining original historical documents instead of basing their studies on the old Western predecessor sources. It is a relatively new field. The old mythology is just now being questioned.

Besides, history abounds with examples of all kinds of people inventing nasty tales about their perceived enemies. It is simply human nature. In order to defend their ideology against this new threat to their worldview, and in accordance with the worldwide practice of defaming one's enemy, non-Muslims in the West set about inventing an entire mythology—comprising at times totally incorrect, virulent, and fantastical tales—surrounding Islam and its prophet and its teachings.

Much of medieval Western polemic focused on Muhammad, the Prophet of Islam. He was accused variously of being a false priest, an idol-worshipper, an eater of pork, licentious, the anti-Christ, the devil, an evil spirit or false god (the word used for Muhammad in English was *Mahounde*), a lecher, an epileptic (still insisted upon by some academics, despite Muhammad's lack of symptoms),[42] and an exiled Catholic Cardinal who had fled to establish a church of his own when he could not become the Pope.[43] Often, these alleged attributes were totally antithetical to Islamic beliefs.

Sometimes these distortions were based upon fact: Christians in the West beheld Muhammad's plurality of wives with morbid fascination, even though polygyny was practiced by many people at the time, including

236 THE MUSLIM NEXT DOOR

Jews. Divorce was actually allowed in Islam, whereas it was not allowed in Christianity; that meant women could remarry in Islam, whereas in Christianity a second husband would have been considered an adulterous affair. [44]

What is surprising and troublesome is that over the centuries, this Western mythological body of misinformation regarding Islam *grew*. It did not grow because more information was added to it. Rather, it grew because new scholars over the centuries continued to repeat and elaborate upon the same polemical arguments with very few additions. New tall tales were built on the old tall tales.

As the centuries passed and the world grew smaller, Europe was decreasingly entitled to excuses for its misguided beliefs. Norman Daniel examines the body of Western mythology concerning Islam, tracing the constructing of the image, and finds the same distortions recurring century after century. He states:

> The themes of hostile medieval misinterpretation of Islam were constantly reiterated with the total assurance with which one would teach the alphabet or multiplication tables, and by major writers using old information, often without direct reference to such sources as were available. If they did look at them, they did so through the eyes of their predecessors…[45]

Even for the first few hundred years after the birth of Islam we can allow for fear and a threatened worldview to account for the total misconceptions pervading Western scholarship. But what is the excuse for the continuing and growing mass of misconceptions after that?

Perhaps, for some, it was shock value. In the mid-1700s, Voltaire used the old medieval legends about Islam in his writings and invented others when the originals were not shocking enough, accusing Muhammad of bloody, gory, monstrous crimes. Actually, as much as anything else, Voltaire seems to have been repulsed by Muhammad's having been a *merchant of camels* and not even at least a proper prince of some sort.[46]

Travelers to Muslim countries "preferred the ideas that they had brought with them to what they might observe."[47] Even faced with reality, Europeans preferred to believe the myths. The really frightening thing is that too often people *still* prefer to believe the myths:

> [E]ven when we read the most detached of scholars, we need to keep in mind how medieval Christendom argued, because it has always

been and still is part of the make-up of every Western mind brought
to bear upon the subject.[48]

And so they are still there, even today, the roots of those misconceptions
and distortions that started flowering more than a thousand years ago.
Western media today teems with nonsensical misstatements about Islam
that are disquietingly similar to the polemical spirit of a thousand years
ago, such as: Christianity contains the concept of forgiveness but Islam
does not; Muhammad was a violent man; Muslim women are third-class
citizens; Islam sanctions all forms of violence; Islam was supposed to be
spread by the sword; and (updated polemic for our computer age) husbands
can divorce their wives by email messages reading "I divorce you."[49]

One would think that at least scholars would know better. But even
well into the twentieth century scholars were referring to Islam as "Mohammedanism." Academics today make unsubstantiated generalizations
about, among other things, "the Muslim mind" as if it were a single, solid,
tangible object. I find this particularly revolting—my mind, thank you, has
nothing to do with Osama bin Laden's mind. John Esposito writes:

> These stereotypes of a static, irrational, retrogressive, antimodern
> religious tradition were to be perpetuated by scholars and develop-
> ment theory in the twentieth century.[50]

As Edward Said pointed out, the West came up with a self-sufficient,
internal view and definition of Islam that was never corrected and has
still not been corrected.[51] The medieval European concept of Islam was
like an enclosed space of misconceptions without any doorways leading
out or leading in; the wall expanded to house more misconceptions but
never opened.[52] So the West, having assembled these nonsensical views of
Islam, not only clung to them over the centuries but detailed them and
expanded them without adding to them any new information.

Amazingly enough, resistance against admitting new information on
Islam is still strong. Instead of trying to learn more about Muslims and
the Middle East, I find the opposite is happening in the United States,
to the point where even academic freedom is assaulted. I was stunned
when I learned that the religious right sued the University of North
Carolina in 2002 for assigning a book about the Qur'an (never mind
that countless universities require their college students to read the
Bible). The case was dismissed at both the trial court and the appeals
court levels.

But that is not all. Some right-wing critics have demanded that Middle East studies programs in universities be precluded from receiving federal funding—presumably because they are committing the reprehensible crime of teaching Americans about various aspects of the Middle East.[53] Daniel Pipes constructed a website containing "dossiers" of academicians who have shown sympathy toward the Palestinians or Islam and urging college students to report other "sympathizers." This was an unveiled attempt to stifle free debate on Middle Eastern issues and prevent the exchange of ideas. It pressured young untenured professors, who could thus be lambasted until their universities considered them too much trouble and dispensed with their careers, and it pressured academic experts to teach only a narrow, one-sided view of the world.

This attitude of "not seeing" even with the facts before us is nothing new. The medieval and subsequent Western historical attitude toward Islam was the same:

> It was with very great reluctance that what Muslims *said* Muslims believed was accepted as what they *did* believe. There was a Christian picture in which the details (even under the pressure of facts) were abandoned as little as possible, and in which the general outline was never abandoned.[54]

Whether a thousand years ago or today, the attitude remains the same. Muslims insist that Islam is a religion of tolerance (just look at history as proof), that bin Laden and his ilk are a very miniscule minority (just look at the numbers as proof), and that Islam does not condone terrorism (just look at Islamic law as proof). Nevertheless, the picture of Muslims is remarkably the same as it was in the Middle Ages.

We need not look far for examples. In 2006, the Pope remarked: "He said, and I quote, 'Show me just what Mohammed brought that was new, and there you will find things only evil and inhuman, such as his command to spread by the sword the faith he preached.'"[55]

For the Pope to disingenuously claim he was only citing a quotation is to hide behind semantics. The original medieval quotation was slanderous. So why spread lies? Why, indeed, perpetuate and promulgate the ignorant and bigoted arguments of medieval Christendom? And yet, when Muslims reacted angrily to the Pope's words, their legitimate reaction was portrayed by the media as irrational and overblown.

Instead, it is common for scholars as well as lay persons to simply ignore history and the facts of world culture. Muslims have been portrayed as "incapable of learning" and Islam as "incompatible with science."[56] Lord Cromer pronounced in the late nineteenth century, "Accuracy is abhorrent to the Oriental mind."[57] Daniel Pipes, who typically vilifies Muslims, has called for entire Muslim populations (whom he calls "fundamentalists") to be treated as "barbarians," and as "potential killers," stating that "[m]any of them are peaceable in appearance, but they all must be considered potential killers....however non-violently they might conduct their own lives, the fact that they back a barbaric force means they too are barbarians and must be treated as such."[58]

Europeans like Lord Cromer did come into contact with Islamic societies, but because they came as adversaries or potential colonizers, much of European scholarship retained the medieval prejudices. In fact, the Europeans added more of their own prejudices in order to justify ruling another society. For example, when local Muslim populations rose up against their European colonizers, this was considered further proof that "Muslims were violent."

Americans generally never came into direct contact with Islamic societies and cultures before World War II. Islam was only discussed in America after WWII and in the context of some political crisis or another, *not* as a study of one of the world's largest religions.[59] Islam became relevant to America only because of issues like the Iranian revolution, the Soviet invasion of Muslim Afghanistan, oil interests, terrorism, the Gulf Wars, and the September 11th attacks.

Moreover, the study of Islam even in the twentieth century was not encouraged by American universities and lacked American scholars in the field. Those Americans and Europeans who did study pre-eighteenth-century Islam were studying a kind of static "classical" Islam that never changed and that had little to do with the modern reality. Those studying modern Islam in America after the second World War were doing so in the context of government policy: which countries were stable and our allies? If they were stable, they were ignored. One consequence was that upheavals that had been fomenting for years because of economic problems, social discontent, social dislocations, poverty, corruption, and post-colonization came as a complete shock. The Lebanese civil war and the Iranian revolution are cases in point.[60] The other consequence: American focus remained only on the violence and political crises involving Muslims.

Finally, very few experts writing about Islam knew the language, so they were endlessly writing about the same things that had been written before, in their own languages. And that is why the prejudices and medieval stereotyping are still an ingrained part of popular and scholarly culture. The result is that "academic experts on Islam in the West today ... never (or almost never) [know] about the whole civilization of Islam—literature, law, politics, history, sociology, and so on."[61]

I was talking to my father about this chapter as I was researching it. He was a mathematics professor for four decades and taught everything from the history of mathematics to number theory. I told him about the fascinating endurance of a mythology that could flourish for over a millennium, even in scholarship, even despite our so-called modernity. My father listened with great interest and then said, "Oh, but it is the same in other fields, too, even those unrelated to religion."

For example, he said, the current textbooks on the history of mathematics sometimes leap from discussing the ancient Greeks to the Renaissance Europeans. This jump of some 2,000 years completely ignores Islamic civilization, Indian civilization, and Chinese civilization—to mention a few. By reading such textbooks, we could logically conclude that modern mathematics began with the Europeans in the sixteenth century. Perhaps that is why I have so often heard the question, "Why have Muslims always been backward?"

Yet, scholarship and culture in the Islamic Empire, which lasted a thousand years, flowered because every Muslim has an obligation to seek knowledge. Secular knowledge does not conflict with holy knowledge in Islam, but is a way to it. The eighth- and ninth-century Arabs in the Islamic Empire established centers of learning in the Middle East and gathered knowledge from everywhere else in the world, translating it into Arabic and developing their own scholarly breakthroughs. When Europe stagnated in the Middle Ages, Baghdad, "City of Peace," the capital of modern-day Iraq and the seat of the Islamic Empire, was the cultural and scholarly center of the civilized world.

The Islamic Empire's contributions to the world of science were so profound that Arabic terms like *algorithm, cipher, zenith,* and *algebra* still linger in scientific language.[62] Had the Arabs not gathered, translated, recorded, and preserved knowledge with such enthusiasm, the works of ancient Greeks such as Aristotle and Pythagoras (whose famous theorem every unsuspecting ninth grader encounters) may never have survived.

The concept of *zero,* called *sifr* in Arabic, came to medieval Europe from the Arabs.[63] It confused the Europeans, who did not have the concept of zero and pronounced *sifr* "cipher." The result of this confusion was that a common saying arose: "Oh, he's saying something totally incomprehensible and abstract, like a *cipher*."[64] Cipher was the European pronunciation of *sifr*, and cipher in turn came to mean a baffling message, a coded communication not easily understood.[65]

In fact, it was the Arab Muslims who invented cryptanalysis, the science of code-breaking, or unscrambling secret messages. Before the Arabs, no one had come up with a method for this. Relatively simple ciphers had remained unbroken for centuries.[66]

But in the ninth century, Arabs began to analyze *hadith*, or quotations of the Prophet Muhammad. They needed to authenticate each of the Prophet's quotations to determine its validity. Therefore, they analyzed the language of each quotation to date it and prove whether or not it could be attributable to the Prophet.[67] This sort of linguistic analysis, coupled with the Arabs' knowledge of mathematics and statistics, all led to the invention of cryptanalysis.

The first known available treatise on cryptanalysis was written by the Arab philosopher al-Kindi and is entitled, *A Manuscript on Deciphering Cryptographic Messages*.[68] This book dates from the ninth century and was only found and published in the 1980s. It refers to another Arab treatise on the subject dated a century earlier, but that manuscript has not been found.[69] Simon Singh writes,

> Cryptanalysis could not be invented until a civilization had reached a sufficiently sophisticated level of scholarship in several disciplines, including mathematics, statistics, and linguistics. The Muslim civilization provided an ideal cradle for cryptanalysis, because Islam demands justice in all spheres of human activity, and achieving this requires knowledge, or *ilm*.[70]

The pursuit of this knowledge resulted in the establishment of libraries, bookshops, and centers of translation and research. In the early 800s, the ruling caliph established a research institute in Baghdad called the "*Bait al-Hikmah*," or the "House of Wisdom."

The Muslims gathered texts in Chinese, Armenian, Hebrew, Greek, Latin, Persian, Coptic, Syriac, and Sanskrit and translated them into Arabic. One of the stories of how exactly they gathered these texts startled me into laughter when I read it:

> So much emphasis did the Arabs place on acquiring other cultures' knowledge that Greek manuscripts were obtained from the Byzantine Empire through peace treaties in return for maintaining the status quo.[71]

In other words, the Arabs said to the Romans, "Okay, here's the deal: we won't take over your country if you give us all your books."

They got the books. The Arabs had centers for copying texts—they had learned the art of making paper from the Chinese—and published tens of thousands of books a year.[72] At a time when books were rare and precious in other parts of the world, streets in Baghdad were lined with hundreds of bookshops. By some accounts, the tenth-century ruler of Cordoba, in Muslim Spain, possessed more books in his library—about 400,000 volumes—than those in all the other libraries of Europe combined.[73]

Among the subjects studied in the ninth-century Islamic Empire were philosophy, astronomy, mathematics, linguistics, physics, chemistry, and medicine. Vast amounts of knowledge may have been lost forever had it not been for the scholarly zeal and the pursuit of knowledge by the rulers, who engaged not only the best Muslim scholars but the best non-Muslim ones, too.

The Arabs expounded on the knowledge they gathered and produced some of the world's greatest philosophers and scientists at a time when Europe was illiterate and unlearned. For instance, Muslim mathematicians developed algebra in the ninth century. The Arabs are responsible for the widespread use of Arabic numerals today. Arab physicians first realized in the twelfth century that blood circulated throughout the body, and their medical texts were used for hundreds of years. They developed the science of optics and made ophthalmological advances such as the removal of cataracts.

The arts flourished, as well; Arab artists fashioned and collected ceramics, paintings, and some of the most intricate textiles in history. The words *alkali, saffron, taffeta, damask,* and *organdy* come from Arabic.[74] Because Islamic textiles were prized above any others in the world, they often shrouded the bones of Christian saints.

Papers are only now being published showing that many mathematical results had been established centuries before Western scholarship took credit for them. The first writings in statistics appeared in Arabic some 800 years before Pascal and Fermat.[75] The Arabs used combinatorics 1,200 years ago.[76]

To my husband's brother-in-law, a philosophy professor, the news that the philosophical treatises of the ancient Greeks, including Aristotle, would have been lost but for the Arabs' preserving and translating them was *huge.* (His words.) Surprisingly enough, this is not common knowledge, even in scholarship. The treatises of Arab philosophers like Ibn Sina (Avicenna) and Ibn Rushd (Averroes) who expounded on Greek philosophy and developed their own seem to be relatively unknown in the West.

Why are we only now discovering gaps in scholarship? The original manuscripts were sometimes lost or archived on some dusty shelf in ancient vaults or made inaccessible by political problems. Sometimes, mathematical results were named after the Europeans who presented them, without credit given to the non-European people who had first discovered them.[77] And sometimes the language problem was so extreme that Europeans, lacking knowledge of Arabic, simply did not understand the extent of Arabic scholarship.

It is only recently that Western scholarship has begun to fully realize the contributions of Islam and the East in general to the world of knowledge. Without this realization, it is easy to think of Islam as backward and ignorant, and that completely colors understanding:

> The academic experts whose specialty is Islam have generally treated the religion and its various cultures within an invented or culturally determined ideological framework filled with passion, defensive prejudice, sometimes even revulsion; because of this framework, *understanding* of Islam has been a very difficult thing to achieve.[78]

In other words, those medieval distortions that formed the basis for the whole Western mythology surrounding Islam have always prevented those living in the West from understanding Islam. And until we move away from that framework, we will continue to prevent understanding. Unfortunately, given media domination, we seem to be burrowing further *into* that historical framework rather than discarding it.

As for misconceptions surviving in our present-day common wisdom regarding Islam, my history teacher's remark about Islam being spread by the sword and by force is a perfect example of the thriving health of the medieval picture. The rapid spread of such a "false religion" staggered the medieval West. Obviously, Islam must have spread by force, because who would convert to it otherwise? Islam's use of armed struggle was condemned, while the wars of the Crusades were justified because they "restored" Christianity and defended the love of God.

Take another modern-day example of the old mythology. In chapter six, we discussed *The Satanic Verses*, as well as the savagery of Khomeini's unfounded death sentence on Rushdie. The death sentence was, beyond doubt, unjustified. Iran was the only country (Islamic or otherwise) that accepted it.

But what I found interesting was that *The Satanic Verses* simply reworks into a modern novel the same medieval, polemical accusations of the West against Islam. Rushdie even resorts to some of the old name-calling, using terms such as "Mahounde" instead of Muhammad. *The Satanic Verses* exemplifies the centuries-old polemic that has not yet been put to rest and which was resurrected, this time, by someone with a Muslim, Asian background.

After September 11th, I read an article in which the journalist compared holy war in Islam and holy war in Christianity. He made Islam to be much more militant and at the same time more religiously driven than Christianity, though the rules of war in both Islam and Christianity were virtually the same.[79] For example, he referred to Muhammad as a military commander and asserted that the Crusaders did not quote the Bible, even though they wore crosses. He neglected to mention that Muhammad was a merchant by profession, not a military commander (except sometimes by necessity); that most Crusaders were illiterate; that the Pope initiated the Crusades; that Muhammad was no more a warrior than the Pope was; and that Christians who died fighting Muslims were considered martyrs who went straight to heaven.[80]

We need only listen to the media or read books (from textbooks to modern fiction) or watch movies and the same stereotypes leap out to be caught by those of us who recognize them. From *Back to the Future* to *True Lies* to *Delta Force*, movies have portrayed Muslims and people from the Middle East as violent. Professor Jack Shaheen identifies over 900 films in the twentieth century that vilify Arab Muslims (Arab Christians are never portrayed). He attributes this to greed (because Arab-bashing sells well at the box office) and sometimes to a purposeful attempt to influence policy in the Middle East.[81] Because the U.S. exports these films, it is global culture—not just American culture—that receives the repeated images of Arabs as nothing more than violent terrorist thugs. Repetition is an effective way of teaching, and filmmakers are teaching their viewers to hate an entire culture of people.

What scares me most, as an American Muslim, is that so many images in the mass media perpetuate the centuries-old misconceptions with a sort of sensationalist, complacent satisfaction that allows no reception of any other view. When the causes of animosity toward the West remain unexamined and are dismissed as irrelevant and when racial and religious hatred becomes socially acceptable, what is before us but the same tightly walled, doorless, and windowless circle of misconceptions that has been securely in place for a millennium?

The idea that medieval myths could stay in place for over a thousand years, despite global communications and education, was unpleasantly epiphanous for me. To be fair, people in Muslim countries also harbor misconceptions about America and Europe. Muslims in the Middle East have been conditioned to have certain views of Israel and Jews in the same way that Americans have been conditioned to have certain views of Islam. Writing from within Western culture, I hear educated, reasonable people on both sides voice ridiculously malignant statements about the other, and it is agonizing to me that neither side sees that both sides are right inasmuch as both sides are ridiculous. Consider this statement, written years before September 11, 2001, but with echoes of premonition:

> If the history of knowledge about Islam in the West has been too closely tied to conquest and domination, the time has come for these ties to be severed completely....otherwise we will not only face protracted tension and perhaps even war, but we will offer the Muslim world, its various societies and states, the prospect of many wars, unimaginable suffering, and disastrous upheavals, not least of which would be the victory of an "Islam" fully ready to play the role prepared for it by reaction, orthodoxy, and desperation.[82]

As our "war on terrorism" and current war on Iraq (which had nothing to do with terrorism) continues, I cannot help thinking that this prophecy has already begun to be fulfilled.

Conclusion

After the September 11th attacks, I was hopeful that non-Muslims in Western countries would be more genuinely interested in learning about Islam. I hoped that the historical framework could be unzipped like a body bag and crumpled into a drawer and that sincere dialogues could finally be established. When I heard a few voices in the media analyzing the causes of September 11th and demanding a reexamination of U.S. foreign policy, I hoped that, especially with new global communications, we would finally be stepping toward a sincere effort to understand one another.

Instead, new global communications have given us ready access to vent our prejudices; we have proximity without understanding. Whereas hatefulness and hostility used to require some effort to disseminate, they now require no effort at all.

Instead of encountering a desire to understand Islam, I encounter best-selling books with titles like *Why I am Not a Muslim* and *President G. W. Bush Is a Moron: Islam Is Not Peace.* This attitude, to me, is less excusable than the medieval polemical tall tales, because today it is much easier to ascertain the truth than it was in the Middle Ages. Throughout the media I hear voices taking refuge in the prejudicial presumptions and learning only what can be used to support those presumptions. The likes of Daniel Pipes, Robert Spencer, and Stephen Emerson grope for every scare tactic available to frighten people and convince them of the evil of Islam and all Muslims, whereas if the very same generalizations they use about Islam were to be directed at anyone else, the result would be resounding cries of "bigotry!" or "Anti-Semitism!"

Indeed, Carl W. Ernst, Professor of Religious Studies at the University of North Carolina, remarked, "This [lawsuit against UNC and accompanying prejudice] is part of a long history of anti-Islamic bias that is akin to anti-Semitism or even racism."[83] Any effort to get past that historical prejudice is resisted. Were we to see the truth, we would no longer have a convenient enemy. It is much easier to entertain lazy, one-dimensional delusions of a monolithic and terrorizing Islam on which to blame the entirety of life's problems than to sift through the complicated picture that Islam presents.

I have two Christian friends who tell me they are afraid to say anything positive about Islam because of the angry reactions such simple statements ignite in their acquaintances. Any suggestion of an actual reason for animosity toward the United States (besides jealousy), they tell me, is seen as unpatriotic and exculpatory of the September 11th hijackers. Another friend informed me disgustedly that for several months after the September 11th attacks, her pastor urged his congregation to convert all Muslims, citing the Dallas Mosque as the source of (almost) all evil. I cannot see much difference between the medieval perception and much of modern public perception of Islam.

If we add media stereotyping to all this negative medieval mythology about Islam, the result is a picture that resists erasure. Add also the confusion about what is religious, as opposed to cultural or socioeconomic. Add the tangible language barriers. Add the extremists who use Islam to commit horrifying crimes. The sum total is an impregnable misunderstanding of Islam and Muslims. And that means not just a profound misunderstanding of Muslims in the "East," *out there*, but also Muslims in the United States and Europe.

The propaganda, the rhetoric, the history, and the media can all be powerful enough to lead to violence. Socially acceptable defamation in the media can lead to self-glorification, persecution of others, and sometimes genocide. Perhaps that is why the Prophet said, "The true Muslim does not defame or insult others."

I included this chapter because, without discussing how the common perception of Islam is so removed from *my* Islam, it was impossible to answer the question, "Why do you live inside your religion?" Throughout this book, I have tried to present the Islam which I and millions of Muslims cherish. Throughout this book, I have tried to answer my friend's question in the hope that this may be a sort of antidote to the spiraling religious hatred against Islam in my country.

I live inside my religion because it is sensible, simple, and it teaches good things like forgiveness, generosity, tolerance, and compassion. I live in America because I believe it can be a nation of many faiths. As people of all religions have urged, it is time for genuine understanding and dialogue, not media hysteria and anti-Islamic racism. If we can separate the daily distortions from the reality, perhaps we can break out of that medieval framework of domination and hostility. Instead of propelling ourselves inexorably toward a "clash of civilizations," perhaps we can avoid a "clash of ignorances."

Questions for Discussion

1. What is religion? What is the purpose of religion? What is the difference between religious doctrine and what religionists do in practice?

2. What is culture? How is it intertwined with religion? Is it so intertwined in the United States? Why or why not?

3. What was your perception of Islam before reading this book and has it been transformed or confirmed after reading *The Muslim Next Door*? In what ways, if any, has it transformed?

4. What information or argument or perspective in the book did you find especially surprising or compelling?

5. Did this book inspire you to read more about the history of Islam and Muslims? Is there anything you learned about this history that you wish to investigate further?

6. Samuel Huntingdon and others insist that a "clash of civilizations" is inevitable. What do you think?

7. Do you adhere to a religion that has a religious text? If so, how old is that text? Do you know what every word means? Would you take every word literally? If not, why not?

8. The author claims that we in the United States grow up with the white, Western viewpoint. Do you agree? Give examples supporting your view.

9. Why does the Muslim head covering provoke such reflexive reactions in many non-Muslims? Is it different from nuns' habits? Jewish orthodox head coverings? What are the issues involved in religious dress?

10. What are the parameters of dress and modesty in our own world, religious or non-religious?

11. Are the words "objective," "apologist," and "biased," appropriate to a discussion of religion? How are they used in the public discourse? Is there an objective view or only different points of view?

12. Can you think of aspects of your own traditions or cultures or religions that could be misunderstood or that other people could point to in a negative light?

Chronology

ca. 570: Muhammad, the Prophet of Islam, is born in Mecca in what is now Saudi Arabia.

595: Muhammad marries Khadija.

608: The Ka'ba is rebuilt. Muhammad is chosen to put the Black Stone in its rightful place. This occurs before Muhammad's prophethood. The story is an important one for Muslims as it reveals signs of Muhammad's special destiny even before his first revelation. As mentioned in chapter one, Muslims believe God gave the Black Stone to Adam when he was expelled from heaven.

610: Muhammad has his first revelation in the Cave of Hira during the month of Ramadan.

615: A group of Muslims escapes Meccan persecution by fleeing to Abyssinia (now Ethiopia).

619: Khadija, Muhammad's wife of nearly 25 years, dies. Abu Talib, Muhammad's uncle who never converted to Islam but protected Muhammad from the Meccans, also dies.

622: After Abu Talib's death, Mecca becomes increasingly dangerous for the Prophet and his followers. They escape to Yathrib, later called Medina. This is the first year of the Islamic calendar.

630: The Meccans surrender the city, without bloodshed, to Muhammad and his 10,000 followers. All the idols in the Ka'ba are destroyed.

632: The Prophet Muhammad dies and Abu Bakr is appointed Caliph.

634: Abu Bakr dies and Umar becomes Caliph.

637: Umar conquers Jerusalem from the Roman Byzantines.

644: Umar is assassinated and Uthman becomes Caliph.

650: The Qur'an is compiled into one book.

656: Uthman is assassinated and Ali, later considered the first Shi'i Imam, becomes Caliph. The Prophet's widow, Aysha, revolts against Ali, leading an army against him. She and her followers are defeated.

661: Ali is assassinated and Mu'awiyah becomes Caliph in the beginning of the Umayyad dynasty, which endures nearly one hundred years.

661–750: The Umayyad caliphate.

670: Ali's son, Hasan, dies.

680: (10 Muharram) Ali's son, Husayn, refuses to swear allegiance to Yazid, who has become Caliph after his father, Mu'awiyah, dies.

This date is called *Ashura*. Yazid became Caliph after his father without the usual election, and many were displeased by this. The early Shi'a in Mecca persuaded Husayn to travel to Kufa and assured him of their support. Husayn and some six hundred followers began the journey to Kufa, but were intercepted by Yazid's troops at Kerbala and massacred there. This is a sorrowful event for all Muslims—Husayn was the Prophet's grandson—but particularly for the Shi'a, who feel guilt on behalf of the early Shi'a who neglected to help Husayn. The date of his death, 10 Muharram on the Islamic calendar, is a day of mourning for the Shi'a.

691: The Dome of the Rock and al–Aqsa Mosque are built in Jerusalem.

750: The Abbasid dynasty is founded.

750–1258: The Abbasid caliphate: This is the golden age of Islam, during which Islamic law is developed; knowledge is acquired, translated, and preserved; and arts and culture are encouraged.

762: The Abbasids establish Baghdad as their capital.

765: The sixth Shi'i *Imam* and founder of the Jafari school of Islamic law, Jafar al–Sadiq, dies. There's a dispute over which descendant should succeed him, and this results in the Sevener Shi'a breaking off from the Twelver Shi'a.

830: Caliph al–Ma'mun establishes the *Bayt al–Hikmah*, or "House of Wisdom," in Baghdad.

874: The line of twelve Shi'i *Imams* ends, the twelfth to return one day as the *Mahdi*.

1095: Pope Urban II calls for a crusade against Islam.

1099: Jerusalem falls to the first crusade.

1111: Abu Hamid al–Ghazali dies. He was a theologian, legal scholar, and mystic who brought Sufism solidly within the realm of mainstream Islam.

1187: Salah al–Din (Saladin) reconquers Jerusalem.

1198: Ibn Rushd (Averroes) dies. He was a noted philosopher, theologian, legal scholar, grammarian, physician, and astronomer.

1227: The leader of the Mongols, Jenghiz (Gengis) Khan, dies.

1256: The Mongol dynasty in Persia begins.

1258: Baghdad falls to Mongol invaders. This is the real end of the Abbasid dynasty, and Baghdad never becomes as illustrious a city as before the Mongol invasion. The Mongols were nature–worshipping tribal nomads from Central Asia and were not Muslim. They eventually become Muslim after ruling Muslim populations for a few generations.

1288: Osman Gazi, a regional leader in the western Islamic Empire, begins to expand his territory.

1326: Osman Gazi becomes the first *Osmanli* Sultan. English speakers will call his descendants the Ottomans. The Osmanli (Ottoman) Turks capture Bursa and begin expansion of their rule.

1369: Timur (Tamerlane) captures Khorasan, which is now part of Iran, and Transoxiana, which is now modern-day Uzbekistan, Tajikistan, and southwest Kazakhstan.

1453: The Ottomans capture Constantinople (once called Byzantium, now called Istanbul). The seat of the Eastern Orthodox Church remains there to this day.

1491–1492: Ferdinand and Isabella capture Granada from the Arabs. The Spanish Inquisition ensues, and tens of thousands of Muslims and Jews flee Spain and settle in the Ottoman Empire.

1520: Suleiman the Magnificent rules the Ottoman Empire at its height; the empire encompasses Turkey, Syria, Iraq, Egypt, Cyprus, Tunisia, Algeria, parts of eastern Europe, and western Arabia.

1526: Babur, a descendant of Timur, establishes his capital at Delhi and Agra, founding the Mughal empire in India.

1542: Akbar the Great becomes the Mughal emperor of India, founding the House of Worship, to which he invites people of all religions to gather and discuss their faiths.

1553: Queen Mary I ascends the throne in England.

1609: The remaining Jews and Muslims are expelled from Spain, and Islam is banned in Spain until Franco's rule (1939–1975).

1643: The Taj Mahal is built in India by the Mughal emperor Shah Jahan.

1658–1707: Auranzeb becomes the Mughal emperor, and he introduces Islamic basis for law and government in India.

1722: The Safavid dynasty in Iran ends.

1745: Beginning of Wahhabi movement in Arabian peninsula.

1775: Jane Austen is born in England.

1779: The Qajars begin their rule of Iran, enduring until 1924.

1798: Napoleon occupies Egypt.

1817–1898: Sayyid Ahmad Khan leads the modernist Islamic movement in India.

1830: The French occupy Algeria.

1833: The Greeks attain independence from the Ottoman Empire.

1837: Queen Victoria begins her sixty-four-year reign of the British Empire.

1850: The beginning of the Baha'i religion. The Baha'i were an offshoot of the Babi, who were an offshoot of the Shi'a. They broke off from Islam but are no longer part of it.

1857: The end of the Mughal dynasty in India. As of this date, the British rule India officially, although they have been ruling in practical terms for decades.

1881: The French occupy Tunisia.

1882: The British invade Egypt.

1901: The French invade Morocco.

1918: The end of World War I; the colonial powers divide the Ottoman Empire. Kemal Ataturk manages to save the modern-day state of Turkey as an independent state.

1924: Turkey, with a population of 95 percent Muslims, becomes a secular democracy and transitions the whole country from the Arabic script to the Roman script in six weeks. The caliphate and the *shari'a* court system are abolished. For the first time in over half a millennium, the tie between Turks, Arabs, and Islam is severed.

1925: Reza Pahlavi becomes Shah of Iran.

1932: The kingdom of Saudi Arabia is founded and remains a monarchy to this day.

1947: India is partitioned into India and Pakistan, which in turn has two geographical sections: East Pakistan and West Pakistan, with about a thousand miles of India in between.

1948: The State of Israel is established.

1949: British and Soviets force Reza Shah to abdicate. His son succeeds him and rules for thirty years.

1950: Indonesia gains independence from the Netherlands.

1953: Mossadegh, the popular Iranian prime minister, criticizes the Shah of Iran and advocates nationalizing oil interests. The CIA and British intelligence back a coup that topples the prime minister and his government. The Shah then flees, but the Americans and British restore him to his throne. The Shah is thereafter seen as a Western puppet.

1954: The Muslim Brotherhood is founded in Sudan, advocating an Islamic social and political order.

1956: Tunisia attains independence from the French.

1962: Algeria attains independence from the French.

1971: East Pakistan revolts and becomes the independent country of Bangladesh.

1977: General Zia ul–Haq overthrows Zulfikar Ali Bhutto's government in Pakistan and takes power. He introduces "Islamization," which vaguely means basing state policies on "Islamic values."

1979: Iranian revolution: The Shah is overthrown and Khomeini seizes power. Iran becomes a theocratic democracy.

1980: Hizbullah is founded in Lebanon and Islamic Jihad is founded in Palestine.

1988: Benazir Bhutto is elected prime minister of the Islamic Republic of Pakistan, the first female elected head of state in the Muslim world.

1989: Ayatollah Khomeini dies.

1990–91: The Persian Gulf War.

2001: Al–Qaeda attacks in New York and Washington. U.S. bombing of Afghanistan.

2003: United States invades Iraq.

NOTES

Chapter One—*Everyday Islam*

1. "Women and Islam" in *The Oxford Dictionary of Islam* (Oxford University Press, 2003), ed. John L. Esposito, p. 339. Hereafter, *The Oxford Dictionary of Islam*.

2. Ibid, p. 339.

3. John Alden Williams, *The Word of Islam* (Austin: University of Texas Press, 1994), p. 43. Hereafter, Williams, *The Word of Islam*.

4. Ibid; see also Edward Said, *Orientalism: Western Conceptions of the Orient* (1978; rpt. Penguin, 1991), pp. 68–70. Hereafter, Said, *Orientalism*.

5. Surah 2, verse 185.

6. Surah 2, verse 271.

Chapter Two—*Some Basic Islamic Concepts*

1. Catholic Encyclopedia (www.newadvent.org) entry on "crusades," as of August 26, 2007.

2. Huston Smith, *The World's Religions* (HarperSanFrancisco, 1958), p. 222. Hereafter, Smith, *The World's Religions*.

3. Surah 29, verse 46.

4. Surah 19, verse 21; see also Surah 19, verses 16–21.

5. Surah 4, verse 157.

6. Geoffrey Parrinder, *Jesus in the Qur'an* (Oxford: Oneworld, 1965), pp. 114–115.

7. Surah 3, verse 55.

8. Surah 3, verse 55; Surah 4, verses 155–159.

9. Surah 11, verse 37.

10. Surah 11, verses 38–40.

11. Surah 11, verses 41–48.

12. Surah 28, verses 29–31.

13. Genesis 3:16–18.

14. For a survey of this notion of woman as evil, see Alvin J. Schmidt, *Veiled and Silenced: How Culture Shaped Sexist Theology* (Macon: Mercer University Press, 1989), Chapter 3. Hereafter, Schmidt, *Veiled and Silenced.*

15. John L. Esposito, *Islam: The Straight Path* (Oxford: Oxford University Press, 1988; rpt., 1998), p. 27. Hereafter, Esposito, *Islam.*

16. Surah 2, verse 112.

17. Muhammad Asad, *The Message of the Qur'an* (Gibraltar: Dar al-Andalus, 1980), Appendix III, pp. 994–95. Hereafter, Asad, *The Message of the Qur'an.*

18. Ibid.

19. Ibid., Surah 15, verses 17–24, note 8.

20. Michael Sells, *Approaching the Qur'an: the Early Revelations* (Ashland; White Cloud Press, 1999), p. 42. Hereafter, Sells, *Approaching the Qur'an.*

Chapter Three—*The Story of an Arab, an Angel, and the God of Abraham*

1. G. M. Trevelyan, *English Social History: a Survey of Six Centuries, Chaucer to Queen Victoria* (Longmans, Green, 1942; rpt., Pelican 1974), p. 245. Hereafter, Trevelyan, *English Social History.*

2. Surah 96, verses 1–5.

3. Surah 112.

4. H.A.R. Gibb, *Mohammedanism* (Oxford University Press, 1949; rpt., 1969), p. 30. Hereafter, Gibb, *Mohammedanism.*

5. Esposito, *Islam*, p. 15.

6. Smith, *The World's Religions*, p. 256, quoting Ameer Ali, *The Spirit of Islam*, p. 212.

7. Gibb, *Mohammedanism*, p. 29.

8. Ibid, p. 32.

9. Andrew Rippin, *Muslims: Their Religious Beliefs and Practices (Volume 1: The Formative Period)*, (London; Routledge, 1990), p. 40. Hereafter, Rippin, *Muslims.*

10. Edward Said, *Covering Islam: How the Media and the Experts Determine How We See the Rest of the World* (New York, 1981; Rev. Ed. Vintage, 1997), p. 84. Hereafter, Said, *Covering Islam.*

11. *60 Minutes*, October 6, 2002, CBS News.

12. See, e.g., Khaled Abou El Fadl, "Terrorism is at Odds with Islamic Tradition," in The *Los Angeles Times*, October 11, 2001. Hereafter, Abou El Fadl, "Terrorism is at Odds with Islamic Tradition." See also Rudolph Peters, *Jihad in Classical and Modern Islam* (Princeton: Marcus Weiner Publishers, 1996), p. 1. Hereafter, Peters, *Jihad in Classical and Modern Islam.*

13. Karen Armstrong, *Muhammad: a Western Attempt to Understand Islam* (London: Victor Gollancz Ltd., 1991), p. 25.

Chapter Four—*The Qur'an*

1. See, e.g., Walter Ruby, "Pro-Israel Political Correctness Leads to Harm Jewish Community," in *The New Jersey Jewish News*, July 22, 1999. See also, Pat McDonnell Twair, "Gephardt Drops Only Muslim Panel Appointment Under Pressure From Extreme Zionist Groups," in *The Washington Report on Middle East Affairs*, September 1999, pp. 14–15.

2. Seyyed Hossein Nasr, *Ideals and Realities of Islam* (George Allen & Unwin, 1966), p. 32. Hereafter, Nasr, *Ideals and Realities of Islam.*

3. Mahmoud M. Ayoub, "Qur'an: History of the Text," in *The Oxford Encyclopedia of the Modern Islamic World,* Vol. 3 (Oxford: Oxford University Press, 1995), p. 386. Hereafter, *The Oxford Encyclopedia of the Modern Islamic World.*

4. Vincent J. Cornell, "Qur'an: The Qur'an as Scripture," in *The Oxford Encyclopedia of the Modern Islamic World,* Vol. 3, p. 388.

5. Akbar S. Ahmed, *Islam Today* (London: I.B. Tauris, 1999), p. 29. Hereafter, Ahmed, *Islam Today.*

6. A.J. Arberry, *The Koran Interpreted* (New York: George Allen & Unwin Ltd., 1955; rpt. New York: Touchstone, 1996), Vol. II., p. 12. Hereafter, Arberry, *The Koran Interpreted.*

7. Sells, *Approaching the Qur'an,* p. 184.

8. Arberry, *The Koran Interpreted,* Vol. I, p. 28.

9. Idib, p. 24.

10. Arberry, *The Koran Interpreted,* Vol II, p. 8.

11. Asad, *The Message of the Qur'an,* pp. iv–v.

12. Ibid.

13. Ibid.

14. Ibid, p. vi.

15. Idries Shah, *The Sufis* (New York and London: Doubleday, 1964), p. 441.

16. Thomas Cleary, *The Essential Koran: The Heart of Islam* (HarperCollins, 1994), p. xiii. Hereafter, Cleary, *The Essential Koran.*

17. Ibid.

18. Sells, *Approaching the Qur'an,* p. 202.

19. Ibid.

20. Ibid, p. 186.

21. Ibid.

22. Ibid.

23. Ibid, p. 185

24. Ibid, p. 204

25. Ahmed, *Islam Today,* p. 31.

26. Fazlur Rahman, *Major Themes of the Qur'an* (Minneapolis: Bibliotheca Islamica, 1980; rpt., 1989), p. 1. Hereafter, Rahman, *Major Themes of the Qur'an*.

27. See generally Rahman, *Major Themes of the Qur'an*.

28. Surah 2, verse 255.

29. Surah 6, verse 108.

30. Surah 109.

31. Surah 42, verse 15.

32. Surah 2, verse 191.

33. Surah 2, verse 191.

34. Surah 2, verse 190.

35. Surah 2, verses 192–193.

36. See generally Asad, *The Message of the Qur'an*.

37. See, e.g., Rudolph Peters, "Jihad," in *The Oxford Encyclopedia of the Modern Islamic World*, Vol. 2.

38. Rahman, *Major Themes of the Qur'an*, pp. 18–19.

39. Surah 114.

40. Rahman, *Major Themes of the Qur'an*, p. 91.

41. Surah 1.

42. Khaled Abou El Fadl, "Islam and the Challenge of Democracy," in *Boston Review: a Political and Literary Forum*, April/May 2003. Hereafter, Abou El Fadl, "Islam and the Challenge of Democracy."

43. Andy Rooney, "Why Islam Has a Hold on Muslims," on *60 Minutes*, CBS News, Dec. 16, 2001. http://www.cbsnews.com/stories/2001/12/14/60minutes/rooney/main321447.shtml

Chapter Five—*Who's Who in Islam*

1. Esposito, *Islam*, p. 47.

2. William C. Chittick, "Sufism: Sufi Thought and Practice," in *The Oxford Encyclopedia of the Modern Islamic World*, Vol. 4, pp. 102–3.

3. See Nasr, *Ideals and Realities of Islam*, p. 116.

4. Ibid, pp. 116–117.

5. Ibid, p. 130.

6. Surah 2, verse 115.

7. William C. Chittick, "Sufism: Sufi Thought and Practice," in *The Oxford Encyclopedia of the Modern Islamic World*, Vol. 4, p. 106.

8. Ibid, pp. 106–107.

9. Michael Sells, *Stations of Desire: Love Elegies from Ibn Arabi and New Poems* (Jerusalem: Ibis Editions, 2000; rpt., 2004), pp. 72–73. Hereafter, Sells, *Stations of Desire*.

10. Ibid, p. 109.

11. Frederick Mathewson Denny, *An Introduction to Islam* (New York: Macmillan, 1985; rpt., 1994), p. 355. Hereafter, Denny, *An Introduction to Islam.*

12. Jane I. Smith, *Islam in America* (New York: Columbia University Press, 1999), pp. xiv, 77. Hereafter, Smith, *Islam in America.*

13. Denny, *An Introduction to Islam*, p. 355.

14. Smith, *Islam in America*, p. 78.

15. Clifton E. Marsh, *The Lost-Found Nation of Islam in America* (Maryland: Scarecrow Press, 1996; rpt., 2000), p. 31. Hereafter, Marsh, *The Lost-Found Nation.*

16. Ibid.

17. Ibid.

18. Marsh, *The Lost-Found Nation*, p. 35.

19. Ibid.

20. Ibid.

21. Marsh, *The Lost-Found Nation*, p. 38.

22. Ibid, p. 42.

23. Ibid, p. 39.

24. Ibid, p. 50.

25. Smith, *Islam in America*, pp. 85–86.

26. Marsh, *The Lost-Found Nation*, p. 55.

27. Ibid.

28. Ibid, p. 61.

29. Ibid, pp. 62–63.

30. Ibid, p. 64.

31. Esposito, *Islam*, pp. 209–215.

32. Ibid.

33. Ibid, p. 215.

34. As quoted in Ahmed, *Islam Today*, p. 21.

35. Michael Sells' lecture at Stanford University, "Islam and the West in the Wake of September 11th," May 2, 2002.

36. Cyril Glassé, *The New Encyclopedia of Islam* (Walnut Creek: AltaMira Press, 1989; rev., ed., 2001), p. 471.

Chapter Six—*Religious Hierarchy*

1. *The Economist*, 6-12 October, 2001, p. 16.

2. For various compilations of statements by Muslims condemning the attacks of September 11, 2001, see: Omid Safi, Colgate University, "Scholars of Islam & the Tragedy of Sept. 11th," http://groups.colgate.edu/aarislam/response.

htm; Charles Kurzman, Dept of Sociology, University of North Carolina at Chapel Hill, http://www.unc.edu/~kurzman/terror.htm; Tim Lubin, Washington and Lee University, "Islamic Responses to the Sept. 11 Attack," http://home.wlu.edu/~lubint/islamonWTC.htm; and The Council on American-Islamic Relations, http://www.cair.com/AmericanMuslims/AntiTerrorism/IslamicStatementsAgainstTerrorism.aspx.

3. Khaled Abou El Fadl, "Fatwa on Women Leading Prayer," at http://www.scholarofthehouse.org/.

4. Ibid.

5. Ibid.

6. Amina Wadud, *Inside the Gender Jihad: Women's Reform in Islam* (Oxford: Oneworld, 2006), p. vii.

7. Barbara Ferguson, "Woman Imam Raises Mixed Emotions," in *Arab News*, Mar. 20, 2005, at http://www.arabnews.com/?page=4&section=0&article=60721&d=20&m=3&y=2005.

8. Ibid.

9. *The Economist*, 6–12 October 2001, p. 16

10. Norman Calder, "Law: Legal Thought and Jurisprudence" in *The Oxford Encyclopedia of the Modern Islamic World*, Vol. 2, pp. 451–452. Hereafter, Calder, "Law."

11. Ibid.

12. "Accent on Southern," Letter from the Editor, *Bon Appetit*, Nov. 1992, p. 14.

13. Jean Calmard, "Ayatollah," in *The Oxford Encyclopedia of the Modern Islamic World*, Vol. 1, p. 163.

14. Reinhard Schulze, *A Modern History of the Islamic World* (Munchen: C.H. Beck'sche Verlagsbuchhandlung, 1995; trans. New York: I.B. Tauris, 2000), p. 223. Hereafter, Schulze, *A Modern History of the Islamic World*.

15. Esposito, "Contemporary Islam," in *The Oxford History of Islam* (Oxford: Oxford University Press, 1999), p. 663.

16. Sharough Akhavi, "Iran," in *The Oxford Encyclopedia of the Modern Islamic World*, Vol. 2, p. 230.

17. Ibid.

18. Salman Rushdie, *The Satanic Verses* (New York: Viking, 1989), pp. 381–82. Hereafter, Rushdie, *The Satanic Verses*.

19. Ibid, p. 381.

20. Ibid, p. 394.

21. John L. Esposito, *The Islamic Threat: Myth or Reality?* (New York: Oxford University Press, 1992), p. 191. Hereafter, Esposito, *The Islamic Threat*.

22. John L. Esposito, *What Everyone Needs to Know About Islam* (New York: Oxford University Press, 2002), p. 138.

23. Mehdi Mozaffari, "The Rushdie Affair," in *The Oxford Encyclopedia of the Modern Islamic World,* p. 445. Hereafter, Mozaffari, "The Rushdie Affair."

24. Ibid.

25. See, e.g. Mohammed Talbi, "Religious Liberty" in *Liberal Islam: a Sourcebook* (New York: Oxford University Press, 1998), pp. 165–67.

26. Abdullahi Ahmed an-Naim, *Toward an Islamic Reformation: Civil Liberties, Human Rights, and International Law* (New York: Syracuse, 1990), p. 84. Hereafter, an-Naim, *Toward an Islamic Reformation.*

27. Ibid, p. 183.

28. Mozaffari, "The Rushdie Affair," p. 444.

29. Ibid.

Chapter Seven—*Women in Islam*

1. Joseph Schacht, *An Introduction to Islamic Law* (Oxford: Clarendon Press, 1964; rpt., 1991), p. 188. Hereafter, Schacht, *An Introduction to Islamic Law.*

2. Carolyn Fluehr-Lobban, *Islamic Society in Practice* (Gainsville: University of Florida Press, 1994), p. 82. Hereafter, Fluehr-Lobban, *Islamic Society in Practice.*

3. Mary Jo Lakeland, trans., *The Forgotten Queens of Islam,* by Fatima Mernissi (Cambridge: Polity Press, 1993), p. 3.

4. Fluehr-Lobban, *Islamic Society in Practice,* pp. 82–83.

5. Ibid, p. 147.

6. Susan Sachs, "In Iran, More Women Leaving Nest for University," in *The New York Times,* July 22, 2000.

7. Frances Harrison, "Women Graduates Challenge Iran," in *BBC News,* Sept. 19, 2006, http://news.bbc.co.uk/go/pr/fr/-/2/hi/middle_east/5359672.stm.

8. Eugene A. Hecker, *A Short History of Women's Rights* (Westport: Greenwood Press, 1914), p. 161. Hereafter, Hecker, *A Short History.*

9. Ibid.

10. Ibid, p. 162.

11. Schmidt, *Veiled and Silenced,* pp. 156–159.

12. Hecker, *A Short History,* p. 132.

13. Olwen Hufton, *The Prospect Before Her (Vol. 1)* (Vintage Books, 1998), p. 263. Hereafter, Hufton, *The Prospect Before Her.*

14. Hecker, *A Short History,* pp. 125–127.

15. Amina Wadud, *Qur'an and Woman: Rereading the Sacred Text from a Woman's Perspective* (New York: Oxford University Press, 1999), p. 35. Hereafter, Wadud, *Qur'an and Woman.*

16. Surah 33, verse 35.
17. Wadud, *Qur'an and Woman*, p. 40.
18. Ibid.
19. Ibid, p. 39.
20. Ibid.
21. Surah 28, verse 7.
22. For a discussion of the traditional view of woman as evil, see Schmidt, *Veiled and Silenced,* chapter three.
23. Wadud, *Qur'an and Woman*, p. 25.
24. Surah 49, verse 13.
25. Asad, *The Message of the Qur'an*, p. 794, footnote 16.
26. Norman Daniel, *Islam and the West: The Making of an Image* (Oxford: Oneworld, 1960; rpt., 2000), p. 314. Hereafter, Daniel, *Islam and the West.*
27. Wadud, *Qur'an and Woman*, p. 2.
28. Ibid.
29. Sells, *Approaching the Qur'an*, pp. 183-204.
30. John L. Esposito and Natana DeLong-Bas, *Women in Muslim Family Law* (Syracuse: Syracuse University Press, 1982; rpt., 2001), p. 11. Hereafter, Esposito, *Women in Muslim Family Law.*
31. Ibid.
32. "Islam and the Media" on *Forum*, KQED Radio, April 29, 1999.
33. Ibid.
34. Schmidt, *Veiled and Silenced*, pp. 131–37.
35. Hecker, *A Short History*, p. 109.
36. Schmidt, *Veiled and Silenced*, p. 135.
37. Surah 24, verses 30–31.
38. Asad, *The Message of the Qur'an*, p. 538, footnote 37.
39. Surah 24, verse 31.
40. Asad, *The Message of the Qur'an*, pp. 538–539, footnote 38.
41. Ibid.
42. Ibid.
43. Ibid.
44. Surah 33, verse 53.
45. Asad, *The Message of the Qur'an*, p. 650, footnote 69.
46. Surah 33, verse 59.
47. Asma Barlas, *"Believing Women" in Islam: Unreading Patriarchal Interpretations of the Qur'an* (Austin: University of Texas Press, 2002), p. 55. Hereafter, Barlas, *Believing Women.*
48. Ibid.
49. Ibid.

50. See Barlas, *Believing Women,* pp. 57–58.

51. See Eating Disorders Coalition, www.eatingdisorderscoalition.org.

52. See American Society of Plastic Surgery, www.plasticsurgery.org.

53. "Islam and the Media" on *Forum,* KQED Radio, April 29, 1999.

54. "The Pastor's Wife" in *Islamic Horizons* January/February 2002, p. 58.

55. Esposito, *Women in Muslim Family Law,* p. 108.

56. Ibid.

57. *Islamic Horizons,* May/June 1423/2002, p. 16.

58. Ibid.

59. Surah 4, verse 130.

60. See, e.g., Deuteronomy, 21:15–17, which begins, "If a man has two wives, the one loved and the other disliked, and they have borne him children, …"

61. Daniel, *Islam and the West,* p. 158.

62. Surah 4, verse 3.

63. Wadud, *Qur'an and Woman,* p. 83.

64. Surah 4, verse 129.

65. Daniel, *Islam and the West,* p. 160.

66. Geoffrey Parrinder, *Mysticism in the World's Religions* (Oxford: Oneworld, 1976; rpt., 1996), p. 121.

67. Trevelyan, *English Social History,* 1974), p. 80.

68. Ibid.

69. Ibid, p. 242.

70. Ibid, p. 81.

71. Ibid, p. 84.

72. Hecker, *A Short History,* pp. 155–56, 168.

73. Esposito, *Women in Muslim Family Law,* p. 101.

74. Ibid, p. 103.

75. Ibid, p. 32, referring to Surah 2, verse 228.

76. Asad, *The Message of the Qur'an,* p. 50, footnote 218.

77. Esposito, *Women in Muslim Family Law,* p. 29.

78. Ibid, p. 32.

79. N. J. Coulson, *Succession in the Muslim Family* (Cambridge University Press, 1971), p. 239.

80. Peter Kolchin, *American Slavery 1619-1877* (New York: Hill and Wang, 1993; rpt., 1999), p. 4. Hereafter, Kolchin, *American Slavery.*

81. See, e.g., Ephesians 6:5–9; Exodus 21:26–27; and Titus 2:9–10.

82. See, e.g., Ephesians 6:5–9 and Titus 2:9–10.

83. Kolchin, *American Slavery,* p. 4.

84. Schacht, *An Introduction to Islamic Law,* p. 130.

85. Rahman, *Major Themes of the Qur'an*, p. 48, discussing Surah 24, verse 33, and noting that some Muslim scholars, interpreted this as a "recommendation" and not a "command."

86. Asad, *The Message of the Qur'an*, p. 540, footnote 47.

87. Schacht, *An Introduction to Islamic Law*, p. 128.

88. Ibid, p. 130.

89. Noel Malcolm, *Bosnia: a Short History*, p. 46.

90. Jonathan Bloom and Sheila Blair, *Islam: a Thousand Years of Faith and Power* (New Haven: Yale University Press, 2002), p. 48. Hereafter, Bloom and Blair, *Islam*.

91. Surah 24, verse 33. See also Asad, *The Message of the Qur'an,* p. 540, footnote 49.

92. Surah 24, verse 33.

93. Kolchin, *American Slavery*, p. 126.

94. Mary Jo Lakeland, trans., *The Veil and the Male Elite,* by Fatima Mernissi (New York: Addison-Wesley, 1991), p. 150. Hereafter, Lakeland, *The Veil and the Male Elite.*

95. See generally, Alex Haley, *Roots* (Doubleday, 1976). It's apparent from page 1 that Kunta Kinte's family is Muslim.

96. Esposito, *Women in Muslim Family Law*, p. 11.

97. Surah 24, verse 33; surah 4, verse 24; Asad, *The Message of the Qur'an*, p. 540, footnote 49.

98. Surah 24, verse 33. See also Asad, *The Message of the Qur'an,* p. 540, footnote 49.

99. Ahmed, *Islam Today*, p. 75.

100. Schacht, *An Introduction to Islamic Law*, p. 127.

101. Ibid.

102. Leila Ahmed, *Women and Gender in Islam* (New Haven: Yale University Press, 1992), pp. 175–76. Hereafter, Ahmed, *Women and Gender.*

103. Surah 81, verses 7–14.

104. See Surah 16, verses 57–59.

105. Surah 2, verse 282.

106. Hufton, *The Prospect Before Her*, p. 55.

107. Ibid.

108. Wadud, *Qur'an and Woman*, p. 86.

109. Ibid, p. 85.

110. Rahman, *Major Themes of the Qur'an*, p. 49.

111. Ibid.

112. Asma Barlas, p. 55, quoting Kenneth Cragg, *The Event of the Qur'an: Islam in its Scripture* (Oxford: Oneworld, 1994), p. 114.

113. Surah 4, verse 34.

114. Khaled Abou El Fadl, *Conference of the Books: The Search for Beauty in Islam* (Lanham: University Press of America, 2001), p. 172. Hereafter, Abou El Fadl, *Conference of the Books.*

115. Wadud, *Qur'an and Woman*, p. 77.

116. Abou El Fadl, *Conference of the Books*, p. 172.

117. Ibid.

118. Ibid.

119. Wadud, *Qur'an and Woman*, p. 76.

120. Ibid.

121. Ibid.

122. Ahmed Ali, *Al-Qur'an: a Contemporary Translation* (Princeton: Princeton University Press, 2001), pp. 78–79. See also Abou El Fadl, *Conference of the Books*, p. 179. Hereafter, Ali, *Al-Qur'an.*

123. Ali, *Al-Qur'an*, p. 78.

124. Hecker, *A Short History*, p. 125.

125. Barlas, *Believing Women*, p. 188.

126. Asad, *The Message of the Qur'an*, pp. 109–110, footnotes 44–45.

127. Abou El Fadl, *Conference of the Books*, p. 169.

128. Lakeland, *The Veil and the Male Elite*, p. 157.

129. Asad, *The Message of the Qur'an*, pp. 109–110.

130. Abou El Fadl, *Conference of the Books*, p. 172.

131. Bloom and Blair, *Islam*, p. 139.

Chapter Eight—*Jihad and Fundamentalism*

1. Khaled Abou El Fadl, *The Place of Tolerance in Islam* (Boston: Beacon Press, 2002), p. 19. Hereafter, Abou El Fadl, *The Place of Tolerance in Islam.*

2. an-Naim, *Toward an Islamic Reformation*, p. 145.

3. Peters, *Jihad in Classical and Modern Islam*, p. 1.

4. Ibid.

5. Surah 25, verse 52.

6. Surah 9, verse 20.

7. Surah 4, verse 75.

8. an-Naim, *Toward an Islamic Reformation*, p. 145.

9. Majid Khadduri, *War and Peace in the Law of Islam* (Baltimore: Johns Hopkins University Press, 1955; rpt., 1962), pp. 56–57. Hereafter, Khadduri, *War and Peace in the Law of Islam.*

10. Abou El Fadl, *The Place of Tolerance in Islam*, p. 23.

11. Surah 2, verse 256.

12. Surah 2, verse 190.

13. Surah 2, verses 192–193.

14. Surah 4, verse 90.

15. Asad, *The Message of the Qur'an*, p. 41, footnote 168.

16. Peters, *Jihad in Classical and Modern Islam*, p. 3

17. Abou El Fadl, "Terrorism is at Odds with Islamic Tradition."

18. an-Naim, *Toward an Islamic Reformation*, pp. 149–50.

19. Surah 59, verses 7–9.

20. Surah 2, verse 190.

21. an-Naim, *Toward an Islamic Reformation*, p. 142.

22. James Turner Johnson, *The Holy War Idea in Western and Islamic Traditions* (University Park: Pennsylvania State University Press, 1997), p. 70. Hereafter, Johnson, *The Holy War Idea*.

23. Ibid.

24. an-Naim, *Toward an Islamic Reformation*, p. 142.

25. Ibid.

26. Ibid.

27. Peters, *Jihad in Classical and Modern Islam*, p. 1.

28. Sells, *Approaching the Qur'an*, pp. 7–8.

29. Peters, *Jihad in Classical and Modern Islam*, pp. 2–3.

30. an-Naim, *Toward an Islamic Reformation*, p. 158.

31. Peters, *Jihad in Classical and Modern Islam*, pp. 2–3.

32. Khadduri, *War and Peace in the Law of Islam*, p. 62.

33. Arthur Goldschmidt, Jr., *A Concise History of the Middle East*, 7th Ed. (Boulder, CO: Westview Press, 2002), p. 54.

34. Gerald Hawting, *The First Dynasty of Islam: The Umayyad Caliphate AD 661-750*, 2nd ed. (1986; rpt., London: Rutledge, 2000), p. 4. Hereafter, Hawting, *The First Dynasty of Islam*.

35. Ibid, p. 8.

36. Khadduri, *War and Peace in the Law of Islam*, pp. 65–66.

37. Sir Thomas W. Arnold, *The Spread of Islam in the World* (London, 1896; rpt. New Delhi: Goodword Books, 2001), p. 46.

38. Ibid.

39. Khadduri, *War and Peace in the Law of Islam*, p. 71.

40. Ibid, pp. 60, 66–67.

41. Peters, *Jihad in Classical and Modern Islam*, pp. 123–24.

42. Ibid, p. 124.

43. Ibid.

44. Ibid, p. 6.

45. Johnson, *The Holy War Idea*, p. 169.

46. Ibid, p. 170.

47. Surah 5, verse 32.

48. *NOW with Bill Moyers*, PBS, Feb. 15, 2002.

49. Surah 5, verse 69; surah 2, verse 62.

50. Surah 5, verse 51.

51. an-Naim, *Toward an Islamic Reformation*, p. 144.

52. See K.Theodore Hoppen, *The Mid-Victorian Generation: 1846–1886* (Oxford: Clarendon Press, 1998), pp. 442–447. See also Patrick Allit, *Victorian Britain, Part I* (Course guidebook and lecture recording) (The Teaching Company Limited Partnership, 2002), p. 34.

53. Martin E. Marty and R. Scott Appleby, ed., *Fundamentalisms Observed* (University of Chicago Press, 1994), p. 35. Hereafter, Marty and Appleby, *Fundamentalisms Observed*.

54. Bloom and Blair, *Islam*, p. 238.

55. Abou El Fadl, *The Place of Tolerance in Islam*, p. 6.

56. Ibid.

57. Michael Sells, *The Bridge Betrayed: Religion and Genocide in Bosnia* (Berkeley: University of California Press, 1996), p. 199. Hereafter, Sells, *The Bridge Betrayed*.

58. Ibid, p. 21.

59. Ibid, pp. 12–14.

60. William Dalrymple, "Scribes of the New Racism," in *The Independent Online Edition*, Sep. 25, 2001.

61. Anna Politkovskaya, "Cleansing Chechnya," Amnesty Now, Fall 2002, p. 14.

62. "India: Justice, the Victim – Gujarat State Fails to Protect Women from Violence," Amnesty International Document Library, Jan. 27, 2005, at http://web.amnesty.org/library/index/engasa200012005; see also "India: Abuse of the Law in Gujarat; Muslims Detained Illegally in Ahmedebad," Amnesty International Document Library, Nov. 6, 2003, at http://web.amnesty.org/library/index/engasa200292003.

63. Karen Armstrong, *The Battle for God* (Ballantine, 2000), p. 363. Hereafter, Armstrong, *The Battle for God*.

64. John Voll, "Fundamentalism," in *The Oxford Encyclopedia of the Modern Islamic World*, Vol. 2, p. 32.

65. Said, *Covering Islam*, p. xvi.

66. John L. Esposito, *Islam and Politics* (Syracuse: Syracuse University Press, 1984; rpt., 1998), p. 349. Hereafter, Esposito, *Islam and Politics*.

67. Ibid., pp. 303–304.

68. Esposito, *The Islamic Threat*, p. 212.

69. Esposito, *Islam and Politics,* p. 304.

70. Ibid, p. 305.

71. Ibid.

72. As of September 2007.

73. an-Naim, *Toward an Islamic Reformation*, p. 156.

74. From an interview on Quantara.de on Oct. 27, 2005. See http://www. scholarofthehouse.stores.yahoo.net/jgowrinwikha.html.

75. Abou El Fadl, "Terrorism is at Odds with Islamic Tradition."

76. Ibid.

77. Ibid.

78. Ibid.

79. Ibid.

80. Thomas J. Nagy, "U.S. Intentionally Destroyed Iraq's Water System," in *Censored 2003: The Top 25 Censored Stories*, ed. Peter Phillips (New York: Seven Stories Press, 2002), pp. 50–52. See also Greg Barnett, "Running Dry: Sanctions Hit Iraq's Young the Hardest," in *The Seattle Times*, August 4, 2002; and Tom Roberts, "Iraq: For the Children, Sanctions are Deadlier than Bombs," in *The National Catholic Reporter*, May 1999.

81. Greg Barnett, "Running Dry: Sanctions Hit Iraq's Young the Hardest," in *The Seattle Times*, August 4, 2002.

82. Surah 109.

83. Surah 2, verse 256.

84. Surah 10, verse 99.

85. Mohamed Talbi, "Religious Liberty," in *Liberal Islam*, p. 163.

86. William Dalrymple, "Scribes of the New Racism," in *The Independent*, September 25, 2001.

87. From "All Things Considered," on National Public Radio, July 31, 2002.

88. See K. Theodore Hoppen, *The Mid-Victorian Generation: 1846–1886* (Clarendon Press, 1998), pp. 442–447. See also Patrick Allit, *Victorian Britain, Part I* (Course guidebook and lecture recording) (The Teaching Company Limited Partnership, 2002), p. 34.

89. M. Cherif Bassiouni, "Sources of Islamic Law, and the Protection of Human Rights in the Islamic Criminal Justice System," in *The Islamic Criminal Justice System* (Oceana, 1982), p. 22. Hereafter, Bassiouni, *The Islamic Criminal Justice System*.

90. Ali Bulac, "The Medina Document," in *Liberal Islam*, p. 173.

91. Daniel, *Islam and the West*, p. 305.

92. Jane I. Smith, "Islam and Christendom," in *The Oxford History of Islam*, ed. John Esposito (Oxford University Press, 1999), pp. 312–313. Hereafter, Smith, "Islam and Christendom."

93. Esposito, *The Islamic Threat*, pp. 40–41.

94. Khadduri, *War and Peace in the Law of Islam*, p. 58.

95. Ibid.

96. Ibid.

97. Peters, *Jihad in Classical and Modern Islam*, p. 3.

98. Khadduri, *War and Peace in the Law of Islam*, p. 58.

99. Deuteronomy 7:1–5.

100. See e.g., Larry Luxner, "Albania;" Muriel Atkin, "Tajikistan;" and James Critchlow, "Uzbekistan," in *The Oxford Encyclopedia of the Modern Islamic World*, Vols. 1–4.

101. Jeremy Henzell-Thomas, "The Language of Islamophobia," presented at the University of Westminster School of Law, London, September 29, 2001. Hereafter, Henzell-Thomas, "The Language of Islamophobia."

Chapter Nine—*Theft and Adultery in Islam*

1. Ali, *Al-Qur'an,* p. 113.

2. Ibid.

3. Ibid.

4. Ibid.

5. Ibid.

6. Abou El Fadl, "Islam and the Challenge of Democracy."

7. Virginia Mackey, "Punishment in the Scripture and Tradition of Judaism, Christianity, and Islam," in *Crime, Values, and Religion* (Norwood: Ablex Pub. Corp., 1987), ed. James M. Day and William S. Laufer, p. 55, quoting Moustafa Kara. Hereafter, Mackey, "Punishment in the Scripture."

8. Ibid, p. 55.

9. Schacht, *An Introduction to Islamic Law*, p. 177.

10. This is the Biblical version: "If any harm follows, then you shall give life for life, eye for eye, tooth for tooth, hand for hand, foot for foot, burn for burn, wound for wound, stripe for stripe." Ex. 21:23-24; also Deut. 19:21 and Lev. 24:20–RSV.

11. Surah 5, verse 45.

12. Mackey, "Punishment in the Scripture," p. 63.

13. Deuteronomy 21:18–21.

14. Trevelyan, *English Social History*, p. 363.

15. Abou El Fadl, "Islam and the Challenge of Democracy."

16. Bassiouni, *The Islamic Criminal Justice System*, p. 5.
17. See Bassiouni, *The Islamic Criminal Justice System*, p. 5.
18. Surah 24, verses 2–3.
19. F. E. Peters, *A Reader on Classical Islam* (Princeton: Princeton University Press, 1994), p. 248.
20. Schacht, *An Introduction to Islamic Law*, p. 177.
21. Surah 24, verses 4–5.
22. Schacht, *An Introduction to Islamic Law*, p. 177.
23. Mackey, "Punishment in the Scripture," p. 54.
24. Calder, "Law," p 453.
25. See Mohammad S. El-Awa, *Punishment in Islamic Law: A Comparative Study* (American Trust Publications, 1982), pp. 135–137. Hereafter, El-Awa, *Punishment in Islamic Law.*
26. Ibid, pp. 136, 137.
27. Surah 5, verse 42.
28. Surah 42, verse 43.
29. Mackey, "Punishment in the Scripture," p. 63.
30. an-Naim, *Toward an Islamic Reformation*, p. 106.
31. Ibid.
32. Bassiouni, *The Islamic Criminal Justice System*, p. 28, quoting Maududi, p. 19.
33. Ibid, p. 42.
34. Ahmad Abd al-Aziz al-Alfi, "Punishment in Islamic Criminal Law," in Bassiouni, *The Islamic Criminal Justice System*, p. 235.
35. Ibid, p. 236.
36. Ibid, pp. 249–250.
37. Mackey, "Punishment in the Scripture," p. 63.

Chapter Ten—*An American Muslim Reaction to September 11th*
1. David Rosenzweig, "2 JDL Leaders Are Indicted by U.S. Grand Jury; Crime: Irv Rubin, Earl Krugel Are Accused of Plotting to Blow Up a Culver City Mosque and a Congressman's Office," in the *Los Angeles Times,* Jan. 11, 2002.
2. Abou El Fadl, *The Place of Tolerance in Islam*, p. 95.

Chapter Eleven—*Why the Misconceptions Persist*
1. *The Economist*, October 6-12, 2001, p. 16.
2. "Islam and the Media," on Forum, KQED Radio, April 29, 1999.
3. Kate Goldberg, "Islam Hijacked by Terror," BBC News Online, October 11, 2001.

4. Jim Muir, "Iran Condemns Attacks on U.S.," BBC News Online, September 17, 2001.

5. Surah 5, verse 32.

6. See website of the Council of American-Islamic Relations, www.cair. com/AmericanMuslims/AntiTerrorism/IslamicStatementsAgainstTerrorism.aspx.

7. CNN, "Victims of Ugandan Cult Massacres to be Mourned Sunday," April 2, 2000.

8. Sells, *The Bridge Betrayed*, p. 128.

9. Ibid, p. 37.

10. Ibid.

11. Paul Hond, "The Great Game," in *Columbia Magazine*, Spring 2007.

12. Allison Keyes, "Woman Leads Muslim Prayer Service in NYC," *NPR News and Notes*, Mar. 28, 2005. http://www.npr.org/templates/story/story. php?storyId=4563514.

13. Robert Scheer, "U.S. Jews Cannot Acquiesce to Sharon's Monstrous Behavior," in the *Los Angeles Times*, April 9, 2002.

14. William Dalrymple, "Scribes of the New Racism," in *The Independent*, Sept. 25, 2001. Hereafter, Dalrymple, "Scribes of the New Racism."

15. Henzell-Thomas, "The Language of Islamophobia."

16. Dalrymple, "Scribes of the New Racism."

17. Henzell-Thomas, "The Language of Islamophobia."

18. Interview with Louise Arbour, U.N. High Commissioner for Human Rights, on *Fresh Air*, WHYY Radio, June 18, 2007. Audio at http://www. npr.org/templates/story/story.php?storyId=11155872.

19. Henzell-Thomas, "The Language of Islamophobia."

20. Ibid.

21. Ibid.

22. Ibid.

23. Ibid.

24. Ibid.

25. See online study, "The Bombing of Afghanistan as Reflection of 9/11 and Different Valuations of Life," by Marc W. Herold, University of New Hampshire, September 11, 2002.

26. Dalrymple, "Scribes of the New Racism."

27. Said, *Covering Islam*, p. li.

28. Ibid, p. xi.

29. Ibid, p. xvi.

30. Ibid, p. 9.

31. Larry Luxner, "Albania," in *The Oxford Encyclopedia of the Modern Islamic World*, p. 66.
32. Ibid.
33. Sells, *The Bridge Betrayed*, p. 4.
34. Smith, "Islam and Christendom," pp. 312–313.
35. Esposito, *The Islamic Threat*, pp. 40–41.
36. Bloom and Blair, *Islam*, p. 95.
37. Said, *Covering Islam*, p. lii.
38. Mackey, "Punishment in the Scripture," p. 58.
39. Smith, "Islam and Christendom," p. 321.
40. Esposito, *Islam*, p. 57.
41. V.S. Naipaul, *Beyond Belief* (Vintage, 1998), p. 18.
42. Geoffrey Parrinder, *Mysticism in the World's Religions*, p. 125.
43. Esposito, *The Islamic Threat*, p. 38.
44. Daniel, *Islam and the West*, p. 160.
45. Ibid, p. 307.
46. Ibid, p. 311.
47. Ibid, p. 307.
48. Ibid, p. 326.
49. Henzell-Thomas, "The Language of Islamophobia."
50. Esposito, *The Islamic Threat*, p. 46.
51. See generally, Said, *Orientalism*; also p. 60.
52. See generally, Daniel, *Islam and the West*; Said, *Orientalism*; R.W. Southern, *Western Views of Islam in the Middle Ages* (Cambridge: Harvard University Press, 1962).
53. Zachary Lockman, "Behind the Battles over U.S. Middle East Studies," Jan. 2004, in *Middle East Report Online,* http://www.merip.org/.
54. Daniel, *Islam and the West*, p. 291.
55. NPR, "Pope's Remarks on Islam, Violence Spur Anger," Sep. 15, 2006. http://www.npr.org/templates/story/story.php?storyId=6084194.
56. Esposito, *The Islamic Threat*, p. 46, quoting Ernest Renan.
57. Said, *Orientalism*, p. 38.
58. Daniel Pipes's posting on http://www.campus-watch.org/, June 22, 2003. See also Nigel Parry and Ali Abunimah, "Campus Watch: Middle East McCarthyism?" in *The Electronic Intifada,* Sep. 25, 2002.
59. Said, *Covering Islam*, pp. 14–21.
60. Ibid.
61. Ibid.
62. Victor J. Katz, *A History of Mathematics*, (HarperCollins College Publishers, 1993), p. 227. Hereafter, Katz, *A History of Mathematics.*

63. Ibid.

64. Ibrahim al-Kadi, "Origins of Cryptology: The Arab Contributions," in *Selections from Cryptologia* (Artech House, Inc., 1998), ed. C.A. Deavours, pp. 98–99. Hereafter, al-Kadi, *Selections from Cryptologia*.

65. Ibid, pp. 98–99.

66. Simon Singh, *The Code Book: The Science of Secrecy From Ancient Egypt to Quantum Cryptography* (New York: Anchor, 2000), pp. 14–19. Hereafter, Singh, *The Code Book*.

67. Ibid, p. 16.

68. Ibid, p. 17.

69. al-Kadi, *Selections from Cryptologia*, p. 94.

70. Singh, *The Code Book*, pp. 15–16.

71. al-Kadi, *Selections from Cryptologia*, p. 95.

72. Singh, *The Code Book*, p. 16.

73. Ahmed, *Islam Today*, p. 62.

74. Bloom and Blair, *Islam*, p. 111.

75. al-Kadi, *Selections from Cryptologia*, p. 116.

76. Ibid.

77. See, e.g., Katz, *A History of Mathematics*, p. 451.

78. Said, *Covering Islam*, pp. 6–7.

79. Daniel, *Islam and the West*, p. 305.

80. Esposito, *The Islamic Threat*, p. 41.

81. See "Dr. Jack Shaheen Discusses *Reel Bad Arabs: How Hollywood Vilifies a People*," in *The Washington Report on Middle East Affairs*, July 2001, p. 103.

82. Said, *Covering Islam*, pp. 172–73.

83. Alan Cooperman, "A Timely Subject—and a Sore One," in *The Washington Post*, August 7, 2002.

Suggested Reading List

In addition to the works I have cited throughout this book, I recommend the following as some of the more readable books relating to Islam and Islamic history. Many books and histories published in Western countries have a Eurocentric bias, and I have tried to choose those that are more balanced (with the exception of Stanley and Hillenbrand, but see the explanation alongside those citations).

On History

Reza Aslan, *No god But God: The Origins, Evolution, and Future of Islam* (Random House, 2005)

Jonathan Bloom and Sheila Blair, *Islam: a Thousand Years of Faith and Power* (Yale, 2002).

The Oxford History of Islam, John L. Esposito, editor (Oxford University Press, 1999).

Arthur Goldschmidt, *A Concise History of the Middle East*, 7th edition (Westview, 2002).

Carole Hillenbrand, *The Crusades: Islamic Perspectives* (Routledge, 2000). This is not a chronological survey of the Crusades but an attempt to present (as a matter of policy) the Muslim perspective by using Muslim sources. This does not purport to be an objective rendering of events but, as the back cover reads, "given the cumulative impact of centuries of Eurocentric scholarship in this field … it should help to create a more balanced picture" of the period.

Albert Hourani, *A History of the Arab Peoples* (Belknap Harvard, 1991). This is longer and drier than the others but thorough.

Stephen Humphreys, *Between Memory and Desire: The Middle East in a Troubled Age* (University of California Press, 1999). This is a history of the modern Middle East.

Zachary Karabell, *Peace Be Upon You: The Story of Muslim, Christian, and Jewish Coexistence* (Knopf, 2007).

Hugh Kennedy, *The Prophet and the Age of the Caliphates: The Islamic Near East From the Sixth to the Eleventh Century* (Longman, 1986; rpt., 1991).

Maria Rosa Menocal, *The Ornament of the World: How Muslims, Jews, and Christians Created a Culture of Tolerance in Medieval Spain* (Little, Brown, and Company, 2002).

Michael Sells, *The Bridge Betrayed: Religion and Genocide in Bosnia* (University of California Press, 1996).

Reinhardt Schulze, *A Modern History of the Islamic World* (I.B. Tauris, 2000).

Diane Stanley, *Saladin: Noble Prince of Islam* (HarperCollins, 2002). This is a beautifully illustrated book for 8–12 year olds, but worth reading for everyone. It's the Muslim side of the Crusades story, about Saladin as opposed to Richard the Lionheart. In a way, the author had the same idea as Hillenbrand, above.

On Stereotyping

Norman Daniel, *Islam and the West: The Making of an Image* (Oneworld, 1960; rpt., 2000).

Edward Said, *Covering Islam: How the Media and the Experts Determine how We See the Rest of the World* (Pantheon, 1981; rpt., Vintage, 1997). The introduction alone is worth the price of this book.

Edward Said, *Orientalism: Western Conceptions of the Orient* (Rutledge & Kegan Paul Ltd, 1978; rpt., Penguin, 1991). This book influenced new scholarship in the West regarding "the East."

Jack Shaheen, *Reel Bad Arabs: How Hollywood Vilifies a People* (Arris, 2003).

Islam Generally and Islam in America

Akbar Ahmed, *Islam Today: A Short Introduction to the Muslim World* (I.B. Tauris, 1999).

John L. Esposito, *Islam: The Straight Path* (Oxford University Press, 1988; rpt., 1998).

Frederick Mathewson Denny, *An Introduction to Islam* (Macmillan, 1985; rpt., 1994).

The Oxford Dictionary of Islam, John L. Esposito, editor-in-chief (Oxford University Press, 2003).

Islam in the Political Arena

John L. Esposito, *The Islamic Threat: Myth or Reality?* (Oxford University Press, 1992).

John L. Esposito, *Islam and Politics* (Syracuse University Press, 1984; rpt., 1998).

Fred Halliday, *Islam and the Myth of Confrontation* (I.B. Tauris, 2003).

The New Crusades: Constructing the Muslim Enemy, Emran Qureshi and Michael Sells, editors (Columbia University Press, 2003).

Stephen Zunes, *Tinderbox: U.S. Middle East Policy and the Roots of Terrorism* (Common Courage Press, 2003).

On Extremism in Islam

Khaled Abou El Fadl, *The Great Theft: Wrestling Islam From the Extremists* (HarperSanFrancisco, 2005). This is an excellent book that explains clearly, profoundly, and intelligently the rise of extremists, or "puritans," in Islam.

John L. Esposito, *Unholy War: Terror in the Name of Islam* (Oxford, 2002).

Sufi Poetry

Coleman Barks and Michael Green, *The Illuminated Prayer:The Five-Times Prayer of the Sufis* (Ballantine, 2000). This beautifully illustrated book presents not only Sufi poetry, but a very thorough, inspiring explanation of the Muslim prayer, or *salat*.

Coleman Barks, John Moyne, and A.J. Arberry, trans., *The Essential Rumi* by Jelaluddin Rumi, New Ed. (Penguin, 2004).

Michael Sells, *Stations of Desire: Love Elegies from Ibn Arabi and New Poems* (Jerusalem: Ibis Editions, 2000; rpt., 2004).

Michael Sells, trans., *Desert Tracings: Six Classic Arabian Odes by 'Alqama, Shanfara, Labid, 'Antara, Al-A'sha, and Dhu al-Rumma* (Wesleyan University Press, 1989).

Recommended Translations of the Qur'an

Ahmed Ali, *The Qur'an: a Contemporary Translation*, rev. ed. (Princeton University Press, 1994).

A.J. Arberry, *The Koran Interpreted* (George Allen and Unwin, 1955; rpt., Touchstone, 1996). Poetic, but no footnotes.

Muhammad Asad, *The Message of the Qur'an* (Dar Andalus, 1980). Great footnotes and clear meaning; this is my favorite translation.

Michael Sells, *Approaching the Qur'an: the Early Revelations* (White Cloud Press, 1999). This is not the Qur'an but a very readable introduction on how to read the Qur'an; includes a CD so you can hear the sing-song chanting of the Qur'an and its rhythm.

Women and Islam

Carol L. Anway, *Daughters of Another Path: Experiences of American Women Choosing Islam* (Yawna Publications, 1995; 5th rpt., 2001).

Asma Barlas, *"Believing Women" in Islam: Unreading Patriarchal Interpretations of the Qur'an* (University of Texas Press, 2002).

John L. Esposito and Natana DeLong-Bas, *Women in Muslim Family Law* (Syracuse University Press, 1982; rpt. 2001).

Amina Wadud, *Qur'an and Woman: Rereading the Sacred Text from a Woman's Perspective* (Oxford University Press, 1999).

Index

Related Titles from White Cloud Press

Approaching the Qur'án
The Early Revelations, 2nd Edition
Translated with an Introduction by Michael Sells
Paperback $22.95, ISBN: 978-1-883991-69-2

The Green Sea of Heaven
Fifty *ghazals* from the Díwán of Háfiz
Translated by Elizabeth T. Gray, Jr.
Paperback $15.95, ISBN: 978-1-883991-06-7

Letters to America: a chance for us to listen
Edited by Erica Geller
Photographs by Mark Brecke
Paperback $18.95, ISBN: 978-1-883991-95-1

Quarreling with God
Mystic Rebel Poems of the
Dervishes of Turkey
Translated and compiled by
Jennifer Ferraro with Latif Bolat
Paperback $19.95, ISBN: 978-1-883991-68-5

Welcome to the Family!
Opening Doors to the Jewish Experience
by Lois Shenker
Paperback $15.95, ISBN: 978-1-883991-41-8